RECONSTRUCTING CHRISTIAN ETHICS

Reconstructing Christian Ethics

Selected Writings

F. D. Maurice

Edited by
Ellen K. Wondra

 Westminster John Knox Press
Louisville, Kentucky

© 1995 Westminster John Knox Press

All rights reserved. No part of this book may be reproduced or transmitted in any form or by any means, electronic or mechanical, including photocopying, recording, or by any information storage or retrieval system, without permission in writing from the publisher. For information, address Westminster John Knox Press, 100 Witherspoon Street, Louisville, Kentucky 40202-1396.

Book design by Publishers' WorkGroup

First edition

Published by Westminster John Knox Press
Louisville, Kentucky

This book is printed on acid-free paper that meets the American National Standards Institute Z39.48 standard. ♾

PRINTED IN THE UNITED STATES OF AMERICA

95 96 97 98 99 00 01 02 03 04 — 10 9 8 7 6 5 4 3 2 1

Library of Congress Cataloging-in-Publication Data

Maurice, Frederick Denison, 1805–1872.
    Reconstructing Christian ethics : selected writings / F.D. Maurice edited by Ellen K. Wondra. — 1st ed.
        p.   cm. — (Library of theological ethics)
    Includes bibliographical references.
    ISBN 0-664-25601-5 (alk. paper)
    1. Christian ethics —Anglican authors.   I. Wondra, Ellen K.
II. Title.   III. Series.
BJ1251.M43 1995
241'.043'092—dc20   95-20191

CONTENTS

LIBRARY OF THEOLOGICAL ETHICS

General Editors' Introduction

The field of theological ethics possesses in its literature an abundant inheritance concerning religious convictions and the moral life, critical issues, methods, and moral problems. The Library of Theological Ethics is designed to present a selection of important texts that would otherwise be unavailable for scholarly purposes and classroom use. The series will engage the question of what it means to think theologically and ethically. It is offered in the conviction that sustained dialogue with our predecessors serves the interests of responsible contemporary reflection. Our more immediate aim in offering it, however, is to enable scholars and teachers to make more extensive use of classic texts as they train new generations of theologians, ethicists, and ministers.

The volumes included in the Library will comprise a variety of types. Some will make available English-language texts and translations that have fallen out of print; others will present new translations of texts previously unavailable in English. Still others will offer anthologies or collections of significant statements about problems and themes of special importance. We hope that each volume will encourage contemporary theological ethicists to remain in conversation with the rich and diverse heritage of their discipline.

ROBIN W. LOVIN
DOUGLAS F. OTTATI
WILLIAM SCHWEIKER

INTRODUCTION

I was sent into the world that I might persuade men to recognise Christ as the centre of their fellowship with each other, that so they might be united in their families, their countries, and as men, not in schools and factions. . . .[1]

Today's discussions of how theological ethics ought to understand the human character, the person as a relational self, and the contexts of human life as formative have a long, rich, and complicated lineage. The lifework of F. D. Maurice (1805–1872) was to illuminate these and other concerns of theology and ethics in a way that would recall persons to their true identity as children of a loving God whose being is grounded in relation. Maurice took up this vocation in a context of increasing religious and cultural pluralism and of tremendous social and intellectual turmoil, all of which Christians often found baffling and even paralyzing. This volume presents selections from Maurice's major writings in moral theology, not only because of Maurice's importance in his own time, but also in order to bring into contemporary view some of the options available for understanding and responding to situations of challenge such as he—and we—face.

LIFE

Frederick Denison Maurice's personal life illustrates the challenges and insights typical of Victorian Christianity.[2] Many of the religious controversies of the early nineteenth century were present in Maurice's family. His father, Michael Maurice, was a biblically conservative and politically liberal Unitarian minister who suffered the financial and social disabilities that accompanied dissent at that time. In addition to his pastoral duties, Michael supported his large family by teaching private pupils who lived with the Maurice family. Michael's wife, Priscilla Hurry Maurice, was for much of Frederick's youth a Unitarian, but in a time of crisis she found evangelical Calvinism better able to address the challenges presented by ordinary life. Under the influence of her elder daughters, she converted, although she thought she was not among the elect. These conversions caused great upset and controversy within the family and were an unfortunate influence on young Frederick, who, by his own account, suffered from "moral confusion and contradiction" during his adolescence and young manhood.[3] The intense religious atmosphere within the family also had a lasting effect on Maurice's theology—as is apparent in his emphases on "the Fatherhood of God, divine unity, opposition to the penal substitutionary view of the atonement, rejection of contemporary views of original sin, and everlasting punishment"—as well as on his social vision.[4]

F. D. Maurice went up to Cambridge University as an agnostic, intending to take a degree in law, but he left without a degree because he would not subscribe to the Church of England's Articles of Religion—a requirement for receiving a degree at that time. While at Cambridge, Maurice was greatly influenced by the religious writings of Samuel Taylor Coleridge (to whom he later dedicated *The Kingdom of Christ*) and by the philosophy of Plato as interpreted by Julius Hare. He was also a journalist and participated actively in political debates, often taking radical positions.

At the conclusion of his university studies, Maurice moved to London to study for the bar, but he soon returned to writing and journalism, editing both *The Westminster Review* and *The Athenaeum.* However, journalism did not satisfy him. As he spent hours with a favorite sister who was dying, reading to and discussing with her sections of his autobiographical novel *Eustace Conway,* Maurice increasingly embraced the Christianity of the Church of England. He went up to Oxford University to study divinity, was rebaptized in the Church of England, and sought ordination. Prior to his ordination in 1834, Maurice served as lay assistant to Joseph Stephenson, whose Millenarian eschatology significantly influenced Maurice's conviction that the Kingdom of Christ has been inaugurated with the Incarnation and is the reality to which the church is called to witness.[5]

After a curacy in a village near Coventry, Maurice returned to London as chaplain of Guy's Hospital, working there among the poor and the sick. This ministry further reinforced his basic theological convictions and insights:

> It seemed to me that except I could address all kinds of people as members of Christ and children of God, I could not address them at all. Their sin, it seemed to me, must mean a departure from that state; it must be their true state, which Christ had claimed for them. I thought I had no Gospel for the sufferers in Guy's Hospital, if it was not that.[6]

In 1838 Maurice wrote and published *The Kingdom of Christ,* substantially revising it for republication in 1842. It is with this work that the selections in the present volume begin. *The Kingdom of Christ* set out the theological and ecclesiological positions that Maurice developed over the rest of his life. In this work, and contrary to much of the prevailing sentiment in the Church of England, Maurice advocated religious tolerance and appreciation of both dissent and secular developments as contributors to the church's quest for truth. He also pursued these themes in a number of tracts that commented on current controversies concerning the allowable breadth of doctrine and ecclesiology in the Church of England.

In the latter half of the 1840s, Maurice's life changed significantly. He became friends with Charles Kingsley; developed a closer relationship with his Oxford mentor Julius Hare; undertook the chaplaincy of Lincoln's Inn; and became Professor of Theology at King's College, London, where he was in charge of candidates for ordination in the Church of England. During this time and subsequently, Maurice also taught at the Working Men's College (where he gave the lectures published as *The Epistles of St. John*), helped found Queen's College (for women), and was active in various other educational, organizational, and journalistic endeavors on behalf of the poor. His association with Kingsley (who had publicly supported the Chartist Movement in 1848) drew criticism from the Council of King's College, as did Maurice's leadership of the Christian Socialists. His position at King's College again became the subject of controversy following the 1853 publication of his *Theological Essays,* and he was finally dismissed from that position. This controversy arose directly from the content of Maurice's theological ethics.

The Christian Socialism of the mid-nineteenth century was an attempt by middle- and upper-class Christians to overcome the breaches and hostilities between the prosperous classes and the working poor in industrial England. The group gathered around Maurice, attracted and motivated by his teaching that

> the truth is that every man is in Christ; the condemnation of every man is, that he will not own the truth; he will not *act* as if this were *true,* he will not believe that which is the truth, that, except he were joined to Christ, he could not think, breathe, live a single hour.[7]

This teaching provided the basis for the Christian Socialists' critique of prevailing social arrangements and gave the vision of what their practical programs sought to achieve.

Maurice and his colleagues offered Bible studies for working men (a practice that grew into the Working Men's College, founded in 1854). The Christian Socialists launched two series of publications, *Politics for the People*, and *Tracts on Christian Socialism*, neither of which endured for long. Numerous practical schemes were proposed, and some production cooperatives were established under the leadership of J. M. Ludlow and W. V. Neale.[8]

Maurice, however, often opposed the practical proposals advanced by members of the group, fearing that they would lead to further divisiveness among the classes at a time when fear of social revolution was high. The group ultimately disbanded, at least in part because the fundamental theological assumptions that Maurice held differed from those of Ludlow and some of the others. In an exchange of letters in which they attempted to overcome their differences, Maurice told Ludlow "I am only a digger," not a builder.[9] Ludlow's response shows his own theological construal of the task at hand:

> I don't believe you, thank God, I won't and I can't. . . . Surely the whole work of Christianity is building and not digging,—just as digging was the work, the

only true work of the heathen philosopher, until the corner-stone should be laid. . . . I do not notice that St. Paul's conviction that he had a "building of God, an house not made with hands, eternal in the heavens," aye, nor his "groaning" for it, prevented him at all from taking up the character of a wise master-builder, laying the foundation stone, and both building himself and warning others how they should build. For myself, I am perfectly prepared to build with wood and hay and stubble, seeing that I feel I have little else to build with.[10]

Maurice in response explains

what I meant by calling myself a digger merely. If I had not been afraid of your mistaking me, I should have given myself the grand title of a theologian. . . . But such a statement would have been misleading, unless I had impressed you with my own deep conviction that theology is not (as the schoolmen have represented it) the climax of all studies, . . . but is the foundation upon which they all stand. . . . My business, because I am a theologian, and have no vocation except for theology, is not to build, but to dig, to show that economy and politics . . . must have a ground beneath themselves, that society is not to be made anew by arrangements of ours, but is to be regenerated by finding the law and ground of its order and harmony, the only secret of its existence, in God. This must seem to you an unpractical and unchristian method; to me it is the only one which makes action possible, and Christianity anything more than an artificial religion for the use of believers. . . . The Kingdom of Heaven is to me the great practical existing reality which is to renew the earth and make it a habitation for blessed spirits instead of for demons.[11]

As the Christian Socialists faltered, Maurice turned his attention from practical economics to education, concentrating his efforts in the Working Men's College and in founding Queen's College for Women. During this time, his *Theological Essays* was published.

In *Theological Essays,* Maurice did not directly take up the Christian Socialist banner. However, in the concluding essay "On Eternal Life," he argued that eternal life and eternal death (or eternal punishment) have nothing to do with temporality, but rather with the presence or absence of God.[12] This notion prompted strong criticism from the Evangelicals,[13] who read Maurice's argument as a denial of divine justice and so an undercutting of morality. Maurice had argued that humanity leads a prodigal existence, in willful selfishness straying from a loving Father who nevertheless welcomes his children home with open arms. For Maurice, the constancy and strength of God's love was more significant than all of human sin with all of its devastating effects. Maurice's critics argued that in emphasizing God's loving Fatherhood, Maurice had obscured God's righteousness, sovereignty, and hatred of sin, thus removing religion's power to deter immoral and criminal behavior, a power associated by Maurice's contemporaries with the doctrine of eternal punishment (or hell).

Maurice responded to his critics by addressing the relationship between God's love and human awareness and repentance of sin in *The Doctrine of Sacrifice* (1854), writing:

We have seen beneath all the evil, beneath the universe itself, that eternal and original union of the Father and the Son . . . which was never fully manifested till the Only Begotten by the eternal Spirit offered Himself to God. The revelation of that primal unity is the revelation of the ground on which all things stand. . . . It is the revelation of that which sin has ever been seeking to destroy, and which at last has overcome sin. It is the revelation of that perfect harmony to which we look forward when all things are gathered up in Christ.[14]

He also clarified his position on eternal life and salvation, denying the charges that he believed in universal salvation.[15] Even so, the Principal and the Council of King's College found Maurice's views of questionable orthodoxy, "of dangerous tendency, and calculated to unsettle the minds of the theological students" for whose training Maurice was responsible.[16]

These two controversies point out both the strengths and the weaknesses of Maurice's theology and ethics. On the one hand, his belief in the unalterable love of God for humanity led him to declare that "every man is [already] in Christ." This being the case, differences among persons on the basis of economic or social class cannot legitimately give rise either to competition between classes or to distinctions of moral requirements on the basis of social circumstances. Social arrangements and theological arguments that favor one class of persons over another serve to perpetuate that separation from God and from other persons, which Maurice understood to be the very stuff of sin. And emphasis on human depravity rather than God's love undercut the basic message of the Gospel of Christ.

On the other hand, Maurice's belief that the Kingdom of Heaven is an already existing reality, and that God has established an enduring order of creation, which—however badly distorted—nevertheless continues to exist in history, kept him from advocating systemic social change. Instead, what Maurice felt was needed (as Ludlow observed) was "tearing away the cobwebs of human systems that conceal" that reality.[17] Maurice's emphasis on education rather than social change reflects this fundamental presupposition: Once human beings become convinced of the fact that they are already in union with God, they will "arise and go to the Father."[18] In the same instant, their communion with each other becomes possible. Competition—the social form of self-centeredness—can be put aside in favor of cooperation, without significant social upheaval. Therefore, concerted and conflictual change directed toward large social systems is not necessary.

Despite the relatively short life of the group of Christian Socialists that Maurice led, the group's—and Maurice's—subsequent influence on Anglo-American social ethics was significant, and primarily theological. It remained for later generations of Christian Socialists—such as Brooke Foss Westcott, Henry Scott Holland (a founder of the Christian Social Union), Stewart Headlam (founder of the Guild of St. Matthew), Walter Rauschenbusch (the American articulator of the Social Gospel), Charles Gore (founder of the Church Socialist League, theologian, editor of and contributor to Lux Mundi), V. A. Demant, and William

Temple—to develop social programs that carried Maurice's theological principles into effective action in British society.

Following his dismissal from King's College, Maurice concentrated his energies in his ministry as chaplain of Lincoln's Inn and in further educational endeavors with working men and women. He was engaged in further theological controversy with H. L. Mansel following the latter's Bampton Lectures on the nature of revelation. (See Mansel's *The Limits of Religious Thought* [1858] and Maurice's *What is Revelation?* [1859] and *Sequel to the Inquiry: What is Revelation?* [1860].) In 1860 Maurice returned to Cambridge as Knightbridge Professor of Casuistry, Moral Theology, and Modern Philosophy. Two courses of lectures he gave there were published as *The Conscience* (1868) and *Social Morality* (1869); selections from each are included in this volume. He also moved his pastoral ministry to St. Peter's, Vere Street. He died on Easter Monday, 1872, his last words being a blessing: "The knowledge of the love of God—the blessing of God Almighty, the Father, the Son, and the Holy Ghost be amongst *you*—amongst *us*—and remain with us forever."[19]

Maurice was a prolific writer. Many of his works originated as sermons, tracts, and letters. During the course of his life, he produced commentaries on virtually every book of the Bible. He was an occasional, rather than systematic, theologian, making use of multiple genres (examples of which are given in this volume) to address a wide range of theological, moral, social, and religious issues. Only two of the present selections—*The Conscience* and *Social Morality*—were conceived as principally academic or scholarly presentations of the topics at hand.

The rest were addressed to a more general public and responded to particular contemporary concerns. The earliest selection, *The Kingdom of Christ,* has two forms: the first edition was a series of letters to a member of the Society of Friends, which was recast as a more formal treatise in the second edition. *The Epistles of St. John* is a course in moral theology that takes its outline and content from biblical material; this work is thus also a commentary on those books of the Bible. *Dialogues . . . on Family Worship* and "A Dialogue between Somebody . . . and Nobody" use a conversational form to resolve a matter of controversy between two persons who typify what Maurice considers significant and differing points of view. "Hatred Necessary to Love" is a sermon preached in the Chapel at Lincoln's Inn, where Maurice held the cure for many years; the topic is shaped by both the appointed lesson and the occasion, the Fifth Sunday in Lent.

This variety of genres displays Maurice's facility with a wide range of sources—from biblical material to the set reading lists for university exams, to the daily *Times,* to the everyday experience of working men. From these sources, he demonstrates a consistent set of premises and claims in moral theology, presented in a mode familiar to his various audiences and appropriate to the situations at hand.

Maurice maintained that revelation from God came in many forms—including writings by secular authors, subscribers to religions other than Christianity, and ordinary human experience. However, divine revelation is summed up and clarified in the Bible, which is "the history of the [gradual] unveiling of God to the creature whom He has made in His image,"[20] "God's revelation to us of ourselves, who are made in His image, and of Himself, who has made us in His image."[21] As noted, he wrote commentaries on virtually every book of the Bible, and his preaching consistently made use of the appointed lectionary or of biblical and credal material found in the *Book of Common Prayer*.

The Bible also played a central role in the writings whose primary audience was not ecclesial. In these instances, Maurice often uses scripture to summarize material he has presented deductively (as in *Social Morality*). This method follows from his conviction that scripture has authority not because some authoritative body has granted it, but because scripture validates and is validated by ordinary human experience.

> I use [the Scriptures] because I conceive they set forth Christ as the Son of God and the Lord of every man. I do not use them because I think they set forth some standard which is good for a set of men called Christians, who are different from other men, and who have not the same God with other men. I use the Scriptures to show us what I believe is the law and the life for all of us. . . . I should not use them if I thought them less universal and more partial than the books of heathens or of later moralists.[22]

To put it another way: Scripture, the revelation of the One who is the source and ground of all that is, speaks authoritatively in human life by showing persons their already existing connection to that ground. Revelation evokes recognition of the true nature of things, and also provides an account of how actual life can be brought into conformity with that true nature.

In addition to the letter to Ludlow quoted at length above, the following sentences from the Introduction to *The Doctrine of Sacrifice* sum up Maurice's own understanding of his vocation:

> My desire is to ground all theology upon the name of God the Father, the Son, and the Holy Ghost, not to begin from ourselves and our sins; not to measure the straight line by the crooked one. This is the method I have learned from the Bible. There everything proceeds from God; He is revealing himself; He is acting, speaking, ruling.[23]

THE SELECTIONS

The selections in this volume span Maurice's lifetime and are drawn from his principal works in theological ethics and moral theology. However, it should be noted that ethics and moral theology play a strong role throughout his entire opus, as Maurice was always concerned with showing the practical application of his view of the Christian faith and the moral life that it shapes.

In *The Kingdom of Christ* (1838 and 1842), probably his best-known book to-day, Maurice endeavors to show that elements or aspects of Truth—which is ultimately one—can be found in each of the sects and denominations that comprise Christianity. Maurice's first letter in the first edition gives the theological bases for his interest in persons outside the Church of England, and it lays out a theological method that not only values what each sect, denomination, or party affirms but shows how each needs all the others. Maurice is convinced that giving up any of these apparently contradictory positions only weakens the whole. He describes his method thus:

> I will consider each of these opinions; I will attempt to show how and wherein each seems to have denied the truth of the others. I will attempt to show how that which each really prizes, that which he feels he cannot part with, will unite in a principle—larger, deeper, more satisfactory, than any of the three, yet freed from the perplexities and contradictions which each has felt in the opinions of the others, and occasionally in his own.[24]

What must be sought is the truth that lies under all positions, of which each position is a partial but nonetheless accurate—and thus indispensable—expression. As one "digs" through each position, one will find how apparent opposites are in fact reconciled and how, when taken together, they provide access to a fuller measure of Truth.[25]

This method works because beneath the rich and various forms of religious and social life there are certain universal structures of human existence; these are outlined in the section from the second edition of *The Kingdom of Christ.* All persons are inherently relational, born into families; they become individuals in that context, but they also long for greater circles of relations. This gives rise to nations. But the "national spirit" itself gives rise and points to a further longing: for a universal society. For Maurice, this universal society is most nearly realized when church and nation are in harmony, both within themselves and with each other. "The kingdom of God begins within, but it is to make itself manifest without. . . . It is to penetrate the feelings, habits, thoughts, words, acts, of him who is the subject of it. At last it is to penetrate our whole social existence."[26] This Kingdom thus far has appeared only partially and fleetingly. Nevertheless, it is possible that this Kingdom will be realized in history.[27]

The Kingdom is manifest wherever human society and individual life cohere with the basic structures of the universe. These structures are at base, according to Maurice, sacramental, which is to say, sacrificial or based in self-giving to a beloved other. In the second selection from the first edition of *The Kingdom of Christ,* Maurice gives his typical description of these structures in abbreviated form. (More is said of these structures below, as they are described in his later *Social Morality.*)

The Kingdom of Christ appeared in the midst of cries for comprehensive reform of the Church of England, expansion of official religious toleration, and considerable resistance from the established Church of England. Maurice's work points a way through the dilemmas presented by this situation. Rather than erecting barriers against religious pluralism and doubt, or resorting to mere tolerance or easy relativism, in *The Kingdom of Christ* Maurice sets out an ecclesiology that is also a theory of religion and its relation to society and culture. The second edition is organized to highlight and detail six "marks of the church," claiming that the Church of England possesses all six. However, they are found, even in the Church of England—indeed, from Maurice's perspective, particularly there—only in flawed, scarred, and distorted form. Sectarianism, "party spirit," emphasis on human sinfulness rather than divine grace: all these turn the Church of England from a church into a "world." As he wrote later in *Theological Essays,*

> The world contains the elements of which the Church is composed. In the Church, these elements are penetrated by a uniting, reconciling power. The Church is, therefore, human society in its normal state; the World, that same society irregular and abnormal. The world is the Church without God; the Church is the world restored to its relation with God, taken back by him into the state for which he created it. Deprive the Church of its Center and you make it into a world.[28]

It is no surprise then, that religious, philosophical, and political movements challenge the church, which has abandoned its identity and mission. These "secular" movements demonstrate that the human desire for union with God will not be squelched, but will appropriate and use a variety of avenues that lead, however haltingly, toward its fulfillment. Better, of course, for the church to recover its own calling, which it may be led to do by seeing itself called into judgment by the social movements around it.

In *The Epistles of St. John,*[29] a series of lectures given at the Working Men's College (published in 1857), Maurice defines ethics or morals as having to do with the human character, that is, with "the manners and habits which belong to us *as human beings*" (37; emphasis added). *Christian* ethics or moral theology has to do with this character as it is revealed in Christ—definitively for all, Maurice thinks. This definition of ethics follows from Maurice's conviction that persons become persons most fundamentally through their relationships with other persons. Principles, maxims, and rules arise from, and point persons back to, these essential relations.

Persons, Maurice insists, are formed in, through, and by their relations with other persons. Therefore, the proper standard of ethics is found through examination of the lives of exemplary persons, in the light of which others measure or evaluate their own lives. In order to serve as an example, a human life must be one to which others find an authentic and compelling connection, and in and through which they find connection to the larger universe and its creator. While this connection is necessarily based in personal experience, it may nonetheless be found through the mediation of others' experiences.

Maurice turns to the Epistles of St. John because they are (he says) the Evangelist's account of how the life that he narrated in his Gospel has served as just such a personal revelation in his own life. This reflection on experienced encounters and events can serve as a revelation and education to others (even across the "ugly ditch" of history) because the Evangelist is recounting his intimate connection to *a* concrete, particular life that is also "*the* Life; the life from which all the life that is in us and in the other creatures is derived" and which all persons long and "feel" after as the grounding for their own lives (48). That is, while any human life may have exemplary elements, the life of Christ, because it is a full human life that is also the incarnate manifestation of the actual life of God, is definitively exemplary for other humans. St. John's intimate relationship with Christ formed his own life, and in his Epistles he explores this in a manner that others may find particularly helpful in their own formation.

St. John gives an experiential account of how human persons come to recognize the reality of both sin and redemption. When we glimpse the Light through a disclosive life, we recognize two things simultaneously: most primarily, our desire to be true to ourselves and in fellowship with others; and consequently, a sense of already being false to this newly discovered desire. These two realizations allow us to acknowledge our sinfulness, which is rooted in separation from the Light and from each other, and to ask how it can be overcome. In Christ's Incarnation, we see that the fellowship for which we long has always been a reality, though we have turned away from it. "You are not looked upon [by God] as a sinful race," Maurice proclaimed, "you are looked upon as a race of which Christ the Son of God is the head. . . . We have no right to count ourselves sinners, seeing we are united in Him. We become sinners when we separate from Him."[30] In Christ's Crucifixion, the way to return to that reality is opened to us. "In Him God meets us; in Him we may meet God. In Him God is satisfied with us; in Him we can be satisfied with God" (69).

In *The Epistles of St. John,* the first aspect of ethics is the revelation of God to humankind, and the second is the possibility of human recovery of our true relationship with God. The third aspect deals with how humans actually make such a recovery. For this, Maurice examines the role of commandments. Commandments certainly provide a measure of our actions relative to our authentic human character, thereby serving as both teacher and judge. However, they have a more significant role than merely setting forth rules. They are a way of formation. That is, they provide the avenue both for becoming intimately acquainted with the character of the God in whose life human life is grounded, and for conforming one's own life to that life. This is not only an internal matter: Love (between individuals and God) and righteousness (between and among persons) are inseparable; our communion with each other in personal relations and large social structures is an expression and mirror of our communion with God. In *The Kingdom of Christ,* Maurice describes this communion as "the resemblance of [God's] character, the fulfillment of his commands, . . . the condition where we can behold His countenance and live, in which we can receive from Him all the power to will and to do" (13). Such resemblance arises from "the Sacramental idea of a holy constitution, and of all evil as a departure from it."[31]

Love of one another, Maurice believes, is implied in the constitution of the universe. However, love turns to hate when we separate ourselves from God. The consequence of broken communion with God is broken communion with others, and restoration of human community comes through restored communion with God. God is always initiating this through self-sacrifice: "Heaven comes down and declares itself to us in acts of love" (*The Epistles of John*; see p. 85), which are, by definition, self-giving. The principal one of these is, of course, the self-giving of God through the Incarnation, Crucifixion, and Resurrection of Christ. This reveals the fundamental pattern of the universe and of human life. "Do you not see," Maurice writes, "that there is an order in the world, and that God is upholding it, in spite—yes, in spite of you and your narrowness and pride, and your wish to be a solitary creature?" When we are confronted with these questions, which are addressed to the conscience, we begin to question our own existence and find the answers to our questions in and through that Life which is fully revelatory of both human and divine life: the life of Christ. At that point, we are able to heed the voice of God speaking to the conscience, turn from our prodigal existence, and arise and go to the one who is "the Father of all" (67).[32]

Maurice deals most directly with this internal voice in *The Conscience,* which deals with the subject of casuistry—that is, with the methods by which dilemmas of conscience are to be resolved. When Maurice was appointed Cambridge University's Knightbridge Professor of Casuistry, Moral Theology, and Modern Philosophy, he proposed a three-part series of lectures that would cover the topics associated with the chair.[33] *The Conscience* (1868) and *Social Morality* (1869) deal with casuistry and moral philosophy. Maurice judged the proposed third part, moral theology, to have constantly "intruded itself" into the other two topics, and so he abandoned the plan to present it separately.[34]

Throughout the first book (abridged rather than excerpted here), Maurice discusses various views of the human person that were prevalent in his day. Of particular interest to Maurice are Bishop Butler's *On Human Nature,* which describes the conscience as a faculty that properly reigns supreme in ethical decision-making, and Jeremy Bentham's theory of utility, which claimed that ethical decisions properly rest on calculation of the pleasure and pain likely to ensue. Through evaluating these and other related views of the person as moral being, Maurice brings out his own understanding of human nature.

Each person, Maurice says, develops a conscience as part of consciousness, which is to say, in the context of concrete, person-making relations (as in *The Kingdom of Christ,* discussed above). The conscience is not merely the individual's appropriation of the rules and expectations of the surrounding society in order to maximize pleasure and minimize pain (as Maurice takes Bentham to mean). But neither is it an abstract faculty whose invariant content can be determined speculatively, "some general human nature which is no man's [*sic*] particular nature" (91) (as Butler claimed).

Rather, the conscience is an internal expression of an authority that is ultimately external to all persons. Maurice thinks this is demonstrated by the fact that the conscience/consciousness persists in raising questions about its own response to external factors—including social rules and conventions, and senses of right and wrong. Further, such questions prove that there is in each person a consciousness of good and the possibility of personal goodness that is a reflection of the goodness of the ultimate authority. And the fact that persons resist the tyranny of social conventions and of political rulers demonstrates that this ultimate authority is also one that calls persons into freedom.

But the conscience is neither immutable nor infallible. It is cultivated in and through concrete human relations, and under the sway of various social arrangements. Although the conscience has the capacity to view these influences critically, it does not do so perfectly. (This is one of the points of Maurice's extended discussions of Epictetus and Marcus Aurelius, including the latter's persecution of Christianity.) And the conscience is affected by sin, the attempt to separate or turn away from its ultimate source. Because consciousness recognizes this reality, the conscience longs for Law to provide restraints and guides, but also to provide an external witness of the conscience's grounding source. "The more there is of Conscience in me—the more I confess a higher law—the greater will be my degradation and the sense of it. . . . This self-consciousness attests the grandeur of which the man is capable" (122).

The role of the casuist, then, is to assist the individual in the lifelong project of living in accord with the ultimate order or purpose to which the conscience witnesses. "The Conscience asks for Laws, not rules; for freedom, not chains; for Education, not suppression. It is the Casuist's business to give it aid in seeking for these blessings" (123). In this effort, rules may serve as guides, but no more. They cannot provide the energy or motivation that spur the conscience on. These come, rather, through persons in relation to whom we feel certain obligations that provide motivation—such as members of our family and persons with whom we have regular social and economic interaction. It is also the casuist's role to remind us that our criticisms of others are most properly directed first and foremost toward ourselves; only then can we ethically address the ills of others.

Maurice's focus in *The Conscience* is more primarily on the nature of persons as such, rather than on their social relations. Still, in the course of his discussion he makes observations on various social phenomena throughout history. In Lecture 4, he gives a typology of asceticism, in the course of which he gives his evaluation of the recently achieved abolition of slavery in the United States—a case where conscience rightly brought about a needed change in an otherwise legitimately established and functioning national order. And, as already noted, he cites the example of Marcus Aurelius—in Maurice's estimate a good man who did much good but also much evil. In both instances, Maurice suggests that conscience and society are interlocked, with ambiguous results which demonstrate that neither can be considered supreme.

His considerations of moral theology in these lectures are incomplete, focusing as they do on the person with little consideration of the group. "Begin with Casuistry," he reminds himself; "go on to Moral Philosophy. First make it clear what you mean by a Person; that you will do when you make it clear what you mean by a Conscience; then treat these persons as if they did form real bodies, and tell us out of history, not out of your own fancy, what these bodies are" (128). Thus he turns to his discussion of *Social Morality*.

In this series of lectures, the subject matter is the manners, standards of behavior, habits, apprehensions, and dispositions of members of society, both great and humble—precisely *as* members of society. Social morality, as a field in ethics, also has to do with character; in this case, the character of particular human societies, that is, the ethos that forms manners, habits, and dispositions. This common ethos can be discovered by looking at the three most basic areas of human life: domestic life, national life, and "a more general human Society than those names suggest" (133). Maurice's lectures are then divided into these three parts.

Maurice further divides each part in order to devote a lecture each to what he understands to be the most important relationships or aspects which, taken together, constitute that arena of life. By studying the "facts" of each of these relationships or aspects, the ethos or characteristic proper to each becomes apparent. The "facts" themselves emerge from the examination of multiple and various examples drawn from concrete common life in light of certain principles—original tendencies or fundamental qualities—in order to discover a truth or reality that is already present.

Thus, to arrive at the definition of social morality as ethos, Maurice explicitly draws on literary, philosophical, and historical texts. These sources are deliberately varied and even conflicting because, for Maurice, it is not possible to discover truth or recognize reality until we have seen how diverse experiences and views are related to (but not identical to) our own. Having ranged widely and uncovered certain commonalities, Maurice then sums them up by appealing to the Sermon on the Mount, which shows that

> acts are nothing except as they are fruits of a state, except as they indicate what the man is; that words are nothing except as they express a mind or purpose. Nor need I add that it is a Society—a Human Society—in which the preacher of that Sermon assumes that this *ēthos* is to be exhibited. (138)

The beginning point of social morality is found in family life. "At my birth I am already in a Society. I am related, at all events, to a father and mother. This relation is the primary fact of my existence. I can contemplate no other facts apart from it" (139). Still, relationality is not the only truth about human beings; they are also persons in their own right: "But since my brother is a being in himself, and not only a brother, since every father is a being in himself, and not only a father,—the actual relation, the living relation, drives us to seek for an Absolute, which lies beyond and behind the Relation."[35] The family is the beginning of all social harmonies and all social contradictions. Starting here will show how persons become persons through relationships, and also how and why they seek to be separate from these fundamental relations.

Family life exemplifies certain fundamental characteristics of social morality: from the relationship between parents and children come the characteristics of authority and obedience (Lecture 2; below, 139ff.); from the relationship between husbands and wives, the ethos of trust (Lecture 3); from that of brothers and sisters, consanguinity and fraternity (Lecture 4); from that of masters and servants, reciprocal reverence (Lecture 5). But each of these also becomes distorted in these same relationships: authority becomes tyranny, trust becomes domination, fraternity becomes competition. The way to restoration of the fundamental characteristics is not through abolishing the relationships, but by returning to the principle that underlies every *ēthos*—to which Maurice will come in Lecture 20 (IV.5). The second lecture, on Parents and Children (below, 139ff.), illustrates Maurice's development of this type of discussion.

National life, like family life, has certain enduring relationships and structures: persons live as neighbors (Lecture 7) under Law (Lecture 8; below, 149ff.) and Government (Lecture 10), joined by language (Lecture 9) and at times assailed by External Threat (Lecture 11). Certain characteristics are found in these structures and relationships, which are discussed or hinted at in the lecture on Law included in this volume. Through living in discrete societies (civilizations or nations), we recognize ourselves as bound together by certain obligations that set the line between right and wrong and so provide basic levels of care. Law—the ordering of these obligations—also makes us conscious of that in ourselves which runs against our own sense of obligation. Law evokes our obedience because we know it as just—fair to both ourselves and our neighbors—but we also find ourselves under its judgment insofar as we are prone to covetousness and selfishness. Law, thus, is linked with the other characteristics of national life: regard of neighbor, loyalty, mutual understanding, and group identity and cohesion.

Even as family life moves out of itself into national life, so national life pushes toward a more general human society that will encompass all of humanity and show human beings to be a unified "kind." Part III of *Social Morality*, "Universal Morality," addresses this area. By considering human impulses for a universal empire together with desires for a universal family, Maurice uncovers the ethos of charity, or universal fellowship, for which both of these social structures strive. Under Empire, however, universal fellowship comes to mean loss of family and national (or ethnic) grounding (Lecture 13). These valuable, person-making relations reach their fulfillment through a universal fellowship that resembles a universal family (Lecture 14). Historically, this universal fellowship first appears after the capital of the supposedly universal empire, Rome, is destroyed. The universal fellowship is headed by a King who is also a Father, one in whom are summed up all the various characteristics that constitute human life. Thus in this universal fellowship all the disparate elements of human life and morality are unified, showing the ethos of "Brotherhood for men as men" (158).

Modern conceptions of humanity (Lecture 19; below 157ff.) seek in various ways to recover the sense of humanity as a "kind" that was present in early Christianity but has since become clouded, fragmented, and distorted. Among modern thinkers, Maurice finds the work of Auguste Comte the most intriguing. Comte, he thinks, believes that whatever is good among humans is not the exception but the rule. He also claims "the human characteristic, that which all are to strive for because it is human, to be not selfishness but love; only when each man seeks not his own interest, but the interest of the whole society, is he truly human" (163). Modern philosophies are at their most helpful when they bring this truth to the fore once again.

But they do so, Maurice claims, by presenting a picture of a humanity without a head. This leaves morality without the ground it seeks, where all the various characteristics of human life are brought together. Today, as at the fall of Rome, what persons long and strive for is membership in a universal family, where "indeed there is a Father in Heaven who adopts men of all nations and kindreds into His Family, and teaches them what are their places in it" (167). A "Fatherly Will is at the root of Humanity and upholds the Universe" (168). This truth still holds today, despite the brutalities of Christianity itself, which arise not from this verity, but from imperfect and confused human apprehension of it.

Maurice then uses the rest of Lecture 20 (below, 167ff.) to show how Christianity meets the needs and desires of modern humanity, even as it met the needs and desires of the humanity of the first century of the Common Era. He uses the Sermon on the Mount to show how the counsels of Christianity are not only applicable to, but possible for, all. God gives us not only commandments, but a living example of what it means to be perfect as God is perfect, giving bread rather than stones to those who ask to be fed. The manner of God's provision of this example—the self-giving of the Father through a perfectly obedient Son—shows that the cardinal virtue upon which all others hinge is self-giving love, what Maurice calls sacrifice. "Sacrifice leads us again to the original principle of the Discourse—'Be like your Father in Heaven.' Men are only bidden to exhibit this grand principle of morality in their acts, they are only able to exhibit it, because He has given the example of it" (180). In his concluding lecture (Lecture 29), Maurice shows how Christian worship enacts this sacrifice, and so contains principles that undergird universal morality.

In joining conscience/consciousness and the existence provided by social structures, Maurice indicates that it is not possible to engage in moral philosophy or theology without considering self-awareness *and* social arrangements, inner *and* outer worlds, persons as individuals *and* as constitutive members of groups. The two phenomena, conscience/consciousness and social existence, together witness to an ultimate order and purpose beyond either the human person or social structures; both draw their own order and purpose from this ultimate and so reflect it.

> All the intricate interrelations of love in the Godhead, of the Father's love of men and of Christ's, of the human and divine natures of the Son, of the Creating and Redeeming Word, of man's love of neighbor in God and of God in the neighbor, or family, nation, and church, have their place. But the center is Christ.[36]

The Kingdom of Christ reconciles these relations to itself. Therefore, studying conscience/consciousness and social morality together gives a full picture of the human person as such, and as related to God.

This volume concludes with shorter selections from three of Maurice's other works. The first of these, *Dialogues between a Clergyman and a Layman on Family Worship* (1862), deals with the relation between Christianity and everyday life in the modern world. In Dialogue 4 (below, 181ff.), Maurice discusses the significance of baptism in a time of acute awareness of religious and cultural pluralism. Maurice had dealt with dawning Victorian awareness of world religions in a series of popular lectures earlier in his career (his 1847 Boyle Lectures, *The Religions of the World and Their Relations to Christianity*). Now he deals with the specific problem of whether the fact of baptism means that Christians are in some sense better than those who are not baptized in the name of the Trinity. Baptism, Maurice claims, "ought continually to keep the truth of my own state in my remembrance" (182). As the Catechism says, each baptized person is "a member of Christ, a child of God, an inheritor of the kingdom of heaven." Baptism is a sign that the baptized are God's witnesses. And the content of the witness is that all good that is done is done by the work of the Holy Spirit, whether such good is done by the baptized or not. This, Maurice notes, should spur moral vigilance, rather than prompting feelings of moral or spiritual superiority. "The blessing of Baptism is that it refers all to His will and choice, nothing whatever to our judgment. If I set up my judgment or presume to measure His acts by it, I contradict the witness of my baptism. It is no longer the sign of His purpose; it is merely the badge of my profession" (184).

Dialogue 11 (below, 187ff.) relates the Lord's Prayer to the particular circumstances facing Christians in urban Victorian England, where conflicts of belief and widespread social problems are seen by many to be driving ordinary Christians away from relying on the mysteries of their faith. Maurice takes a different tack. It is, he says, when the Lord's Prayer is *not* the standard for "the weekday work of the world" that we give in to appearances and worldly standards (191). Further, it is when we pass from praying from "thy kingdom come" to the reading of the daily newspaper that we realize that there is "no preparation for that reading which will avail us except that prayer, as I know no commentary on that prayer so wonderful and so awful as that reading" (192).[37]

Maurice then goes on to consider the individual petitions of the Lord's Prayer, suggesting that if "Each petition ought to be realized in its own power and significance," then much will change within individuals, among individuals, and in human social, economic, and political arrangements (189). The prayer for daily bread, for example, reminds the well-off that what they need is sufficiency, not excess. When this petition is prayerfully considered in conjunction with reading the daily newspaper, "I am driven to pray, *Father, give us all day by day our daily bread*" (193).

By the time he wrote *Dialogues on Family Worship,* Maurice had long been actively involved in addressing the social, economic, educational, and religious disparities between the classes in Victorian England. His "Dialogue between Somebody (a Person of Respectability) and Nobody (the Writer)" was the first of the series Tracts on Christian Socialism (published in 1850) and gives Maurice's most succinct discussion of what he means by Christian Socialism. The principle of socialism, and of Christianity, is cooperation rather than competition. "Any one who recognises the principle of co-operation as a stronger and truer principle than that of competition, has a right to the honour or the disgrace of being called a Socialist" (197).

In this brief dialogue, Maurice describes how the socialism of the Christian Socialists departs from that of Owen, Fourier, and Blanc. The most important difference is that Christian Socialism finds Christianity to be the root and ground of the principle of cooperation. Other modern socialists have either rejected Christianity or set it aside because it has been presented as the foundational warrant by those who see competition as the rule of human existence. This is possible only because Christianity has become "mingled with that maxim of selfish rivalry which is its deadly opponent. So the two have blended themselves together in strange disorder. So men have identified the one with the other" (201). However, the true basis of Christianity, says Maurice, is not "a great strife of individual competitors," but a divine family becoming a divine nation that is opening into a divine universal society (202).

Both socialists and Christians would do well to reassess. As matters stand at mid-century, socialists have yet to find "a power which is adequate to resist the power of competition" (200). This power is and always has been available in Christianity. Christians, on the other hand, have allowed their religion to devolve from a fellowship with a divine constitution into "a scheme or method for obtaining selfish prizes which men are to compete for, just as they do for the things of earth" (201). Christians tend, then, to "love the poor as poor; as means, that is to say, of calling forth and exhibiting the virtues, the self-sacrifice, the saintship of the rich," when they should be living in fellowship with them as actual human beings (203–204).

By reclaiming Christianity's identity, Christians can join with socialists to bring to light the foundational principle of cooperation, which, Maurice claims, is "the only possible condition of society" (202). Once it is recognized that Christian Socialism seeks not to make society anew, but to return it to its original ground, its goals are clear: to raise the poor to the status of full humanity, and to "deal with the commonplace details of human misery, to inquire . . . how you and I may buy our coats without sinning against God, and abetting the destruction of our fellow-creatures" (206).

The Tracts and other Christian Socialist publications were intended to interpret the group's activities in ways that would appeal to ordinary people and inspire them to develop "habitual acts of deliberation and reflection upon our relations to our brethren [that] may avert or relieve wretchedness, which grand charities, magnificent subscription-lists leave untouched or perhaps aggravate" (206). However, the Tracts, the earlier series Politics for the People, and other publication ventures were short-lived and gave few signs of reaching their intended audience. The cooperative producers' associations that Maurice and his colleagues formed continued, and there were ten still in existence in 1854. However, the overarching organizational group ceased meeting in 1855 and was supplanted by the Working Men's College, where Maurice gave the series of lectures published as The Epistles of St. John.

The final selection in this volume, a sermon titled "Hatred Necessary to Love," makes a crucial distinction between tolerance and the animosity appropriate to the Christian life. Maurice preached this sermon on the Fifth Sunday in Lent, 1859, as a general election approached, and his concluding exhortations denounce the fraudulent claims and promises all too typical of election campaigns.

Taking as his text a verse from Psalm 139, Maurice contends that David (the putative author) quite properly hated the "principalities of spiritual wickedness" that are manifested as "untruth and unrighteousness" in the actions of concrete individuals and institutions. What David hated in the specific groups he opposed was precisely their untruth and unrighteousness, characteristics he also recognized in himself—and hated there as well. "The more sure he was that God is, and that He is the Lord of man, and that He seeks to establish righteousness and truth in the earth, the more vehemently and savagely he abhorred whatever he saw which denied God and aimed at keeping the earth an abode of deceit and wrong" (209). Christians tend to claim that they love all persons because Christ commands them to. But, Maurice suspects, the actual disposition at work is tolerance born of resignation to and familiarity with wickedness, both of which are viewed as inevitable.

At the same time that Christians tolerate wickedness, they also cherish hate against those who differ from themselves on grounds less than ultimate. This inappropriate hatred nurtures "pride and malice or cruelty" within individuals, "scandals and abominations in the nation," and "fierce party-spirit [and] lying, in the Church" (210). Maurice contends that the latter improper hatred will be overcome only as Christians increasingly recognize the nature and reality of God. "The acknowledgment of a God who beareth all things, hopeth all things, endureth all things,—who has been long-suffering with all His creatures and long-suffering with us,—will make us tremble to deal harshly with the struggles and doubts—how much more with the convictions—of our fellow-beings" (210–211).

SUMMARY OF MAURICE'S MORAL THEOLOGY

The preceding discussion of the selections included in this volume can yield a summary of Maurice's moral theology as a relational ethics that focuses on the development of character in both individuals and social groups. The theological basis of this moral theology is in Maurice's doctrine of God. God is One, perfect Charity. At the same time, God is Trinity, inherently interrelated, dynamic, and diverse, and this relationality and diversity are likewise an inherent and good part of historical existence. By definition, love is self-giving, self-communicative, reciprocal, and other-directed—in Maurice's terms, sacrificial. Sacrifice, can, therefore, be taken to be the ground of all truth and goodness, and to find correspondence in that in which it issues—that is, in creation. Humanity in all its diversity is created in the image of this dynamic relational love.

As God is One, so Truth is one. But in history, Truth is to be found only through examination of the partial truths expressed in and through multiple, differing perspectives. Thus all positions are to be appreciated and their proponents cherished, even while different and differing positions must be examined critically. Such examination leads to the reconciliation of opposites at a level deeper than appearances because, through inquiry into opposites, a common underlying ground can be discerned.

As God is relational while One, so unity or communion with that One is the source, end, and foundation of historical existence; and such unity is found in and through actual relationships. Persons are inherently relational, born into families and seeking their individuality and their larger spheres of relationship from that basis. Finally, all relationships drive toward a universal society of harmony and order that is also integrally and evidently connected to the One who is the source of all.

This universal society ought to have the same character as the one who is its source and goal: the self-giving love that Maurice calls sacrifice. Insofar as historical existence reflects this love, it participates in the Kingdom of Christ. The church is intended by God to be the sign of this Kingdom, the institution through which the Truth of the divine is most fully revealed and through which persons are brought into communion with God and community with each other. However, through sectarianism, party strife, and other manifestations of faithlessness, the church allows itself to devolve into a "world"—a structure that seeks to be separate from God and to guide itself by its own lights instead of being guided by the Divine Light. When this happens, Truth manifests itself elsewhere, in movements and ideas in the "secular" world. This phenomenon puts the church under present judgment, and draws attention to the church's historically evident tendencies to defensiveness, retrenchment, and division. Nevertheless, Maurice maintains, the church has a specific calling, and the challenges it faces historically call the church to reclaim its identity and heritage.

The church's calling is to be both manifestation of and witness to communion between creation and God, the communion for which humanity has been created. In the Incarnation, that Creator is fully manifest also as Deliverer. And in the Incarnation, the relation of humanity to divinity is both restored and vindicated from its anomalous separation from God through sin. Humankind is in constant union with the complete self-expression of that love, the Christ, who reveals the loving character of God *and* the true constitution of humanity as a race that is rightly related to God in trust.

Maurice's moral theology follows consistently from these fundamental theological convictions. Although fellowship or communion between God and humanity has been damaged, it may be restored through humanity's ordering of common and individual life in accord with the God-given "facts" of historical existence: the birth of all persons into families, their becoming both individuals and members of societies, and their gradual incorporation into the universal society of which the church is the truest form. While the particularities of these sorts of relations vary according to individual and collective character, historical diversity is rooted and grounded in God's own unity, and the moral life seeks to move toward this unity through the formation and cultivation of human character that is the image of the divine character. Character is expressed, of course, through structures and individual dispositions and behaviors, but underlies these. Rules, maxims, and principles then are useful only insofar as they point back to character.

Because persons are formed relationally, their best moral character is formed in and through relations with exemplary persons, the most important one of whom is Christ (whom Maurice often calls our "Elder Brother"). Relationship with Christ illumines all other relations and allows us to confront our sinfulness, embrace our righteousness, and "arise and go to the Father," that is, to reclaim the communion with God in and for which we were created.

This reclaiming is both an internal and an external process. Internal development or formation is facilitated by the conscience, the internal voice connected to external authority, both proximate and ultimate. Because the conscience is connected to proximate external authority—social structures and conventions—it can be led astray. But such prodigality cannot break the connection to the ultimate authority, God, who always wills to be connected to creation. Rather, through its resistance to injustice and unrighteousness in society, the conscience witnesses to the enduring presence and power of God.

Formation toward the divinely intended character is not, for Maurice, a process that involves individuals and their personal lives only. The historically variable structures of human social existence are divinely endowed with particular characters as well. Examining larger structures and relations—be they familial (personal) or national (social)—yields a picture of humanity as a "kind" or species, and gives some hints and clues as to how humanity ought to be related to God. What is evident in rich variety at every stage of history, and in the modern world, is the human longing for a universal harmonious communion (in contemporary terms, community) in which all persons are related as brothers and sisters under a single headship. While this headship can accurately be described in terms of sovereignty, Maurice greatly prefers familial metaphors, because they better convey the intimacy, self-giving, and love that are characteristic of the divine life and the relationship of God to creation.

The means of fulfillment of the human desire for communion or unity with others can be expressed as a principle: sacrifice understood as self-giving love. Such love finds the well-being of the individual unbreakably connected with the well-being of others, not only those one knows personally, but also those to whom one is connected by social, economic, and political structures. In actuality, however, historical existence is characterized not by unity, but by the selfishness and competition that are its perversion. Seeking out and participating in modes of cooperation in every aspect of life is necessary for persons and groups to overcome the power of competition and move toward actual unity in the structures of everyday life.

Self-giving love, embodied in social structures of cooperation as well as in the ordering of one's personal life, requires and fosters certain dispositions: abhorrence of untruth and unrighteousness coupled with self-criticism and true charity toward others, especially in times of conflict, controversy, and apparent social fragmentation.

> To detect the right meaning, the sound faith, the divine inspiration which is latent under confused, rough angry words, directed against ourselves,—even against principles which are dearer to us than ourselves,—will be a duty which we learn at the Cross,—a faculty which only Christ can impart to us. We shall exercise it just because we believe Truth to be all-important, falsehood accursed; just because we love the one and hate the other. (211)

Maurice's theological ethics remains suggestive today, although his views and recommendations cannot be adopted either completely or uncritically. As was clear to some of Maurice's contemporaries, his grounding of all things in a foundational order that is always making itself manifest combines with his emphasis on unity and harmony to inhibit recognition of the extent to which human arrangements—and so both human limitation and human sin—contribute to our characters, our community with each other, and our understanding of our communion with God. With these fundamental presuppositions, it is difficult to see how the conversion of individuals and the transformation of culture for which one longs—as Maurice undoubtedly did—can be brought about through other than essentially educational endeavors.

Still, Maurice gives us "hints" that have been, and continue to be, worth heeding. As has often been noted, his work points out the wisdom of constant openness to the possibility that those of differing experience, belief, and life situation have attained indispensable insight into human life and purpose. The appropriate responses to difference, then, are first and foremost appreciation and dialogue, the goal of which is not merely understanding but also the deepening of that communion with God and common life with each other.

Christians may ground such openness in the conviction that all creatures are created by one God. On this ground, difference can be seen not as fragmentation, but as the manifestation of the rich variety of creation itself. Human particularity can be treasured without sacrificing the desire for harmony. Recognizing all as springing from and grounded in the divine unity allows and encourages what Maurice called "digging" for the ground upon which all stand, even while particularities remain, in both one's own and others' life and community.

Such an orientation toward difference is of inestimable importance in contexts of pluralism such as contemporary Christians face globally, ecumenically, and within our own particular churches or religious communities. In our time and contexts as in Maurice's, the phenomena of pluralism can prompt defensiveness, despair, and even domination. But they need not. "Every [one] is in Christ," Maurice wrote. That is, all persons are in constant relationship with a God whose basic character is love. And so all are related to each other. It remains for those who orient their lives around this conviction to witness to it with a hope that is both informed and active.

Without the encouragement of a number of people, and their interest in bringing some of Maurice's work back into print and discussion, this volume would not have come into being. I am particularly grateful to Timothy F. Sedgwick for suggesting the inclusion of Maurice in the Library of Theological Ethics and for urging me to edit the volume. The selection of material was made after consultation with a number of Maurice scholars, including James M. Gustafson, Carter Heyward, Frank M. McClain, and Timothy F. Sedgwick, and to them I am also grateful. (Any idiosyncracies evidenced by the final choice are mine alone, however.) I have also been encouraged by the ongoing conversation about Maurice I share with my colleague William H. Petersen and with many of my students at Colgate-Rochester Divinity School/Bexley Hall/Crozer Theological Seminary (to whom this volume is dedicated).

Collecting copies of Maurice's works has been a challenge, made easier by Newland Smith (Garrett-Seabury Union Library), David Siegenthaler (Weston-Episcopal Divinity School Library), and Ken Sawyer (Jesuit-Kraus-McCormick Library). Susan Block patiently photocopied material at the Library of Congress. Ralph A. Pugh graciously provided me with a copy of his recent excellent doctoral dissertation. And Frank M. McClain lent me his photocopies and microfilms of unpublished Maurice correspondence and other material housed in libraries in England.

Most especially, thanks go to Linda Sniedze of the Ambrose Swayze Library of the Divinity School in Rochester, New York, for her endless patience, good humor, and imagination in pursuing my numerous interlibrary loan requests while also handling a very busy circulation department.

It has been estimated that Maurice published more than ten thousand pages. This volume obviously represents only a very small portion of that corpus. It is my hope that this book will stimulate readers to explore those remaining pages.

NOTES

1. Frederick Maurice, ed., *The Life of Frederick Denison Maurice, chiefly told in his own letters* (London: Macmillan and Co., 1884), 1:240.
2. The following biographical sketch draws significantly on William H. Petersen's excellent short biography and classification of Maurice's writings ("Frederick Denison

Maurice as Historian: An Analysis of the Character of Maurice's Unsystematic Theology, Attempting to Disclose a Method Capable of Reconciling Secular and Ecclesiastical Historiography" [Ph.D. diss., Graduate Theological Union, 1976]). Frederick Maurice's *The Life of Frederick Denison Maurice* is indispensable to understanding the man's theology as well as his life. On the crises in Victorian culture and religion, see, for example, Walter E. Houghton, *The Victorian Frame of Mind, 1830–1870* (New Haven, Conn.: Yale University Press, 1957); and Charles D. Cashdollar, *The Transformation of Theology, 1830–1890: Positivism and Protestant Thought in Britain and America* (Princeton, N.J.: Princeton University Press, 1989).

3. See Maurice's two autobiographical letters, written to his biographer son in 1866, published in *Life*, 1:12–21.

4. David Young, *F. D. Maurice and Unitarianism* (Oxford: Clarendon Press, 1992), 92.

5. See Frank M. McClain, *Maurice: Man and Moralist* (London: SPCK, 1972), for a discussion of Stephenson's ideas and influence.

6. *Life*, 1:236.

7. Ibid., 1:155; italics in the original. Maurice wrote this letter to his Calvinist mother in response to her conviction that she might not be among the elect. Maurice's language not surprisingly reflects the androcentric use of masculine pronouns; unless otherwise noted, I have maintained his original language throughout.

8. The literature on the Christian Socialists of the 1840s and 1850s is voluminous. The major published works are Charles Raven's *Christian Socialism, 1848–1854* (London: Macmillan and Co., 1920), and Torben Christensen's *Origin and History of Christian Socialism, 1848–54* (Aarhus: Universitetsforlaget, 1962). Christensen's finally negative assessment of Maurice is challenged and corrected in Ralph A. Pugh's "The Constitutive Principles of Early Victorian Christian Socialism, 1848–1854" (Ph.D. diss., University of Chicago, 1994).

9. *Life*, 2:132.

10. Ms. letter, 13 September 1852, Cambridge University Library ADD 7348, art. 17, no. 3. I am grateful to Frank McClain for loaning me his microfilm copy of this letter.

11. *Life*, 2:136–37.

12. This essay was substantially revised for the second edition of *Theological Essays* (1854), and the passages that excited the controversy were revised or removed.

13. The two criticisms of Maurice's views on eternal life that are best known today are Robert S. Candlish's "On Maurice's *Theological Essays*," in *Exeter Hall Lectures, 1853–54* (London: James Nisbet and Co., 1854), and James H. Rigg's *Modern Anglican Theology: Chapters on Coleridge, Hare, Maurice, Kingsley, and Jowett, and on the Doctrine of Sacrifice and Atonement* (London: Alexander, Heylin, 1857). At the time, Maurice was also roundly and continuously attacked in the Evangelical press, in terms much less measured than those used by Candlish and Rigg.

14. *The Doctrine of Sacrifice Deduced from the Scriptures: A Series of Sermons* (London: Macmillan and Co., 1854), 194.

15. *The word "Eternal" and the Punishment of the Wicked: A Letter to the Rev. Dr. Jelf* (London: Macmillan and Co., 1853).

16. Quoted in William J. Wolf, "Frederick Denison Maurice," in *The Spirit of Anglicanism*, ed. William J. Wolf (Wilton, Conn.: Morehouse-Barlow, 1979), 66.

17. Ms. letter, 13 September 1852.

18. Maurice writes, "When a man knows that he has a righteous Lord and Judge, who does not plead His omnipotence and His right to punish, but who debates the case with

him, who shows him his truth and his error, the sense of Infinite Wisdom, sustaining and carrying out Infinite Love, abases him rapidly. . . . A feeling of infinite shame grows out of the feeling of undoubting trust. The child sinks in nothingness at its Father's feet, just when He is about to take it to His arms" (*Theological Essays* [London: James Clarke and Co., 1957], 59).

19. *Life,* 2:641.

20. *The Epistles of St. John: A Series of Lectures on Christian Ethics* (Cambridge: Macmillan and Co., 1857), 9.

21. Ibid., 13.

22. Ibid., 14.

23. *The Doctrine of Sacrifice,* xli.

24. *The Kingdom of Christ; or Hints on the Principles, Ordinances, and Constitution of the Catholic Church in Letters to a Member of the Society of Friends,* 3 vols. (London: Darton and Clark, 1838), 1:75. See also "Hatred Necessary to Love" (p. 207 in this volume).

25. On Maurice's retrieval of the coincidence of opposites, see David Newsome, *Two Classes of Men: Platonism and English Romantic Thought* (London: J. Murray, 1984), especially chapter 3.

26. F. D. Maurice, *The Lord's Prayer* (London: J. W. Parker, 1848), 41f. and 44.

27. See H. Richard Niebuhr's *Christ and Culture,* where Maurice's work provides the principal exemplar of the type "Christ transforming culture." As Niebuhr indicates, the central emphases of this type spring from the Gospel of John, with its insight that "the Christ who comes into the world comes into his own" and "exercises his kingship" directly, not through intermediaries (H. Richard Niebuhr, *Christ and Culture* [New York: Harper & Brothers, 1951], 220). Others whom Niebuhr places in this type include Augustine (in some interpretations), Wesley, and Jonathan Edwards; this is also Niebuhr's own preference.

28. *Theological Essays,* 276–77.

29. Numbers in parentheses refer to page numbers in this volume.

30. *The Epistles of St. John,* 131.

31. *The Kingdom of Christ* (1838), 1:295–96.

32. Maurice's reference to the parable of the Prodigal Son is typical of his account of human coming to consciousness of relationship with God: it recurs in various forms in many of his works.

33. *Casuistry, Moral Philosophy, and Moral Theology: An Inaugural Lecture* (London: Macmillan and Co., 1866).

34. *Social Morality: Twenty-One Lectures Delivered in the University of Cambridge* (London: Macmillan and Co., 1869), xii.

35. *What is Revelation?* (Cambridge: Macmillan and Co., 1859), 276.

36. Niebuhr, *Christ and Culture,* 221.

37. In 1848, Maurice was preaching a series on the Lord's Prayer at the Chapel at Lincoln's Inn as revolution was brewing across the continent of Europe. He reached the petition "Thy Kingdom come" less than a week after revolution broke out in France.

CHAPTER 1

The Kingdom of Christ; or Hints on the Principles, Ordinances, and Constitution of the Catholic Church

LETTER TO A MEMBER OF THE SOCIETY OF FRIENDS (1) (1838)*

My Dear Friend,

If the books and pamphlets which you so kindly forwarded to me had been all written by members of your Society, I should not have offered a word of comment upon the subjects discussed in them. As a private Christian, and as a student of ecclesiastical history, I must have been deeply interested in the controversy; but I should have feared to take part in it, lest I might excite your alarm, and render your own inquiries less manly and less effectual.

But I find that I should not be the first intruder. . . . I do not approve of the method which these writers have adopted in addressing you. I dislike it from taste, from experience, from principle. To inspire men with contempt or indifference for those whom they have been taught from their infancy to admire and love—from the accounts of whose deeds and whose sufferings they have acquired their first perceptions of moral courage, and beauty and dignity of character,—from whose teaching they have probably first learnt to love their brethren, and revere the operations of their own spirits,—seems to me at all times a most heartless proceeding. I know the phrases that are used to defend it. I know what they say about the paramount worth and preciousness of truth. In my heart of hearts I own that preciousness, and hope that I may die rather than part with the sense of it. But I believe a tender and reverent spirit is inseparable from the love of truth. I never saw the last permanently strong where the other was wanting; and

*From *The Kingdom of Christ; or Hints on the Principles, Ordinances, and Constitution of the Catholic Church in Letters to a Member of the Society of Friends,* 1st ed. (London: Darton and Clark, Holborn Hill, 1838), Letter no. 1, 1:1–61 (abridged).

I believe that anything which tends to weaken either, weakens both of them. I do not believe that those of your Friends, who are tempted by their own hearts, or the sneers of others, to think scornfully of their ancestors, will be half so zealous and affectionate in their determination to risk everything for the truth's sake, as those who retain a fond admiration for their beauties, and are willing to throw a veil over their deformities. I cannot forget that Ham was cursed though Noah was drunk. I cannot forget what his curse was;—the most affronting to the proud spirit of independence which dictated his crime—"A servant of servants shall he be." And a servant of servants—the slave of every fanatic, who is himself the slave of his own delusions—do those high-minded persons most generally become, who, after his example, commence their career of free inquiry with detecting and exposing the absurdities of their earthly or spiritual fathers.

A moral instinct would lead me to the conclusion; all the experiments that I have seen or heard of abundantly confirm it.

I have known persons, brought up in your Society, . . . to join our church. I saw no reason to question their sincerity or their zeal. But I observed that their views were always more negative than positive; that they were led to embrace a doctrine, not so much because they believed that to be true, as because they perceived its opposite to be false; that they could perceive what was inconsistent much more quickly than they could recognize what was orderly; that their minds were unquiet, unharmonious, and ricketty. In a few years our proselytes departed, gone, as we ought to have expected beforehand, to join or establish some newer sect, denouncing us now, as they have denounced you before; destined shortly to become as discontented with their present notions as with either. I say it in sorrow, not in bitterness; in reproach to *us* for seeking converts, by exciting unhallowed feelings, not that I dare to pass uncharitable judgment upon them. There are instances equally recent and better known, of some, high in cultivation, and, as I am well assured, in feeling and in honesty, who had fled to us, from what most would consider, a much worse faith than yours,—a faith which almost every Dissenter, Quaker, and Churchman thinks himself at liberty to scorn and satirize. We raised a shout when they joined us; we listened with delight while they laid bare the gross abominations of the body from which they had escaped; we thought it a mighty compliment to our faith, that such sagacious champions should adopt it; we thought we had a security for the permanence of their convictions, which scarcely any other circumstances could have afforded us. Time showed what sage prophets we were. These learned and able Neophytes were as little constant as those ardent ones; they soon left us, proclaiming to the world as the reason of their departure, the grand discovery, so often made before, (never, perhaps, since the days of the Athenian sophists announced with equal boldness), that that only is true which seems so to each man. Nothing can abate the grief which we feel on their own account for their change. To us they have made abundant compensation for our loss, by leaving us the lesson, never to be conned over or prized too much, that the mind which is continually dwelling on the falsehood of any system, even though it do not in the least exaggerate the amount or evil of that falsehood, contracts an incapacity for welcoming or perceiving truth, in that or any other system.

On these grounds, if on no other, I should have disapproved of the method which several churchmen and dissenters have taken in their recent addresses to you. All seem to make it their business to undermine your respect for your founders, and your belief in the *positive* principles which they taught. I say positive principles, for the [critics] will be ready to exclaim "we agree with George Fox and his friends most entirely, in their denunciations of your church, though their language may seem to us occasionally too uncourteous, and though we may believe that they pushed their objections too far, when they attacked all pecuniary provision for the support of ministers." These were their *negative* doctrines; in these I am perfectly aware that they may find admirers and supporters in every vestry-room and tavern. But I need not inform *you,* that your early Friends rested their opinions on these subjects on certain principles relating to the heart and spirit of man. . . .

Now here is the point on which I join issue with them. I say these principles were not false and heretical, and inconsistent with Christianity. A number of phrases and notions may have been appended to these principles, of which I utterly disapprove. In support of these principles, your friends may have declared themselves at war with everybody, and everybody at war with them. With this conviction on their minds, they may have denounced opinions as inconsistent with theirs, to which I most inwardly and heartily subscribe. They may have used language respecting the persons who maintained these opinions, which I think most extravagant and unreasonable; and a sense of the necessary connection between their doctrines and their denunciations, will have become stronger in their minds in proportion as their opponents identified the two together, and considered themselves as much bound to deny what the Friends asserted, as to assert what they denied. But through all this confusion, I perceive certain great truths maintained by these Friends, with a power and vigour which have scarcely been surpassed, and for the sake of which, I, for my part, can well forgive all the hard language used by them against institutions that I believe to be not only of incalculable benefit, but of divine appointment. Nor do I take any credit for this forgiveness. Every right-minded man must feel that one, who, from a sound and honest heart, directing a somewhat less sound understanding, curses him or that which he supposes to be him, is at all times to be loved rather than disliked. In such days as these, he will find it not only very pleasant, but very useful to compare such men with those who rave at him on no principle at all, or with those, still more odious, who, with a simpering face and civil compliments, are seeking to undermine him, because he is a witness for principles which they hate.

But this is not all. I maintain, that those truths which your early Friends asserted, lie at the foundation of the institutions which I love. In recognising those truths, I believe that I am upholding those institutions, and showing on what an immoveable basis they rest. It is nothing to me that Fox and Penn did not perceive this; it is nothing to me, that those who fought for these institutions against them, did not perceive it. Such contradictions and perplexities are not new. All history—ecclesiastical history most especially—is full of them. One set of men is busy in maintaining certain great and permanent bulwarks for truth, which, if they were taken away, the truth would be left without power, and without a witness. This is their task; they do not perceive exactly what they are defending, or why they are defending it. They often, therefore, fight ignorantly, blindly, passionately; but they do God's work, and future generations have reason to bless them.

On the other hand, it is given to some to perceive, with great power the truth, or at least a portion of it, which is the secret foundation of those institutions, which is the living principle embodied and expressed in them. Such men often conceive a furious rage against the institutions themselves, as if it was they which kept the truth from manifesting itself to men—as if there were no way to exhibit it but to tear them away. For a long while this strife continues; one party doggedly upholding forms, the other vehemently asserting the Spirit independent of these forms. . . .

What if all outward witness should disappear from the world, just at the moment that the inward witness is most weak and ready to die? You have at once the Millennium of infidelity, that to which every man who wishes for the misery of his species—who wishes to see men changed into brutes—is looking forward with prophetic hope and exultation.

You see it must be so. If you look merely to us, you may exclaim with good reason,—"See the hour is approaching, which our great men told us of, when forms shall be universally contemned and trampled under foot." But if you turn your eyes inward, have you not cause to exclaim,—"The hour is coming, the dreadful hour, which those Friends would have contemplated as the Egyptian night of the world, when all apprehension of a spiritual principle is perishing out of the hearts even of us, its appointed witnesses." What if these two facts, apparently so contradictory, should really be the joint indication of our state, and of the will of God concerning us? What if they should be saying to those churchmen who are willing to cast away forms,—"You are despising forms now, because you never knew the principle and the meaning of these forms; because you adopted them merely as traditionary heirlooms; because you did not own that there was a spirit and life in them." What if they are saying to the Quakers,—"You have been fighting all along against that which was the standing witness, the divine scheme for asserting those spiritual truths, and sustaining that spiritual life, of which you thought that your own hearts were the safe depositaries;—now, if you would not see everything that you have accounted most precious wither before your eyes, you must turn to these forms for the preservation of them."

I hope I have explained sufficiently how entirely my views respecting your present position, differ from those of the churchmen and dissenters who have hitherto addressed you. Instead of wishing to dispossess you of your patriarchal faith, I lament to see that that faith is not stronger and deeper. Instead of thinking you too firmly rooted in the principles which George Fox promulgated, I would, if I could, establish you more thoroughly in them. Instead of availing myself of the dissatisfaction which I see prevailing amongst certain members of your body respecting these doctrines, and saying,—"See how nobly we support those other doctrines, to which you suppose they are opposed,"—I would do my utmost to persuade these persons, that the truths which they are just beginning to perceive, and are embracing with such a first-love ardour, are not inconsistent with the views which they are inclined to abandon, but can only be held soundly and firmly when associated with them. I wish to make each one of your parties perceive, that it has hold of a principle, which it must not for all the world abandon; and I wish them to show you by what means only you can uphold each of these principles without mutilation, with real power, and in harmony with the rest. In plain words, I wish not to unquaker you in order to make you churchmen, but to teach you how to be thorough Quakers, that you may be thorough churchmen. And this power of interpreting to you your own position, of leading you to be what each of you in some sort is striving to be, I possess, not in virtue of any talents or insight which belong to me as an individual;—I possess it, because God has been pleased to place me on the high ground of a church polity, from which I can look down and see the directions that you are taking, and show you to what point they are leading. This is the revenge that I wish to take for any little insults that you or your fathers have put upon us; this is the compensation that I wish to render you for the injuries real or fancied which they or you may have endured at our hands.

I consider George Fox a great man and an eminent teacher. Do not mistake me. I do not think George Fox had a commission to preach the Gospel. I do not think that, in the strict sense of the word, he *did* preach the Gospel; but I think that he was raised up to declare a truth, without which the Gospel has no real meaning, no permanent existence. All around him, George Fox heard men preaching the doctrines of Christianity,—preaching justification, sanctification, election, final perseverance, and what not; exhibiting amazing logical subtlety; making nice distinctions, building parties upon them;—his heart required something which none of them could tell him. All these doctrines were about God and man,—all talked of connection between God and man; but all their theological skill, and all their theories on human nature, seemed to George Fox only to make the distance wider between the poor man and his Lord. Impassable gulfs of speculation intervened. There was a voice in the heart of this mechanic which told him that this could not be. As he studied his Bible to understand that voice, he found continual encouragements to believe that it could not be. At the same time, the darkness that was over his mind, his incapacity for realizing that communion which he felt must somehow be possible—told him that the teachers of the day were in some sense right,—that there is a deep fountain of corruption in man, and that man, unless raised out of that corruption, could never apprehend God. The tumult within him becomes more and more awful, till at last the bird of calm lights upon the waters, and the day begins to dawn. He perceives that man is a twofold creature; that there is a power always drawing him down, to which he is naturally subject, and to be subject to which is death; but that there is also a power drawing him up, a light shining in darkness, and that to yield to that power, to dwell in that light, is life and peace. To this conclusion he was brought himself, and this, with the earnest zeal of a lover of mankind, he longed to tell to all the world,—"My brother, there is a light shining in the darkness of your heart—the darkness has not comprehended it. Oh believe in that light, follow in that light, and be happy!" Dare I say that one atom of this belief was deception? Dare I say that he was not taught this truth from above? Not till all the deepest and most sacred convictions of my own heart have been resisted or have perished; not till I become a traitor to God's house, and deny all his discipline; not till truth and error become hopelessly confounded and intermingled in my mind. . . .

[A]ll the personal feelings and faith of man are unsafe, unless they rest upon the ground of an universal atonement. Unless each man feels himself to be a member of a body, reconciled and united to God, in Christ, he has no clear and definite indications of his own relation to Christ: his mind will be continually fluctuating and disturbed. On the other hand, unless this belief of an atonement rests upon the faith of a Trinity, it is unmeaning and baseless. The union of the whole body to the Father, in the Son, by the Spirit, are the very terms of the constitution. Unless there be an Absolute Being, the ground of all being,—unless there be one in whom that Being beholds the church, and in whom it beholds Him,—unless there be a Spirit, uniting together all the members to each other, and to their Head, the source of their faith, the inspirer of their worship, the originator of all their acts, the ruler of all their powers,—the idea of a church has no consistency, the idea of an atonement no possibility. Thus are we driven to this principle, as the ground of our society,—the only bond of our fellowship,—the only foundation for universal communion,—the only source of life, and distinctness to each person in it. And yet this, which is the first ground of all faith, is also the termination of all. This mystery of a Father dwelling with the Son in one Spirit, is the grand resting-place and repose of the reason, the feelings, and all the faculties of man;—that for which they are ever in search, and can have no peaceable home or resting-place until they find it. This is that blessed and perfect unity, for which the announcement,—"Hear, oh Israel! the Lord thy God is one Lord," is only the preparation;—that consummate unity of God, which is the real ground of all unity between men, the real ground of all unity in our own hearts, transcending all things, yet sustaining all things, the perfect love, the ineffable glory in which the saints delight, and yet which compasses the cradle of every baptized child.

I have thus arrived at the point to which all my observations have been tending,—to the connection, I mean, between the constitution and order of a church, the principles of Christianity, and the personal life of each man. . . .

You say that you do not like the doctrines of the Trinity, and the Atonement, and the Incarnation to be turned into mere dogmas. Hear, then, how they have been turned into dogmas. A universal church is found existing, acknowledging the Trinity, acknowledging the Atonement as the foundations of its being. These great truths are expressed in Sacraments; their relation to the constitution of the church and of society gradually unveiled in the written word; their meaning interpreted to the people, by a ministry connecting one generation with another; their meaning expressed in various acts of allegiance, and offices of thanksgiving, intercession, communion. The members of this church become, to a great extent, ignorant of the principle upon which it is founded. They will not suffer the written word to interpret those principles to the people; the idea of a spiritual constitution becomes hopelessly lost in naturalism and sensuality; the principle of an universal kingdom is abandoned, by one of the officers of that kingdom usurping dominion over the whole. Here was conduct, and here were notions so contradictory to the idea of a kingdom, that they must have destroyed it, if God had not been its protector. But he raised up men who perceived the necessity of a written word, to interpret to us the constitution into which we have been introduced, and to interpret each man to himself,—perceived the eternal distinction between the flesh and the Spirit—the right of every man by his spirit to claim union with Christ, the Lord of his spirit—the inconsistency of a visible and mortal head, with an universal and imperishable kingdom. They protested against these principles as subversive of the idea of a catholic church; they affirmed the reality of this church: they affirmed, that in each particular nation or kingdom, constituted under its appointed head, this church must be recognized as the foundation and upholder of all political institutions, or else those institutions would lose their character, and become mere instruments of internal oppression or external aggrandisement. Thus the church, the kingdom of Christ, remained established in its sacraments, its ministry, its forms, with a new witness of the divine protection and government exercised over it. A large portion of its members, however, continued to assert principles incompatible with the universality and unity of the church, and anathematized all who would not acknowledge these principles. With them there could be no communion, for they would not have it; they remained a seceding, separating, apostate body. Other bodies of men, as I have shown you, renounced the idea of an universal kingdom upon other principles. They established voluntary (more properly arbitrary) associations, grounded upon the notion or belief which each member had, that he himself, and the other members, were true believers in Christ; or if not constituted on this ground, constituted on one merely of opposition to some other body, upon the assertion of some particular notion, or the non-assertion of some other notion. Here begins dogmatism. Personal salvation or safety is made the groundwork of the society; just so much of the doctrines asserted by the universal church is to be believed, as seems necessary to that safety. Hence the questions,—How much is to be believed? What portions are to take precedence of the rest? Hence strife, battle, rage; hence also, I am bold to affirm, persecution; for whenever the church catholic has persecuted, it has done so because it has taken itself for a party; because it has not understood that it was standing on certain eternal and

immovable principles. In asserting the doctrine of the atonement, we assert redemption, liberty for mankind, union with God, union with each other. We denounce the denial of that doctrine, because we say, that to deny it is to take away
from man that which in all ages he has been sighing for,—communion with God,
communion with his fellows. When we assert the doctrine of the Trinity, we do
so, because we believe it to be the grand foundation of all society, the only ground
of universal fellowship, the only idea of a God of love. As different notions and
heresies arise respecting these points, we are obliged to exercise the faculties
which God has given us, to draw subtle distinctions, to refer to ancient experience, to call in all aids of philosophy, and philology, and history, But this we do,
because they drive us to it. All we want is to maintain a principle, without which,
we say, men would be divided from each other; a principle which, while we maintain it, enables us to claim fellowship with every man who will not disclaim it
with us. For the sake of the poor man,—for the sake of the denier of these
truths,—for the sake of Jews, Turks, and Infidels, we assert and uphold them; for
we find them to be the key-notes to all the harmonies of the world, and that without them all would be broken and dissonant.

These are my reasons for feeling that you, the assertors of spirituality, the enemies of mere dogmas, if you would uphold those principles of your Society
which your orthodox members are asserting; if you would maintain those principles of unity which your moderate party are asserting; if you would combine
these with the truths and facts concerning the personal life of each man, which
the party that calls itself Evangelical, is asserting, you must manfully cast away
your prejudices, and inquire calmly, rationally, and under the teaching of the
Spirit of God, into the foundations of the catholic church. In this inquiry I am
anxious to assist you. . . .

Yours very faithfully.

LETTER TO A MEMBER OF THE
SOCIETY OF FRIENDS (4) (1838)*

My Dear Friend,

[M]y great wish is to show you, that the Anglican Church was led, not by reason of any peculiar excellence or glory in the members or teachers of it, but by a
course of providential discipline, to put worship and sacraments before *views*, to
make those acts which directly connect man with God the prominent part of
their system,—that which was meant to embody the very form and meaning of
Christianity,—and those verbal distinctions which are necessary to keep the un-

---

*From *The Kingdom of Christ*, 1st ed. (London: Darton and Clark, Holborn Hill, 1838), Letter no. 4,
1:255–332 (abridged).

derstanding of men from error and confusion, as its accessary and subordinate part. Believing the church to be a kingdom, which each nation, from the time of its conversion to Christiantiy had become bound to acknowledge, bound, I mean, for the sake of its own stability and existence; they started at once with the assumption that every English child was to be received into this kingdom by Baptism, and was to be treated as a member of it. It was as much admitted by this rite into Christ's heavenly kingdom of the church, as it was by birth into Christ's earthly kingdom of the nation. It was not cognizant of the privileges belonging to either state, no, not even of the lower, but still mighty privilege, of being the member of a family,—but to each of these blessings were its teachers, confiding in God's promises and help, to awaken its inward eye, as the outward opened upon the face of its parents, upon the hills and vallies of its native land, upon its towns and castles, which testified that it was a land which the Lord God had cared for,—upon its churches, which spoke of its connection with the mysterious and the invisible. The silent education under the eye of its parents, God's ordinance for calling forth the *affections*,—the stern sway of schoolmasters, his ordinance for awakening the *conscience*,—were alike an induction into the full enjoyment of those higher ordinances assumed in both, which showed that the awfulness of disobedience is never so great as when it is committed against a perfectly loving Father. Baptism lay at the commencement of this great scheme of spiritual education; the Divine declaration of the state of the creature before God, and of its relation to its fellow-men, teaching the teacher with what an awful subject he has to deal, what mighty power he has at his command, for what a glorious end he is continually to be working; holding forth to the learner an unfailing hope of ever increasing life, and peace, and knowledge, of which even in his pupilage he enjoys the foretaste, of which only by the sacrifice of self-will he may obtain the fruition. Child, and boy, and man are alike instructed that they have an interest in this kingdom; that all the acts of their life can only be interpreted in relation to it; can be justly performed only while they keep it in remembrance. They are surrounded by it each morning when they awake; they are to rise and give thanks that it is theirs by every title of conquest and inheritance; to confess how little they have cared for its privileges; to plead the assurance which experience has taught them, that they shall fall from all its glories, unless they be upheld with fresh strength that day to receive the promised supply of pardon, encouragement, experience, wisdom, confidence, enjoyment. This kingdom compasses them in as they lie down at night, to bear witness of another day of continued unstartling miracles; of bodily and spiritual nourishment supplied, as much from heaven as if they saw the white flakes on the ground, and went out for the first time to ask what is it, and to inspire the prayer of hope and fear, that the Presence which has been with them through the day, the Angel of the Covenant, who has permitted the cloud to shelter them from the sun's heat, may be a light round about them in the night season. Every act reminds them that they are brought into this kingdom of righteousness, and peace, and love. A marriage cannot be celebrated unless the King be present, to turn the water of an earthly ordinance into the wine of a spiritual mystery; he must be with them on their sick beds; he must go with them to death and the grave, in which he has been before them. Such was the idea of our Reformers, and in expressing this idea, they found they had no occasion to invent, they had only to purify. A kingdom they believed had been set up in the world ages before. Its subjects had been taught to express their wants, their thanksgivings, their hopes in every crisis of sorrow and joy,—in these men had found solace, and hope, and inspiration, excitements to their devotion when they were sluggish; sympathy in it which encouraged, not cramped, their own aspirations when they were cheerful; these reminded them that Christ was the same yesterday, to-day, and for ever; and that there was a golden cord of feelings binding generation to generation. Surely, to invent some cold, and correct, and scholastic formulas of devotional propriety,—surely, to leave it to the chance of individual feeling creating an expression for its own solitary and selfish wants, would not have been so good a way of providing life for that age, strength for those that were to come, as to remove from the ancient forms whatever impurities had crept into them, through the notions and fashions of particular periods, and to give them a permanence which should counteract more effectually than any other measure could, the effect of similar corruptions hereafter, (sure to steal in by means of improvised prayers), upon the mind and theology of the nation. But that which crowned all these services and acts, as the service of Baptism lay at the foundation of them all, and that without which all the rest are unintelligible, is the service of Communion. The prevalence and dignity which our Reformers gave to this word, above all that had been heretofore used to designate the Lord's Supper, though not to the disparagement of any one of them, is a help in interpreting the nature of our services, and, as I conceive, the whole idea of Christianity, which seems to me unspeakably precious. It at once lifts the mind to this one sublime and awful thought, that Communion with God in the largest and fullest sense of that word, is not an instrument of attaining some higher end, but is itself the end to which he is leading his creatures, and after which his creatures, in all kingdoms, and nations, and languages,—by all their schemes of religion, by all their studies of philosophy, by art, by science, by politics, by watching, by weeping, by struggling, by submitting, by wisdom, by folly, in the camp and in the closet, in poverty and in riches, in honour and in shame, in health and in sickness, are secretly longing and crying, and without which they cannot be satisfied. For all are labouring after good or happiness of some kind or other, and all testify by their acts, if not by their words, that this good must be in some sense or other out of themselves; and all testify that this good must some way or other be connected with themselves, and that they must become capable of participating in it. Wherefore there is not a solid pursuit or a vain dream, recorded in the history of man, or felt by him now, or that shall be experienced hereafter, but points to this one object, and tells him he must achieve that, in order that he may attain any of the subordinate objects which he also desires, and must labour after. . . .

If you will consider what I said in my last letter respecting the sacramental doctrine of the early ages, you will see how, without imputing more knowledge to those ages than I did then, or, the least disparaging that light which I supposed the Church to receive by gradual experience respecting the wants of its members, I may yet suppose, that the forms which were preserved in those periods, were the best fitted to prepare us for the full apprehension and enjoyment of the glorious Revelation of God. We described them as considering everything,—a communication from a Father to his adopted family. Every blessing originating with Himself; Himself selecting the channels through which it should flow; Himself securing its transmission to those creatures by whom they were needed. Further than this, we supposed them, sometimes to inquire—not much to apprehend; what these wondrous and supernatural blessings are; how they fit the constitution of those to whom they are sent; what organs have been provided for their reception; these were not parts of the faith delivered to the saints; but it was a knowledge to which the Author of every good and perfect gift intended, by various processes, to bring his children, that they might know him better, and adore him more. Thus much, however, was a part of the faith given once for all, and never to be augmented or detracted from—that there was one Being from whom all blessings proceeded—one Mediator in whom all blessings are contained, and through whom all must come—one Spirit, by whom alone they can be communicated to the church and to all its members. That knowledge so high and wonderful should give birth to more simple and child-like overflowings of confidence, supplication, and love, than were likely to burst forth from the soul after it had begun to pore over its own nature, and qualities and operations, I think a reasonable man will be disposed to admit. But if you have gone along with what I said just now, you will admit something more; you will see that the very same language which expressed in one age a mere sense of the condescension of God, looking down upon his creatures, pitying their infirmities and supplying their wants, may be the most suitable to him who has discovered that the enjoyment of fellowship with God, is the very blessing which his heart most craves after, and is the centre round which all others must revolve; that the very same Mediator, in whom the Father can alone, well-pleased, behold his creatures, must be He through whom the creatures can alone behold their Father; that the Spirit which comes down to dwell among men, must be the only Being who can open the eyes of the creatures, to look upon that Lord and Friend of their hearts, in whom they may at length behold the awful and ineffable Godhead.

I have spoken of language,—but you will see also that all the principles contained in the earlier apprehended truth, wonderfully connect themselves with the later; that all the forms which embody the one, are suitable for the other. Through human hands,—the hands of men,—consecrated and set apart for this office, says the old church, does it please our heavenly Father to give us this sustenance. Men, weak, fallible men, not in virtue of any holiness appertaining to them, though holiness *is* their privilege, and without it every thing they do is a monstrous contradiction,—but in virtue of a separation formally ordained and outwardly signified to the world, have the glory of transmitting to you this amazing gift. Two common elements,—one, the necessary food which sustains the frame of all men, the other, that which most invigorates their life,—are the outward instruments through which it pleases the Author of your bodily as well as spiritual constitution,—the Inspirer of your spiritual as well as your bodily life,—to distribute the amazing boon. The early church, contemplating the deep condescension of the act, scarcely conceiving the possibility of any other instruments, thankfully receives those which it believes to be appointed. The Christian of a later age contemplating the magnitude of the blessing, after which he feels that he and all other men are aspiring—reading the history of the baffled hopes, and profound ignorance, and miserable failures of the men who have striven to reach it, or have thought that they strove, or have pursued something else, when this was that after which they really aimed—reading in history, too, and in his own experience, the danger of looking upon men in any light but as the appointed means of transmitting the gifts of God to man, which is the idolatry of other creatures,—and the misery of refusing to look upon them in that light—of wanting every thing immediately, and for our own purposes, which is self-idolatry—which two evils, have been in every age the great obstacles to finding that whereof we are in search;—reading in history, and in the experience of his own life, the mischief of looking upon natural things as good in themselves, and not looking at them as good and precious when honoured and set apart by God and to Him,—first, is disposed humbly to submit to the method of this institution, because it is a prescribed one; and, secondly, humbly and devoutly to honour it, because God has permitted him some glimpses into its wisdom. But while the idea of the elder church thus beautifully corresponds to all the cravings of a later period, whatever of confusion in those points which concern not the transmitted faith, but arose only from the lack of experience in those who received it, were easily obviated by the English Reformers, instructed in the evils which these innocent confusions had brought forth, and as keenly alive as any men of their times to the necessity of asserting the freedom and justification of the conscience. . . .

By putting the idea of Communion as the final cause of all acts of Christian devotion, our Reformers, however, did much more than merely explain the nature of those acts, and justify the arrangements which the direct words of Christ, or the authority of the church, had settled for the performance of them. They threw a broad and brilliant light upon the connection between these acts and those more transcendent acts, of which He in his own person was the only author and finisher. . . .

Now, by that one simple method of proposing communion with the Holy God, as the end of all Christianity, the object to which all the divine plans have been directed, and to which all human desires must be directed, if man is to realise the purpose for which he is constituted; we say that the church relieves us from both these perplexities, each so deeply rooted in our nature, each sure to present itself in different predicaments of our mind and feelings, each in turn perceived and condemned by those who are the victims of the other, each pitied and justified by those who feel how prone they are to both, and feel inwardly what truth lies hid under both, each needing some kind mother and teacher, instructed and appointed of God to remove it, not by cold rebukes, but by tender and loving instruction.

Can the stoutest Antinomian express himself in stronger language respecting the full, perfect, and sufficient satisfaction for sin, than that which is adopted in our Communion Service?. . . . The church had no need to weaken the statement respecting the freeness of salvation; she had only to state, broadly and plainly, what salvation is; she had no need to say something was left undone on the part of God in order to make His creatures happy; she had only to proclaim what the highest happiness is which God can bestow, or the creature can enjoy. If it be a state of communion with God,—the resemblance of his character, the fulfilment of his commands,—it must be a state of action, and a state of continual obedience. To bring us into the condition in which we can behold His countenance and live, in which we can receive from Him all the power to will and to do, was His act, accomplished once and for ever. To raise up the hearts of man to that contemplation, to bestow upon him that will and power, is His continual act. Now, does it need any balancing phrases, is it any thing but the carrying out of this idea, to affirm that *not* to behold, *not* to will and to do, is to be miserable? . . .

[T]he church has been bearing a calm and steady witness as to the transcendant worth and meaning of sacrifice, which, if they had heeded it, might have saved all her sons,—which has saved numbers of them either from yielding to those dishonourable misrepresentations of that Name, to hallow which is our first duty and our earliest prayer, from yielding to the unbelief, into which some, by indignation at these cold and crude interpretations, have been driven. Without a sacrifice for sins there could be no communion between God and his creatures. His sacrifice removes those impediments to the communion, which the blood of bulls and goats, sacrifices of mere arbitrary appointment, though most precious as instruments of moral and spiritual education, could not possibly have removed. Until One appeared who said, "Lo! I come, in the volume of the book it is written, to do thy will, O God,"—until He offered up himself as a perfect and well-pleasing sacrifice to God, how could there be perfect contentment in the mind of a holy and loving Being, how could a perfect communion exist between Him and man? And thus the church, taking the Epistle to the Hebrews for her classic, and giving, not a literal, but a living exposition of it, teaches us that a sacrifice, a real and spiritual sacrifice, was necessary to the atonement of God and his creatures; that this sacrifice was offered up once for all, and was accepted for the sins of men; that the consciences of those are purified from sin, who by faith receive this sacrifice as their reconciliation to God; that this purification is itself only a means and preparation for our drawing nigh unto God with pure hearts and faith unfeigned, through Him who is the Priest, as well as the sacrifice, the ever-living Mediator of a covenant which is established, not in the law of a carnal commandment, but in the power of an endless life. . . .

IV. But, lastly, I would advert once more to that which is the most remarkable and portentous peculiarity of this age,—the disposition to combine, not on a family or national basis, but in one that aims at being universal. The French Revolution brought out this tendency in all its naked power; it was held back for a while in our own land by the religious feeling which had been recently excited in the poorer classes, by that regard for the forms of our national life, which Burke's writings converted in the minds of thoughtful men into a deep, intelligent reverence; and, lastly, by the atrocities which accompanied the first manifestation of the new principles. But the influence of that religious excitement has passed away; the events of the French Revolution are forgotten or not connected with its creed; national institutions have lost their hold upon the multitude, and the principles which their great defender asserted are little remembered by the statesmen who have succeeded him. Meantime the restless desires which began to put themselves forth at the end of the last century, are becoming stronger every day; if their outward exhibition is checked for a moment, you may see that they are working more securely underneath. Here is another habit of mind, then, which must have tended to produce a great impatience of ordinances; a contempt because they seem to have no outward result,—a hatred because they are fixed forms, and not the work of our own hands.

And yet, if you consider again, where will you find anything so suitable to meet this state of mind, and, if God will, to make it sound and healthy, as a bold declaration of the meaning and power of this Sacrament? We cannot raise again the dormant national feeling; to attempt it seems to be spending our strength for nought. We cannot reproduce that kind of religious excitement which the Methodists were permitted and ordained, for merciful reasons, to be the means of creating; see how abortive and mischievous all attempts of the kind have proved. You cannot excite horror of a past evil. Alas! history had never much influence on men's minds, and we have used the facts of it so dishonestly, for such low, mob purposes, that now it has less than ever. But you can meet men who are longing for a universal fellowship and say,—"Here is one, and here are the symbols of it, and you have a charter of admission to it, signed and sealed in blood. And this universal society is founded by God himself, and it has stood for eighteen centuries, and in this Sacrament the Lord of this society has bound himself to its members, and they to him and to each other; and when they hold it fast, he has enabled them to love him and love one another; and he has never broken this Sacrament to any one man, but many have broken it to him by not obeying him, and helping and serving one another. And this disobedience is dreadful, and shall meet its reward. But none who trust in him, none who really join themselves to him in this Sacrament, shall incur that danger. They shall go from strength to strength; they shall get the better of every thing that divides them from him and from each other, and from the whole family in heaven and earth, till at last they shall all come to know and feel that they are indeed one with him, and one with each other, and that they shall be so for ever and ever." We may declare this to them, and we may tell them, that they have tried other Sacraments, and they have come to nought; they have sought to be brothers, without having a common Lord, and their hugs have been death embraces. There is but this one left; but it is God's Sacrament, and nothing in earth or hell has power to break it. And if we speak to them thus, I believe we shall act more wisely by far, than if we try to rouse their consciences to a sense of sin, or take any other course whatever of our own devising. For surely we are meant to study the course of God's providence; what desires he awakens in man—these we whom he calls to be his fellow-workers are meant to satisfy. The individual consciences of men were alive at the Reformation; to them the Reformers appealed; the desire for union and fellowship is alive now; to that let us appeal. Only let us appeal to it as Christians,— as men who would use what is holy in men to further holy ends, not what is vile,— as men who would do the will of the God of peace and love, and not the will of the spirit of division and enmity.

To turn once more to you. We are full of personal restlessness, of religious dissension, of philosophical pride, of political hatred. But we have within us, if we would use it, that which would make our lives calm, and holy, and orderly; that which would heal our differences; that which would humble us and satisfy us; that which would make us a true and heavenly family. Come, then, not to make us glory in a train of proselytes, but to make us ashamed, as we behold how much they prize that which we have counted worthless. Come and tell them who have thought Baptism an empty name, that there are scales on the eyes of those who do not submit to it; that it is the privilege of those who receive the ordinance, to find them disappear, and to behold their relation to Christ, and to all their brethren in him. Come and tell those who have thought that the gift of the Spirit is not really connected with this divine adoption and fellowship, that there is a mighty difference between the hope of sudden and casual visitations, and the belief of a power abiding with you by night and day, of whose presence sin may make you unconscious, to whose presence repentance may restore you, but of which it is a sin to doubt whether he is with you of a truth. Come and tell them who think that acts of self-appointed devotion may supersede the Holy Eucharist, that it is an incalculable blessing to feel that you are not seeking life to yourself, but that He is providing it for you; that you are not engaged in a solitary exercise, but in an act of holy fellowship; that your whole life, fashioned according to this model, becomes more and more that which the life of a translated saint must be,—a divine Sacrament, a thanksgiving feast, a holy communion.

Believe me,

Yours very faithfully.

INDICATIONS OF A
SPIRITUAL CONSTITUTION (1842)*

When I was speaking of the Quaker system, I noticed one practical inconsistency which seemed to lie at the root of it, and to affect all its workings. The member of the Society of Friends ought to be the conscious disciple of a Divine Teacher. But every child born to a Quaker is actually considered and treated as a Friend till, by some act of rebellion, he has deprived himself of the title. Something of the same anomaly we have traced in the Protestant systems. Consciously justified men ought to constitute the Evangelical Church; persons conscious of a divine Election the Reformed: yet neither of these have had the courage to exclude their children from *all* religious fellowship, to treat them absolutely as heathens. The Anabaptists have made the nearest approach to that practice; but even in them there are very evident indications of timidity and inconsistency.

When we examined the schemes of the world which had been constructed by philosophers, we observed that they had been encountered by a knot, not unlike that which had perplexed the authors of religious sects, and that they had found themselves compelled with more or less of ceremony to cut it. It was next to impossible to organise a universal society, while the distinction of families prevailed. In such a society men must be so many separate units. But there is this glaring fact of family life to prove that they are not units; that they are bound together by a certain law, which may be set at naught, and made almost utterly inefficient, but which cannot be entirely repealed.

I. Now this fact, that men exist in families, which seems so grievously to disturb the inventors of systems, is perhaps the very one which would be most likely to suggest the thought to a plain person, that there must be a moral or spiritual constitution for mankind. We are obliged to speak of every man as being in two conditions. He is in a world of objects which offer themselves to his senses, and which his senses may be fitted to entertain. He is a son, perhaps he is a brother. These two states are equally inevitable; they are also perfectly distinct. You cannot by any artifice reduce them under the same law or name. To describe the one you must speak of what we see, or hear, or handle or smell; to describe the other, you must speak of what we are; "I *am* a son," "I *am* a brother." It is impossible therefore to use the word "*circumstances*" in reference to the one state with the same strictness with which you apply it to the other. All the things which I have to do with, I naturally and rightly call my circumstances—*they stand round me:* but that which is necessary in an account of myself, seems to be entitled to another name. We commonly call it a *relationship.* And this difference soon becomes more conspicuous. We speak of a man *having* a bad digestion or a bad hearing; we speak of his *being* a bad brother or a bad son. By both these phrases

---

*From Part Two, "Of the Catholic Church and the Romish System," *The Kingdom of Christ,* 2d ed. (1842; New York: D. Appleton & Co., 1843), Chapter 2, 1:212–19.

we imply that there is a want of harmony between the man and his condition. But by the one we evidently wish to signify that there need not be this want of harmony, that he is *voluntarily* acting as if he were not in a relation in which nevertheless he is, and must remain. This inconsistency we describe by the term moral evil, or whatever equivalent phrase we may have invented; for some equivalent, whether we like it or not, we must have.

It might seem to follow from these observations, that the family state is the *natural* one for man; and accordingly we speak of the affections which correspond to this state, as especially natural affections. But it should be remembered that we use another phrase which is apparently inconsistent with this; we describe the savage condition, that is to say, the one in which man is striving to be independent, as the natural state of society. And though it may be doubtful whether that should be called a *state of society,* which is the contradiction of all states and of all society, yet there seems a very considerable justification for the application of the word *natural* to it: seeing that we cannot be acquainted with a family, or be members of a family, without knowing in others, without feeling in ourselves, certain inclinations which tend to the dissolution of its bonds, and to the setting up of that separate independent life, which when exhibited on a large scale we name the savage or wild life. These inclinations are kept down by discipline, and the affections which attract us to the members of our family are called out in opposition to them; surely, therefore, it cannot be a mistake to describe them by the name which we ordinarily apply to plants that spring up in a soil, uncultivated and uncalled for.

We have here some of the indications of a spiritual constitution; that is to say, we have the marks of a state which is designed for a voluntary creature; which *is* his, whether he approve it or no; against which, he has a nature or inclination to rebel. But still, most persons would mean something more by the phrase than this; they would ask how you could call that spiritual, which had no reference to religion. Now the histories and mythologies of all the people with whom we are acquainted bear unequivocal witness to this fact, that men have connected the ideas of fathers, children, husbands, brothers, sisters, with the beings whom they worshipped. This is the first, rudest observation which we make upon them. But, when we search further, we begin to see that this simple observation has the most intimate connexion with the whole of mythology; that it is not merely *a* fact in reference to it, but the fact, without which all others which encounter us are unintelligible. You say all kinds of offices are attributed to the gods and goddesses; they rule over this town and that river, they dispense this blessing or send that curse. Be it so; but who are they who exercise these powers? The mythology tells you of relations existing between them; also of relations between them and the objects of their bounty and their enmity. In later ages, when we are studying the differences in the mythology of different nations, it is no wonder that we should notice the character of the soil, the nature of the climate, the beauty or the dreariness of the country, the rains or the inundations which watered it, as circumstances helping to determine the views which the inhabitants entertained of their unseen rulers. And then the transition is very easy to the belief, that by these observations we have accounted for their faith, and that the histories of the gods are merely accidental poetical embellishments. But, if we consider that the worshippers evidently felt that which we call accidental to be essential; that the merging the gods in the objects with which they were connected was merely an artifice of later philosophy; that the circumstances of soil and climate did indeed occasion some important *differences* between the objects reverenced in various nations, but that the circumstance of their being parents, brothers, and sisters, so far as we know, was *common* to all, or only wanting in those which were utterly savage, that is, in which the human relations were disregarded; if we observe that those who endeavour to explain mythology by the phenomena of the world, are obliged to beg what they call "a law of nature," alleging that we are naturally inclined to inquire into the origin of any great and remarkable objects which we see; if we will notice how utterly inconsistent it is with all experience and observation to attribute such a disposition as this to men whose feelings and faculties have not been by some means previously awakened, how very little a savage is struck by any except the most glaring and alarming phenomena, and how much less he thinks about them: if we will reflect upon these points, we may perhaps be led to adopt the opinion that the simplest method of solving the difficulty is the best; that it is not our being surrounded with a strange world of sensible objects which leads us to think of objects with which we do not sensibly converse, but that these perceptions come to us through our family relationships; that we become more and more merely idolaters when these relationships are lost sight of, and the other facts of our condition only regarded; that a world without family relationships would have no worship, and on the other hand, that without worship all the feelings and affections of family life would have utterly perished.

II. But is there no meaning in that savage wish for independence? Is it merely the dissolution and destruction of those family bonds which are meant for men, or is it the indication that men were meant for other bonds than these, not perhaps of necessity incompatible with them? History seems to decide the question in favour of the latter opinion. It seems to say, that as there is a worse state of society than the patriarchal, there is also a better and more advanced one; it declares that the faculties which are given to man never have had their proper development and expansion, except in a *national* community. Now if we examine any such community, taking our specimen from the Pagan world, we shall perceive that the member of it had a more distinct feeling of himself, of his own personality, than the mere dweller in a family could have. It may seem to us very puzzling that it should be so; for if we look at Sparta or Rome—at any commonwealth except Athens—it seems as if the society were imposing the severest restraints upon each man's own taste, judgment, and will. Nevertheless, it is the manifestation of energetic purpose in particular leaders, and the assurance we feel that there was the same kind of purpose, though in a less degree, existing in those who composed every rank of their armies, which gives the interest to the better times of these republics; as it is the feeling of a change in this respect—of the armies having become a body of soldiers merely, not of men, which makes the declining ages of them so mournful. We have evidence, therefore, coming in a way in which it might least be expected, that this personal feeling is connected with the sense of national union.

Of all men the savage* has *least* of the feelings of dignity and personal self-respect; he is most emphatically a mere workman or tool, the habitual slave of his own chance necessities and inclinations, and therefore commonly of other men's also. He who understands the force of the words, "I am a brother," has taken a mighty step in advance of this individual man, even in that respect on which he most prides himself; he is more of a person, more of a freeman. But he is not enough of a person, not enough of a freeman. If he will be more, he must be able to say, "I am a citizen;" this is the true onward step; if he aim at freedom by any other, he relapses into an independence which is only another name for slavery. Now, we may observe several facts, too obvious to escape the most careless student of history, except it should be from their very obviousness, which are closely connected with this. One is, that in every organised nation at its commencement, there is a high respect for family relations, that they embody themselves necessarily in the national constitution; another is, that there is a struggle between these relations and the national polity, although they form so great an element in it; the legislator feeling that each brother, husband, father, is a citizen, and that as such, he comes directly under his cognizance.

In Sparta, we see the principle of family life, though distinctly recognised, sacrificed in a great degree to the Laws. In Athens, we see the legislator, in his anxiety to leave men to themselves, allowing the growth of an independence which proved incompatible both with family relations and with national society. In Rome, we see the legislation so exquisitely interwoven with the family principle, that so soon as that became weak, the commonwealth inevitably fell.

These facts lead us to ask what this legislation means, wherein its power lies, and in what way it comes to be so connected with, and yet diverse from, these relationships? In trying to find the answer to this question we are at once struck with this observation—Law takes each man apart from his fellows; it addresses him with a *Thou;* it makes him feel that there is an eye fixed upon his doings; that there is a penalty overhanging him. It is therefore, in this point of view, the

---

*Of course there is no *ideal* savage in actual existence—no one who is perfectly independent. The North American Indian has so many tribe feelings, that the admirers of savage life, taking him for an example, have been able to contend that it is the very soil for the cultivation of domestic affections. But not to dwell upon the violent exaggerations and distortions of fact which have been necessary for the support of this hypothesis, it is quite obvious that these feelings and affections are just so many departures from savage perfection, so many threatenings of a degeneracy into the social and civilised condition. The true savage is Caliban; the nearest approximation to him is probably to be looked for in New Holland [Australia].

direct opposite of a *relationship* by which we are bound to each other, and are made to feel that we cannot exist apart from each other. But, again, we find that the Law denounces those acts which make union and fellowship impossible, those acts which result from the determination of men to live and act as if they were independent of each other, as if they might set up themselves and make self-pleasing their end. The Law declares to each man that he is in a fellowship, that he shall not do any act which is inconsistent with that position. That therefore which is the great foe to family relationship, the desire for individuality, is the very thing which Law, even while it deals with men as distinct persons, is threatening and cursing. A nation then, like a family, would seem to possess some of the characteristics of a spiritual constitution. If we take the word *spiritual* in that sense in which it is used by modern philosophers, we have abundant proofs that where there is no feeling of national union, there is a most precarious and imperfect exercise of *intellectual* power. If we take it in the sense of *voluntary* we find here a constitution evidently meant for creatures which have wills; seeing that it is one which men do not create for themselves, that is one which may be violated, nay, which there is a natural inclination in every man to violate; and that by the words "bad citizen," we express moral reprobation, just as we do when we speak of a bad father or mother. And if we ask whether there are any *religious* feelings connected with national life, as we found there were with family life, the mythology of the old world is just as decisive in its reply. If the Homeric gods were fathers, brothers, husbands, they were also kings; one character is just as prominent, just as essential as the other. It is possible that the former may have been the most ancient, and this would explain the notion of scholars that traces of an earlier worship are discoverable in the Iliad. In Homer's time the two characters, the domestic and the kingly, were incorporated, and the *offices* of the gods as connected with *nature*, though they might be gradually mingling themselves with these characters, and threatening to become identical with them, are nevertheless distinct from them. The princes of Agamemnon's league felt that there must be higher princes than they; they could use no authority, take no counsel, except that in belief. And though they spoke of these rulers as compelling the clouds and winds, they did not look upon this exercise of power as higher or more real, than that of putting wisdom and spirit into Diomed, and arming Hector for the fight. And hence the leaders were always types of the gods in every country which had attained the forms of a national polity. Wherever these existed, invisible rulers were recognised; a class of men interpreted the meaning of their judgments; they were invoked as the guides in battles; sacrifices were offered to avert their displeasure or to claim their protection.

But a time came, when thoughts were awakened in men's minds of something more comprehensive than either this family or this national constitution. The former belonged to all men; yet in another respect it was narrow, separating men from each other. The latter was obviously exclusive; a nation was limited to a small locality; it actually treated all that lay beyond it, and whom it could not subdue to itself, as aliens, if not enemies. If this exclusion were to continue, there was certainly some nation which *ought* to reign, which had a right to make its polity universal. Great Asiatic monarchies there had been, which had swallowed all tribes and kingdoms into themselves, but these had established a rule of mere physical force.

Might not Greece, the land of intellectual force, show that it was meant to rule over all? The young hero of Macedon went forth in this hope, and in a few years accomplished his dream. In a few more his empire was broken in pieces; Greece was not to be the lord of the world: still in the Egyptian and Syrian dynasties which she sent forth she asserted a mental supremacy. But a nation which paid no homage to art or to philosophy swallowed up all these dynasties, and with them all that remained of Greece herself. A universal polity was established in the world, and the national life, the family life, of Rome, perished at the very moment in which she established it.

Was there a religion connected with this universal polity as there was with the family and the national? We find that there was. The Emperor was the great God. To him all people and nations and languages were to bow. Subject to this supreme divinity all others might be tolerated and recognised. No form of religion was to be proscribed unless it were absolutely incompatible with the worship of a Tiberius and a Vitellius. It has been suggested already, that this Roman Empire answers exactly to the idea of a universal *world*. If there is to be anything different from this, if there is to be a *universal Church*, we ought to know of what elements it is to be composed, we ought to know whether it also sets aside family or national life, or whether it justifies their existence, reconciles them to itself, and interprets the problems of ancient history concerning their mysterious meaning.

THE SCRIPTURAL VIEW OF
THIS CONSTITUTION (1842)*

It is commonly acknowledged by religious persons, that the Bible is remarkably unsystematic. Sometimes this admission is made thankfully and even triumphantly; it is urged as a proof that the Bible is mainly intended to supply the daily wants, and to meet the ever-changing circumstances of the spiritual man. Sometimes it furnishes the ground of an argument for the necessity of that being done by others which is not done here; by those who lived nearest the age of the Apostles, or at the Reformation, or in a more advanced period of civilisation. Sometimes it is alleged as a reason for denying that there is any book possessing the character which Christians have attributed to this one; for asserting that it is

---

*From Part Two, "Of the Catholic Church and the Romish System," *The Kingdom of Christ*, 2d ed. (1842; New York: D. Appleton & Co., 1843), Chapter 3, 1:220–39.

a collection of documents belonging to a particular nation, accidentally strung together, and invested by the superstition of after-times with a fictitious entireness.

All these notions, it seems to me, assume that the words *system* and *method* are synonymous, and that if the first is wanting in the Scriptures the last must be wanting also. Now to me these words seem not only not synonymous, but the greatest contraries imaginable: the one indicating that which is most opposed to life, freedom, variety; and the other that without which they cannot exist. If I wished to explain my meaning, I should not resort to a definition; I should take an illustration, and, of all illustrations, I think the most striking is that which is afforded by the Bible itself. While the systematiser is tormented every page he reads with a sense of the refractory and hopeless materials he has to deal with, I am convinced that the person who is determined to read only for his own comfort and profit is haunted with the sense of some harmony, not in the words but in the history, which he ought not to overlook, and without reference to which the meaning of that in which he most delights is not very certain. And, while this sense of a method exists, the fact that these works were written at different periods, in different styles, and by men of totally different characters, increases the impression that there is something most marvellous in the volume they compose. The most skilful and laborious analyst cannot persuade his disciples to abandon the use of the word *Bible,* he cannot divest himself of the feelings with which it is associated.

I. Perhaps it may be useful for the purpose at which we are aiming, that we should examine a little into this phenomenon. Everyone who reads the Old Testament must perceive that the idea of a covenant of God with a certain people is that which presides in it. In plain history, in lofty prayers and songs, in impassioned denunciations of existing evil, and predictions of coming misery, this idea is still at the root of all others. Take it away, and not merely is there no connexion between the different parts, but each book by itself, however simple in its language or in its details, becomes an incoherent rhapsody. A person, then, who had no higher wish than to understand the character and feelings of that strange people which has preserved its identity through so many generations, would of course begin with examining into the account of this covenant. He would feel that the call of Abraham, the promise made to him and to his seed, and the seal of it which was given him, were the most significant parts of this record. But one thought would strike him above all: This covenant is said to be with a *family;* with a man doubtless in the first instance, but with a man expressly and emphatically as the head of a family. The very terms of the covenant, and every promise that it held forth, were inseparably associated with the hope of a posterity. It is impossible to look upon the patriarchal character of Abraham as something accidental to his character as the chosen witness and servant of the Most High. These two positions are absolutely inseparable. The fact of his relationship to God is interpreted to him by the feeling of his human relations, and his capacity of fulfilling them arose from his acknowledgment of the higher relation. A little further reflection upon the subordinate parts of the narrative (which, when this fact is felt to be the centre, will all acquire a new value and meaning) must convince us, that sensuality, attended of necessity with sensual worship, was the character of the tribes among which Abraham was dwelling; that in this sensuality and sensual worship was involved the neglect of family bonds; that the witness for an invisible and righteous God, against gods of nature and mere power, was, at the self-same moment and by the same necessity, the witness for the sacredness of these bonds. The notion of a Being exercising power over men, seen in the clouds, and heard in the winds, this was that which the *world* entertained, and trembled, till utter corruption brought in utter atheism. That there is a God *related* to men and made known to men through their human relations, this was the faith of Abraham, the beginner of the Church on earth. But this truth could not be exhibited in one individual faithful man; it must be exhibited through a family. The rest of Genesis, therefore, gives us the history of the patriarchs who followed Abraham. But what if these, or any of these, should not be faithful? What if they should not maintain the principle of family relationship, or retain a recollection of the higher principle involved in it? What if the *world* should find its way into the Church? The historian does not wait for the question to be asked him; his narrative answers it. The great majority of the sons of Jacob were not faithful men, they did not maintain the principle of family life, they did not recollect the Being who had revealed Himself through it. Perhaps then, the Joseph, the true believer, separated himself from his godless brethren, and established a new and distinct fellowship. Had he done so he would have acted upon the principle of Ishmael or Esau; he would have founded a society which was built upon choice, not upon relationship. The historian declares, that he followed a different course, that he was indeed separated from his brethren, but by their act, not his: that he continued a witness for God's covenant, not with him, but with Abraham, Isaac, and Jacob; not with an individual, but with a family. Acording then to the Jewish Scriptures, the Abrahamic family, though cut off by their covenant from the other families of the earth, was so cut off expressly that it might bear witness for the true order of the world; for that order against which all sensible idolatry, and all independent choice or self-will, is rebellion; for that order in which alone men can be free, because to abide in it they must sacrifice those inclinations which make them slaves; for that order, in and through which, as we might have guesses from the Gentile records, the idea of God can alone be imparted. The promise of the covenant therefore was, that in the seed of Abraham all the families of the earth should be blessed.

II. But, whatever sentimentalists may say about the patriarchal condition of the world, its essential purity, and the misery of departing from it, the Scriptures give no countenance to such dreams. It was part of the promise that the children of Jacob should enter into another state. They were to possess the Canaanitish nations. They were to become a nation. And although the history, in strict conformity to all experience, describes the middle passage between these two conditions as a grievous one, though the children of Abraham are said to have sunk into moral debasement and actual slavery, yet their redemption is connected with a more awful revelation than any which had been imparted, or, as far as we can see, could have been imparted, to them in their previous state; and leads to new and most wonderful discoveries respecting the relations between men and God. The God of Abraham and Isaac and Jacob declares that He remembers His covenant, and has seen the affliction of His people. But He declares Himself to the appointed guide and deliverer by another name than this—that name upon which the Jewish covenant stands, which is the foundation of all law, I AM THAT I AM. And as soon as the judgments upon natural worship, and upon a tyranny which set at naught all invisible and righteous government, had been accomplished, and the people had been taught to feel that an unseen Power had delivered them, that awful code was proclaimed amidst thunders and lightnings, which spoke straight to the individual conscience of each man, even while it reminded him in the most direct and solemn manner that he was related to God and his brethren. I will not enter here into an explanation of the manner in which the tribe institutions, those which speak of family relationship, were so embodied in the Jewish constitution that they gave a meaning to this law and yet did not deprive it of its awful personal character. That observation must needs strike everyone who studies with the slightest attention the Jewish institutions, as they are described in the Pentateuch. It is more necessary to notice those which led the thoughts of the Jews above the bonds of family and of law, though they were inseparably intertwined with both; I mean the tabernacle, the priesthood, and sacrifices. That these were the shrines of an undeveloped mystery every thoughtful Jew was conscious; but he was equally certain that this mystery was implied in all his acts, in all his family relations, in the national order, in his legal obedience. That there was an awful self-existent Being from whom all law came, was declared by the commandments: the Tabernacle affirmed that this Being was present among His people, and that it was possible in some awful manner to approach Him. The family covenant bore witness that there was a relation between Him and His worshippers; the Priesthood from generation to generation witnessed that this relation might be actually realised, that it might be realised by the whole people, in a representative. The National Constitution and punishments awakened in each person the feeling of moral evil, and taught them that that evil arose from violating his relations with God and his countrymen, and that the effect of it was a practical exclusion from these blessings; the sacrifices intimated that the relation was restored, when he had personally, and through the priest, given up something, not selected by himself as the most appropriate, or the most precious, but appointed by the law; and when he had given up that self-will which caused the separation. Such thoughts were wrought gradually into the mind of every humble and obedient Jew; they were brought directly home to him by the parting instruction of his great Law-giver; they were confirmed and illustrated by all his subsequent experience, and by the teachers who showed him the purpose of it.

The national polity of the Jews was in its essence exclusive. We dwell upon this fact, as if it destroyed all connexion between this polity and that of the Pagans, or of modern Europe. But every *nation,* as such, is exclusive. Athens was exclusive, Rome was exclusive; nevertheless, we have admitted, all persons admit, that more of humanity came out in the exclusive nations of Athens and of Rome, than ever showed itself in the savage tribes of the earth, which have never attained to a definite polity. Before we can ascertain whether the exclusiveness of the Jews was an inhuman exclusiveness, we must find out what it excluded; and here the same answer must be given as before. It excluded the worship of sensible, natural things; it excluded the idea of choice and self-will. The covenant with an invisible Being made it treason for men to choose the objects of their worship. This worship of the one Being was the bond of the commonwealth, and, if this were broken, it was dissolved. The covenant with an invisible Being obliged them to look upon all kings as reigning in virtue of His covenant, as representing His dignity, as responsible to Him; upon all other officers, the priestly, the prophetical, the judicial, as in like manner directly receiving their appointments and commissions from Him. By its first protest it affirmed that there are *not* a set of separate gods over each territory, various, according to the peculiarities of soil and of climate; but that there is one Almighty and Invisible Being, who is the Lord of all. The God of Israel is declared to be the God of all the nations of the earth; the Israelites are chosen out to be witnesses of the fact. By the second protest the exclusive Hebrew witnessed, that no king, no priest, no judge, has a right to look upon himself as possessing instrinsic power; that he is exercising office, under a righteous king, a perfect priest, an all-seeing judge; that, in proportion as he preserves that thought, and in the strength of it fulfils his task, the character of that king, and priest, and judge, and the relation in which he stands to men, reveal themselves to him; that these offices are continued from generation to generation, as a witness of His permanence who is Lord of them all, and who abides for ever and ever.

As then in the patriarchal period the Divine Being manifested Himself in the family relations, and by doing so manifested on what these relations depend, how they are upheld, and wherein their worth consists: so in the national period He was manifested to men through all national offices; thereby explaining their meaning and import, how they are upheld, and wherein their worth consists. But we are not to suppose that the family relations had less to do with this stage of the history than with the former. As they were embodied in the national institutions, as the existence of these institutions depended upon them, so their meaning in connexion with national life and national sins, and with a Being of whom both witnessed, became continually more apparent.

I need not point out to anyone who reads the prophets, what is their uniform method of awakening the conscience of the Jew, and of imparting to him the highest truths. I need not say that the Lord is throughout presented in the character of the *husband* of the nation; that acts of apostacy and false worship are constantly referred to as adulteries; and that the greatest pains are taken to convince us, that these are no poetical flourishes or terms of art, by connecting the actual human relation and human offence with the properly spiritual one. Oftentimes the verbal commentator is at fault, from the apparent confusion of the two. He cannot make up his mind whether it is the infidelity of the nation to her God, or of actual wives to their actual husbands, which the holy man is denouncing. And such perplexity there must needs be in the thoughts of all persons who are determined to separate these two ideas,—who do not see that it is the main object of the prophet to show their bearing upon one another,—who will not enter into his mind, by feeling that human relationships are not artificial types of something divine, but are actually the means and the only means, through which man ascends to any knowledge of the divine; and that every breach of a human relation, as it implies a violation of the higher law, so also is a hindrance and barrier to the perception of that higher law—the drawing of a veil between the spirit of a man and his God.

But how did this idea of a human constitution harmonise, or come into collision, with those attempts at *universal empire,* which appeared to be the necessary consummation or termination of the ancient polities? The Asiatic monarchies have been sometimes called *patriarchal,* and beyond a doubt the patriarchal feeling—the belief that the king was a father—did lie at the foundation of them, and did constitute all that was sound and healthful in the acts of the monarch, or the reverence of the people. But if we are to believe the Bible, the king is not merely a father, he is something more; his position has its ground in the acknowledgment of an unseen absolute Being, whose relations to men lead up to the contemplation of Him in Himself. The effort therefore to make the paternal relation all in all is, according to this showing, a false effort, one necessarily leading to false results. In this case the result is very apparent. The power of the monarch not having any safe ground to rest upon, soon becomes reverenced merely as power. No conscience of a law, which they ought to obey, is called forth in the minds of the subjects or the monarch; he may have kindly affections towards them, which may be reciprocated, but that is all. There is nothing to preserve the existence and sanctity of the family relationship, upon which the sovereign authority is built; nothing to resist the tendency to natural worship, which destroys it; nothing to hinder the monarch from believing that he reigns by his own right. Hence, these so-called patriarchal governments, besides that they awaken neither the energies of the human intellect nor the perception of right and wrong, soon are changed into the direct contraries of that which they profess to be. The father becomes an oppressor of his own people, a conqueror of others; all idea of the invisible is swallowed up in a reverence for him. Ultimately he is looked up to as the God of gods and the Lord of lords. It is no false feeling which leads us to rejoice when these patriarchal kings were driven back by the little national bands at Marathon or Plataea. No one who reveres invisible more than visible strength, will restrain his paeans at that discomfiture. It is a hateful and a godless thing to check them, or to stir up our sympathy on behalf of the Eastern tyrant. He who cherishes such a habit of feeling, will not be able to rejoice, whatever he may fancy, when Pharaoh and his hosts sink like lead into the waters, or when Sisera with his six hundred chariots is put to flight by the prophetess of Israel.

If we look at the history of the Jews, we shall find that their distinct polity was a witness, through all the time it lasted, against all these Babel monarchies; that in them the Jew saw that world concentrated in its worst form, out of which the covenant with the Abrahamic family, and with the Israelitish nation, had delivered him. To be like this world, however, to share its splendours, to adopt its worship, was the perpetual tendency of his evil nature, a tendency punished at length by subjection to its tyranny. But it was not merely by punishment that this inclination was resisted. The wish for fellowship with other nations was a true wish inverted; the dream of a human polity was one which the true God had sent to the Jew, though he had been taught how to realise it by an evil spirit. To bring out the true idea of such a polity, to show how it lay hid in all their own institutions, and how it would at length be brought out into full manifestation, this was the great office of the Hebrew Seer. Side by side with that vision on a Babylonian kingdom, which he taught his countrymen to look upon as based upon a lying principle, the contrary of their own, and as meant to be their scourge if they adopted that principle into their own conduct, rose up another vision of a king who did not judge after the sight of his eyes or the hearing of his ears, but who would rule men in righteousness, and whom the heathen should own. And as each new step in the history of the covenant—the first call of the patriarch which made them a family, their deliverance under Moses which made them a nation—was connected with a fresh revelation of the Divine King through these different relations, neither displacing the other but adopting it into itself; this glorious vision would have been utterly imperfect, if it had not involved the prospect of such a discovery as had not been vouchsafed to any former age. The prophet, trained to deep awful meditation in the law, the history of his land, but above all in the mysterious services of the temple, was able by degrees to see, as one sin after another, one judgment after another, showed him what were the dangers and wants of his nation, that the heir of David's throne must be a MAN, in as strict a sense as David was, capable, not of less but of infinitely greater sympathy with every form of human sorrow than he had been capable of, and yet that in Him, the worshipper must behold GOD less limited by human conceptions, more in His own absoluteness and awfulness, than even in the burning bush, or admidst the lightnings of Sinai. How these two longings could be both accomplished; how idolatry could be abolished by the very manifestation which would bring the object of worship more near to all human thoughts and apprehensions; how the belief of a Being nigh to men, could be reconciled with that of one dwelling in his

own perfection; how unceasing action on behalf of His creatures consists with
eternal rest; how He could be satisfied with men, and yet be incapable of satisfaction with anything less pure and holy than Himself; these were the awful questions with which the prophet's soul was exercised, and which were answered, not
at once, but in glimpses and flashes of light coming across the darkness of his own
soul, and of his country's condition, which even now startle us as we read, and
make us feel that the words are meant to guide us through our own confusions,
and not to give us notions or formulas for disguising them. One part of his teaching must have been derived from that polity which was the great contrast to his
own. The universal monarchs, the Sennacheribs and Nebuchadnezzars, were
Men-gods. They took to themselves the attributes of the Invisible; and just in
proportion as they did so, just in proportion as they hid the view of anything beyond humanity from the eyes of men, just in that proportion did they become
inhuman, separate from their kind, dwelling apart in an infernal solitude.

This black ground brought the perfectly clear bright object more distinctly
within their view; they felt that the God-man, in whom the fulness and awfulness of Godhead should shine forth, might *therefore* have perfect sympathy with
the poorest and most friendless, and might at the same time enable them to enter into that transcendent region which their spirits had ever been seeking and
never been able to penetrate.

III. Now, when we open the first book of the New Testament, the first words
of it announce that the subject of it is the Son of David and the Son of Abraham.
As we read on, we find that, according to the belief of the writer, this person came
into the world to establish a Kingdom. Every act and word which is recorded of
Him has reference to this kingdom. A voice is heard crying in the wilderness that
a kingdom is at hand. Jesus of Nazareth comes preaching the Gospel of the kingdom. He goes into a mount to deliver the principles of His kingdom. He speaks
parables to the people, nearly every one of which is prefaced with, "The kingdom
of heaven is like." He heals the sick; it is that the Jews may know that His kingdom is come nigh to them. His private conferences with His disciples, just as
much as His public discourses, relate to the character, the establishment, and the
destinies of this kingdom. He is arraigned before Pontius Pilate for claiming to
be a king. The superscription on the cross proclaims Him a king.

That there is a difference of character and style in the different Evangelists,
and that a hundred different theories may be suggested as to their origin, their
coincidences, their varieties, no one will deny. But that this characteristic is common to them all, that the most sweeping doctrine respecting the interpolations
which have crept into them could eliminate it out of them, that it would not be
the least affected if the principle and method of their formation were ascertained,
is equally true. The kingdom of Christ is under one aspect or other the subjecct
of them all. But this peculiarity, it will be said, is easily accounted for. The writers of the New Testament are Jews; language of this kind is essentially Jewish. It
belonged to the idiosyncrasy of the most strange and bigoted of all the people of

the earth. To a certain extent, the reader will perceive, these statements exactly tally with mine. I have endeavoured to show that the habit of thinking, which this perpetual use of a certain phrase indicates, is Jewish, and why it is Jewish. But there is a long step from this admission, to the one which is generally supposed to be involved in it, that this phrase is merely connected with particular accidents and circumstances, and has nothing to do with that which is essential and human. According to my view of the position of the Israelite, he was taken out of all nations expressly to be a witness of that which is unchanging and permanent, of that which is *not* modal, of the meaning of those relationships which belonged to him in common with the Pagans and with us, and which, as every Pagan felt, and as every peasant among us feels, have a meaning, and of the ground and purpose of national institutions and of law, which the Pagans acknowledged, and which most of us acknowledge, to be the great distinction between men and brutes. And since beneath these relationships, and this national polity, the Pagans believed, and we believe, that some other polity is lying, not limited like the former, not exlcusive like the latter, I cannot see why we are to talk of the prejudices and idiosyncrasies of the Jew, because he expresses this universal idea in the words which are the simplest and the aptest to convey it. That, say the Evangelists, which we have been promised, that which we expect, is a Kingdom; this Jesus of Nazareth we believe and affirm to be the King. Either proposition may be denied. It may be said, "Men are not in want of a spiritual and universal society." It may be said, "This person has not the credentials of the character which he assumes." But it must, according to all ordinary rules of criticism, be admitted that this was the idea of the Evangelists, and we ought surely, in studying an author, to seek that we may enter into his idea, before we substitute for it one of our own.

I am aware, however, that the objector would be ready with an answer to this statement, and that it is one which will derive no little countenance from the opinions which are current among religious people, and therefore will have no inconsiderable weight with them. It will be said, "We have an excuse for this attempt to separate the inward sense of the Gospels from their Jewish accidents, in the inconsistency which we discover in the use of those very phrases to which you allude. Do not the Evangelists constantly represent this kingdom as if it were an outward and visible kingdom, just like that of David and Solomon, nay, that very kingdom restored and extended? as something to supersede the government of Herod, ultimately perhaps that of the Caesars? And do they not at the same time introduce such words as these and attribute them to their Master, 'The kingdom of God cometh not with observation,' 'The kingdom of God is within you,' 'My kingdom is not of this world'—words which indicate that He taught (at least commonly) another doctrine, which has become leavened with these coarser and more sensual elements? If so, are we not justified in decomposing the mass and taking out the pure ore?"

I think the reader, who has gone along with me thus far, will not be much staggered by this argument. The kingdom of David, the kingdom of Solomon, *was* distinguished from the kingdoms of this world. It did not come with observation. It stood upon the principle which other kingdoms set at naught—the principle that the visible king is the type of the invisible, that he reigns in virtue of a covenant between the invisible king and the nation, that he is subject to a divine law. This principle, which was practically denied in all the great nations of the earth—denied then especially and emphatically when they became *kingdoms* (the ordinary, apparently the necessary, consummation of them all)—the Israelitish kingdom existed to enforce. All through the history, the tendency of the nation and its kings to set at naught the constitutional principle, to forget the covenant, is manifest; but this very tendency proved the truth of the idea against which it warred. If this be so, what contradiction was there in affirming that the new kingdom was the kingdom promised to David, the kingdom of his son, and yet that it was in the highest sense a kingdom not to be observed by the outward eye, a kingdom within, a kingdom not of this world?

Do I mean that there was nothing startling in such announcements to all or to most of those who first heard them? If I did, I should be rejecting the express testimony of the Evangelists. They tell us that the leading members of the Jewish commonwealth, and all the most admired and popular sects whch divided it, were continually perplexed and outraged by this language. But they tell us also, that these same persons had lost the family and national character of Hebrews, that they perverted the express commands of God respecting the honouring of fathers and mothers, that they had no feelings of fellowship with Israelites as Israelites, but glorified themselves in their difference from the rest of their countrymen either on the score of righteousness or of wisdom; that individual self-exaltation, on one or the other of these grounds, was their distinguishing characteristic. They tell us, in strict consistency with these observations, that these men were never so scandalised as when Jesus spoke of His *Father,* of His coming to do His will, of His knowing Him, and being one with Him. The idea of a relation between men and their Maker, which was the idea implied in the Abrahamic covenant, had wholly departed from them; and therefore, the hope of a complete manifestation of the ground upon which this relationship rested, the hope which had sustained every suffering Israelite in every age, which was expressly the hope of Israel, could not be cherished by them. Their idea of God was the heathen one of a Being sitting in the clouds or diffused through the universe, entirely separated from His worshippers, incapable of speaking through men to men, only declaring Himself by signs, like those of the red sky in the morning and the lowering sky in the evening. And therefore the king they expected was the counterpart of the absolute Emperor. It is true that the awful words, "We have no king but Caesar," would not have been uttered at any other moment than the one which called them forth; that it required the most intense hatred and all the other passsions which then had possession of their hearts, to induce the priests formally to abandon the dream of Jewish supremacy; and that they probably

reserved to themselves a right of maintaining one doctrine in the schools, another
in the judgment-hall. Still these words expressed the most inward thought of the
speakers; the king of Abraham's seed whom they wanted was a Caesar and nothing else.

But those who amidst much confusion and ignorance had really claimed their
position as members of a nation in covenant with God; those who had walked in
the ordinances of the Lord blameless, finding in every symbol of the Divine Presence, which seemed to the world a phantom, the deepest reality, and in what the
world called realities, the merest phantoms; those who were conscious of their
own darkness, but rested upon the promise of a light which should arise and shine
upon their land; those who, uniting to public shame a miserable sense of moral
evil, looked for a deliverer from both at once; those to whom the sight of the Roman soldier was oppressive, not because it reminded them of their tribute, but
because it told them that the national life was gone, or lasted only in their prayers;
those who under the fig-tree had besought God that the clouds which hid His
countenance from them might be dispersed, that He would remember the poor,
and that men might not have the upper hand: these, whether or no they could
reconcile in their understandings the idea of a kingdom which should rule over
all with one which should be in their hearts, at least acknowledged inwardly that
only one to which both descriptions were applicable could meet the cries which
they had sent up to heaven. And whatever they saw of Him who was proclaimed
the king, whatever they heard Him speak, tended to bring these thoughts into
harmony, or at all events to make them feel that each alike was necessary. He exercised power over the elements and over the secret functions of the human body,
(of course I am assuming the story of the Evangelists, my object being to show
that the different parts of it are thoroughly consistent, when they are viewed in
reference to one leading idea,) but this power is exercised for the sake of timid
fishermen, of paralytics and lepers. He declares that His kingdom is like unto a
grain of mustard-seed, which is indeed the least of all seeds, but which becomes
a tree wherein the fowls of the air lodge; He declares also that this seed of the
kingdom is scattered over different soils, and that the right soil for it is an honest *heart*. His *acts* produce the most obvious outward effects, yet their main effect is to carry the persuasion home to the mind of the prepared observer, that a
communion had been opened between the visible and the invisible world, and
that the one was under the power of the other. His words were addressed to Israelites as the children of the covenant, yet every one of them tended to awaken
in these Israelites a sense of *humanity,* a feeling that to be Israelites they must be
more. And all this general language was preparatory to the discoveries which were
made in that last supper when, having loved His own who were in the world, He
loved them unto the end,—to the announcements that they were all united in
Him, as the branch is united to the vine, that there was a still more wonderful
union between Him and His Father, to the knowledge of which they might
through this union attain, and that a Spirit would come to dwell with them and

to testify of Him and of the Father. All which discourses to men are gathered up in the amazing prayer, "That they all may be one, as Thou, Father, art in Me, and I in Thee, that they may be one in Us."

Either those words contain the essence and meaning of the whole history, or that history must be rejected as being from first to last the wickedest lie and the most awful blasphemy ever palmed upon the world. And if they do contain the meaning of it, that meaning must be embodied in *acts*. The Evangelists therefore go on to record in words perfectly calm and simple the death of their Master and His resurrection. As events they are related; no comment is made upon them; few hints are given of any effects to follow from them. We are made to feel by the quiet accurate detail, "He certainly died, who, as we believed, was the Son of God, and the King of Israel; He actually rose with His body, and came among us who knew Him, and spake and ate with us: this is the accomplishment of the union between heaven and earth; it is no longer a word, it is a fact." And of this fact, the risen Lord tells His Apostles that they are to go into the world and testify; not merely to testify of it, but to adopt men into a society grounded upon the accomplishment of it. In connexion with that command, and as the ultimate basis of the universal society, a NAME is proclaimed, in which the name that had been revealed to Abraham, and that more awful one which Moses heard in the bush, are combined and reconciled.

To a person who has contemplated the Gospel merely as the case of certain great doctrines or fine moralities, the *Acts of the Apostles* must be an utterly unintelligible book. For in the specimens of the Apostles' preaching which it gives us, there are comparatively few references to the discourses or the parables of our Lord. They dwell mainly upon the great acts of death and resurrection as evidences that Jesus was the king, as expounding and consummating the previous history of the Jewish people, as justifying and realising the truth which worked in the minds of the heathen, "that we are His offspring." On the other hand, a person who really looks upon the Bible as the history of the establishment of a universal and spiritual kingdom, of that kingdom which God had ever intended for men, and of which the universal kingdom then existing in the world was the formal opposite, will find in this book exactly that without which all the former records would be unmeaning.

The narrator of such transcendent events as the ascension of the Son of Man into the invisible glory, or the descent of the Spirit to take possession of the feelings, thoughts, utterances of mortal men, might have been expected to stand still and wonder at that which with so entire a belief he was recording. But no, he looks upon these events as the necessary consummation of all that went before, the necessary foundations of the existence of the Church. And therefore he can quietly relate any other circumstances, however apparently disproportionate, which were demanded for the outward manifestation and development of that Church, such as the meeting of the Apostles in the upper room, and the completion of their number. If the foundation of this kingdom were the end of all the purposes of God, if it were the kingdom of God among men, the human conditions of it could be no more passed over than the divine; it was as needful to prove that the ladder had its foot upon earth, as that it had come down out of heaven. As we proceed, we find every new step of the story leading us to notice the Church as the child which the Jewish polity had for so many ages been carrying in its womb. Its filial relation is first demonstrated, it is shown to be an Israelitic not a *mundane* commonwealth; then it is shown that, though not mundane, it is essentially *human,* containing a principle of expansion greater than that which dwelt in the Roman empire.

And here lies the apparent contradiction, the real harmony, of those two aspects in which this kingdom was contemplated by the Apostles of the Circumcision and by St. Paul. The one witnessed for the continuity of it, the other for its freedom from all national exclusions. These, we may believe, were their respective offices. Yet, as each fulfilled the one, he was in fact teaching the other truth most effectually. St. Peter and St. James were maintaining the universality of the Church, while they were contending for its Jewish character and derivation. St. Paul was maintaining the national covenant, while he was telling the Gentiles, that if they were circumcised Christ would profit them nothing. Take away the first testimony and the Church becomes an earthly not a spiritual commonwealth, and therefore subject to earthly limitations; take away the second, and the promise to Abraham is unfulfilled. In another sense, as the canon of Scripture shows, St. Paul was more directly carrying out the spirit of the Jewish distinction, by upholding the distinctness of ecclesiastical communities according to tribes and countries, than the Apostles of Jerusalem; and they were carrying out the idea of the universality of the Church more than he did by addressing the members of it as of an entire community dispersed through different parts of the world.

But we must not forget that while this universal society, according to the historical conception of it, grew out of the Jewish family and nation, it is, according to the theological conception of it, the root of both. "That," says Aristotle,* "which is first as cause is last in discovery." And this beautiful formula is translated into life and reality in the letter to the Ephesians, when St. Paul tells them that they were created in Christ before all worlds, and when he speaks of the transcendent economy as being gradually revealed to the Apostles and Prophets by the Spirit. In this passage it seems to me lies the key to the whole character of the dispensation, as well as of the books in which it is set forth. If the Gospel be the revelation or unveiling of a mystery hidden from ages and generations; if this mystery be the true constitution of humanity in Christ, so that a man believes and acts a lie who does not claim for himself union with Christ, we can understand why the deepest writings of the New Testament, instead of being digests of doctrine, are epistles, explaining to those who had been admitted into the

---

* *To prōton aition eschaton en tē heuresei.*

Church of Christ their own position, bringing out that side of it which had reference to the circumstances in which they were placed or to their most besetting sins, and showing what life was in consistency, what life at variance, with it. We can understand why the opening of the first of these epistles, of the one which has been supposed to be most like a systematic treatise, announces that the Gospel is concerning Jesus Christ, who was made of the seed of David according to the flesh, and marked out as the Son of God with power, according to the Spirit of holiness, by the resurrection of the dead. The fact of a union between the Godhead and humanity is thus set forth as the one which the Apostle felt himself appointed to proclaim, which was the ground of the message to the Gentiles, and in which all ideas of reconciliation, of a divine life, justification by faith, sanctification by the Spirit, were implicitly contained. We can understand why the great flight of the Apostle with the Corinthians should be because they exalted certain notions, and certain men as the representatives of these notions, into the place of Him who was the Lord of their fellowship, and why pride, sensuality, contempt of others, abuse of ordinances, should be necessarily consequent upon that sin. We can understand why St. Paul curses with such vehemence those false teachers who had denied the Galatians the right to call themselves children of God in Christ in virtue of the new covenant, and had sent them back to the old. We may perceive that those wonderful words in which he addresses the Ephesians, when he tells them that they were sitting in heavenly places in Christ Jesus, are just as real and practical as the exhortations at the end of the same letter, respecting the duties of husbands and wives, fathers and children, and that the second are involved in the first. We may see what connexion there is between the entreaty to the Colossians not to stoop to will-worship and the service of angels, and the assertion of the fact that Christ was in them the hope of glory, and that He is the head in whom dwell all the riches of wisdom and knowledge. We may see how possible it was for some of the Philippian Church to be enemies to the cross of Christ, their god their belly, their glory their shame, not because they had not been admitted to the privileges of being members of Christ, but because they had not pressed forward to realise their claim. We may enter a little into the idea of the letters to the Thessalonians, however we may differ about the particular time or times of its accomplishment, that there must be a coeval manifestation of the mystery of iniquity and of the mystery of godliness; that the two kingdoms, being always in conflict, at certain great crises of the world are brought into direct and open collision. We shall not need any evidence of the Apostolical derivation of the epistle to the Hebrews, to convince us that it unfolds the relations between the national and the universal dispensation, between that which was the shadow and that which was the substance of a Divine humanity; between that which enabled the worshipper to expect a perfect admission into the Divine presence, and that which admitted him to it; between that which revealed God to him as the enemy of evil, and that which revealed Him as the conqueror of it. Nor is it inconsistent with any previous intimation which has been given us, that the writer of this epistle should in every part of it represent the sin of men as consisting in their unbelief of the blessings into which they are received at each stage of the Divine manifestation, and that he should with solemn earnestness, mixed with warnings of a fearful and hopeless apostasy, urge those whom he is addressing to believe that the position into which they had been brought was that after which all former ages had been aspiring, and as such, to claim it. From these exhortations and admonitions, the transition is easy to those Catholic epistles which some have found it so hard to reconcile with the doctrine of St. Paul. And doubtless, if the faith which the epistle to the Romans and the epistle to the Hebrews adjured men, by such grand promises and dire threats, to exercise, were not faith in a living Being, who had adopted men into fellowship with himself on purpose that *being* righteous by virtue of that union they might *do* righteous acts, that having claimed their place as members of a body the Spirit might work in them to will and to do of his good pleasure, the assertions that faith without works saves, and that faith without works cannot save, are hopelessly irreconcilable. But if the idea of St. Paul, as much as of St. James, be, that all worth may be attributed to faith in so far forth as it unites us to an object and raises us out of ourselves, no worth at all, so far as it is contemplated simply as a property in ourselves; if this be the very principle which the whole Bible is developing, one does not well see what either position would be good for, if the other were wanting. If our Lord came among men that He might bring them into a kingdom of righteousness, peace, and joy, because a kingdom grounded upon fellowship with a righteous and perfect Being, the notion that that righteousness can ever belong to any man in himself, and the notion that everyone is not to exhibit the fruits of it in himself, would seem to be equally contradictions. And therefore I believe that without this consideration we shall be as much puzzled by the sketch of a Christian man's life, discipline, and conflicts, in the epistle of St. Peter, and by the doctrine of St. John, that love is the consummation of all God's revelations and all man's strivings, as by any former part of the book. For that men are not to gain a kingdom hereafter, but are put in possession of it now, and that through their chastisements and the oppositions of their evil nature they are to learn its character and enter into its privileges, is surely taught in every verse of the one; and that love has been manifested unto men, that they have been brought into fellowship with it, that by that fellowship they may rise to the fruition of it, and that this fellowship is for us as members of a family, so that he who loveth God must love his brother also, is affirmed again and again in express words of the other. With such thoughts in our mind, I believe we may venture, with hope of the deepest instruction, upon the study of the last book in the Bible. For though we may not be able to determine which of all the chronological speculations respecting it is the least untenable, though we may not decide confidently whether it speaks to us of the future or of the past, whether it describes a conflict of principles or of persons, of this we shall have no doubt, that it does exhibit at one period or through all periods a real kingdom of heaven upon earth, a kingdom of which the principle must be ever the same, a kingdom to which all kingdoms are meant to be in subjection; a kingdom which is maintaining itself against an opposing tyranny, whereof the ultimate law is brute force or unalloyed selfishness; a kingdom which must prevail because it rests upon a *name* which expresses the perfect Love, the ineffable Unity, the name of the Father, and of the Son, and of the Holy Ghost.

CHAPTER 2

The Epistles of St. John:
Lectures on Christian Ethics

INTRODUCTORY*

I have given some lessons on Ethics, or Morals, to a class in the College, which met me on one of the evenings of the week. I have had a Bible class on the Sunday evenings. I propose at this time to give a lecture upon Morals, or Ethics, which shall be drawn from a book in the Bible.

Some of you, I dare say, will wish to ask one or two questions. I have spoken of Morals, or Ethics. First, what do I mean by the word Morals? It is a word derived from the Latin; it signifies Manners. I understand by it the manners and habits which belong to us as human beings. That is the sense I have always given it in my lectures. Do I intend something different by Ethics? No; I intend the same thing. It is a word derived from the Greek. It expresses, I think, a little more delicately and accurately than the other word, that the manners are not outside manners, not mere deportment. It answers more nearly to what we call character. I have, therefore, adopted both expressions; but either will serve our purpose.

If this be the case, then you may ask me, in the second place, why in the programme I have prefixed the adjective Christian to Ethics? Did I not propose to speak of the habits or character of a man? Do I mean that a Christian is to be something different from a man? Do I think that he can be anything better than a man? Or do I suppose there is one kind of morals for week-days and another for Sundays, and that the last is to be got from the Bible, the first somewhere else?

You cannot be more anxious to ask these last questions than I am to answer them. I have little hope that we can understand one another till I have quite cleared my meaning about them. And I feel very confident that I shall be able to make you, the members of this College, understand me even if I fail to make

*From *The Epistles of St. John: A Series of Lectures on Christian Ethics* (Cambridge: Macmillan and Co., 1857), Lecture 1, 1–18.

other people understand me. I think so because I believe you come to study morals, and every other subject, for the sake of work, for the sake of life. I think so further, because I know that my colleagues, and that all who come by accident to lecture among you, cultivate that disposition in you and try to show you that books only exist to make us acquainted with facts and with laws which God has established for us and for the world. Some of you may have listened to a beautiful lecture, which was so kindly given here last night, upon Natural History, by Mr. Huxley. You will have observed how he proceeded. You will remember that he did not give us a system out of a book; that he did not entertain us with an eloquent panegyric on his study. He took a lobster; he explained to us the different parts of its frame, the uses to which each part was applied, the type upon which the whole was constructed. So he led us by degrees to perceive what the objects of Natural History are, how it interprets one and another portion of the Universe to us, how it may cultivate our own minds. I cannot follow an eminent and accomplished man of science, but I should like at least to catch something of his spirit, above all of his modesty. And I should like you to try me by the same kind of test, severe as it is. If I cannot help you better to understand the facts and laws which most concern yourselves, my words ought to go for nothing.

Perhaps I shall be able to explain the plan which I have endeavoured and am endeavouring to pursue in this College of Working Men, if I tell you a little of my own experience when I was a student in a much older and more august society. From what you have heard of the University of Oxford, and of its being confined till very lately to members of the Church of England, you will perhaps fancy that the book on Ethics, or Morals, which is used there, is a book written by some eminent divine. By no means. It is a book written by an old Pagan philosopher. Out of that I learnt lessons on this great subject. What other books I read there on Ethics, were chiefly for the purpose of illustrating the Ethics of Aristotle. How did this answer? I cannot venture to speak for others; but I will for myself. I owe quite unspeakable gratitude to the University of Oxford, for having put this book into my hands and induced me to read it and think of it. I doubt if I could have received a greater service from any University or any teacher. For I will tell you what this book did for me. First, it assured me that the principles of Morals cannot belong to one time or another, that they must belong to all times. Here was an old Heathen Greek making me aware of things that were passing in me, detecting my laziness and my insincerity, showing how little I was doing the things which I professed to do, forcing me to confess that, with all the advantages which I had, he was better than I was. That was one great thing. Whatever takes down a young man's conceit must be profitable to him. This book might have done it much more effectually in my case than it did; that was my fault, not the writer's. Next, I could not but learn from him, for he took immense pains to tell me so, that it is not by reading a book, or learning a set of maxims by heart, one gets to know anything of morality; that it belongs to life, and must be learnt in the daily practice of life. I repeat it, he tells us this very often. English and Christian writers might have told it me also. But I am not sure that their words would have gone as much home to me as Aristotle's did. I might have thought that it was their business, part of their profession, to utter that maxim; and also, there would have been so much in these books which I did not find in Aristotle, that I might have trusted them more, and not have thought that I wanted some inward experience to expound them. For this is the third good that I got from the old Greek; he did *not* satisfy me. He told me a number of things which I believed then, and believe now, to be of continual use. He made me see the worth of habits, the worth of acts, the worth of moral purposes. But when I asked him what was to be the standard of my habits and acts and moral purposes, he did not give me any distinct answer. And the more I questioned him, the less could I extract from him what I wanted. He had made me know that it was not a mere book standard I needed, that all the theories and all the laws in the world would not give it me. For that I was infinitely obliged to him. But I positively wanted to learn where it was, since without it I felt I could not practise the things he wished me to practise, I could not be the worthy man he was trying to make me. Nay, I should have been a very unworthy man; for I had reason to think there was such a standard, and I felt strange twinges for having departed from it, which twinges he could not explain to me.

Of course many people would have said to me at once, "If you want this standard you must turn to the Bible." The common religious opinion of my country said so; the University in which I had been studying this Heathen book said so. But I found a difficulty in practically attending to the recommendation. I had got the conviction thoroughly worked into me, that this standard could not be contained in any letters, though they were the most wonderful letters ever written in the world. It did not signify how good they were, how much authority they had. Aristotle's was an imperfect treatise, a treatise containing plenty of errors. But if there were a perfect treatise, one in which were no errors at all, it would not be the standard that I wanted; still less would it enable me to follow a standard. The standard must be a LIFE. It must be set forth in a living Person. If it is to do me any good, his life must in some way act upon my life. Aristotle had been, as I said, a blessing to me for making me understand that this was so; he had failed from being unable to show me such a life as this. Neither the authority of my country's faith nor of my University, though I had reason to reverence them both, could warrant me in practising a self-deception in so important a matter. If the Bible was merely a book, though it might be the best of all books, though it might be a book without a flaw, I could not hope to find in it that which I was seeking.

There was another lesson I had learnt from Aristotle,—had learnt from that which he did tell me and from that which he did not tell me. He believed that there was one Creator of the Universe. He might pay a sort of reverence to the gods whom his country worshipped, but they evidently did not affect his speculations in the least about Nature or about Morals. All his inquiries as to the course of the world and as to man's life were pursued independently of them. He arrived at the conclusion, that it was most likely there was one Ruler over the whole Universe, by reasonings that were quite independent of any he had received by tradition.

Well, I said to myself, this acknowledgment of a one Ruler in him is very good, I am very glad he was able to make it. But has it anything to do with *me*? *I* dwell in this world. Is there any sort of relation between *me* and the Maker of it? I found from the history of the world that men everywhere had been dreaming that they had something to do with some powers or rulers whom they could not see. I found that these dreams had not been confined to a few people here or there, who might perhaps have leisure for dreaming; that they had affected the condition of all people from the highest to the lowest; that what they thought of their gods, and the worship they had paid to their gods, had influenced their civil life, their opinions about Nature, their notions of what they themselves were to do and to be. It had influenced their conduct to each other, it had influenced their inward characters. Aristotle no doubt had discovered that the honesty of their investigations and the honesty of their practice was very seriously interfered with by the terror with which the gods inspired them, and by the notions they had of the feelings and passions of the gods and of the demands they made upon men. He had little hope that his countrymen would fairly study the facts of nature or the facts of human life, while these confusions about the gods, and their connexion with them, were continually intruding themselves into their minds. So he simply gave all these thoughts the go by. His physical studies and his moral studies were pursued without reference to them.

One could not help admiring Aristotle for taking a course which seemed to him the most honest under his circumstances. It showed him to be a brave man, that he did not profess to understand what he did not understand, and that he tried to make the best of what he did. To those who act thus more will be given in due time. One said so whose words I believe; who never said anything which I do not expect will come to pass. But then I was bound to inquire for my own sake whether this course was a reasonable or a possible one. Certainly the effect of it was to cut off an immense body of facts which had told upon the condition of all generations of men, all tribes of the earth. Certainly the effect of it was to confine the study of the Morality which is for all human beings within a small circle of human beings. But was this all? Could I for myself dispense with thoughts of this kind? No; those twinges of which I spoke, were they not just like what other men had felt in other ages and in other regions of the world? Were they not witnesses to me that I had a common nature with them, that I was not free from their doubts and fears and griefs? Did they not show that I needed what they needed? Could I make up a scheme of morality for myself which should take no notice of these facts in myself? And what did these facts imply? Did not they seem to say, "There *is* some connexion between you and a Being who is higher and better than yourself? He *is* calling you to account for these acts of yours and

these thoughts of yours. If you had nothing to do with Him, you might be easier than you are; but you would be more of a mere animal, you would be less of
a man."

A person who finds this out is likely to be in great perplexity. For he cannot
be satisfied with only talking of a one Creator of the universe. What he is thinking of is of a Being who has something to do with *him,* who is *his* Ruler, who is
the standard of *his* life. And yet he cannot help perceiving that men's opinions
about this Being have often led them to strange crimes and cruelties. He cannot
wonder that Aristotle, and many men since his time, should think it safer to lay
down the plan of their existence without any direct reference to Him. What is to
be done? For to stand still in such a state of mind as this is impossible. The world
does not stand still. Our own years and days do not stand still. We are swept
along, whether along in the right course or in the wrong one.

Then perhaps it may occur to a man to ask, "Was I doing justice to the faith
of my country, when I supposed that it was merely setting up a book, even a divine book, as the standard of man's acts, and life, and morality? Is not that Book
commonly spoken of as a Revelation of God? Is it not spoken of as the Revelation of One who was the Son of God and the Image of God, and who became
Man? Supposing it were this, might it not tell just what Aristotle shows me that
I need to be told? Might it not set forth to me a *Life?* Might it not set forth the
Life that is the standard of my life, the standard of the life of all human beings?
Might it not explain the dreams there have been in all men about the relation be-
tween them and some Being that is above them? Might it not clear those dreams
of that which has been so mischievous in them? Might it not place Ethics, or
Morals, on a true and universal ground?"

Those of you who have attended my Bible class on Sunday evenings, will
know that I have taken some pains to show you that the Bible may be read as a
continuous history, and that it is the history of the unveiling of God to the creature whom He has made in His image. I have tried to show you this by taking
separate books in the New Testament, and examining them chapter by chapter,
verse by verse. I have tried to show it you by beginning at the beginning of the
Old Testament, and tracing the course of its narratives. I have tried to show it
you by comparing the Old Testament with the New. I have not used any arguments to prove that the book was divine or was worthy of our attention. If it was
divine and worthy of our attention, I thought it would make good its claims for
itself, though I could not make them good. All I wanted was that we should find
out what it is saying to us. I believe if we question it, it will answer more honestly than any book in the world. There may be mistakes in our translation of it
which ought to be set right, as all mistakes ought to be set right where they can
be, especially when they have to do with the most important matters. But in our
way of proceeding with the Old Testament, this was not a very serious matter;
for we wanted to find out the upshot of the history, the principle which was
involved in it; and that did not depend much upon the interpretation or the

construing of particular texts. Whenever I could give you any light that I thought might make a passage clearer, especially in those books which we were examining more carefully, I was bound to do so. But what I chiefly desired was, that I might put myself as little as possible between you and the revelation which I was sure the book contained, and that we should question ourselves and each other to see whether it did reveal anything to us, whether it did scatter any darkness that was in us before. That was what I aimed at in this course of lessons. I believe the aim was right and the method was right, whether I have succeeded or not.

In the Lectures which were said to be on Ethics, or Morals, I pursued an entirely different method. I had no text-book; I rather carefully avoided text-books; I was afraid you should think I was delivering a system which was contained in them, not making you acquainted with facts which were in you. I was equally afraid that you should think I was working a system out of my own head. I tried to avoid both dangers by speaking to you of what you all knew. When any of us is born into this world, he is surrounded by objects which he is by degrees to get acquainted with through his senses. But he has also human relations—a mother at all events, a father; perhaps brothers and sisters. He sees their faces, he hears their voices, as he sees the curtains of the bed and hears the noise in the streets. But his relation to them must be something different from this. We all are sure that it is. All the seeing and hearing in the world do not fulfil that relation. We speak of affections. Evidently a man's relation to his fellow-men fails utterly, is not fulfilled, unless he has these affections. They are as necessary to it as seeing and hearing are to his intercourse with any thing that is not human. To these relationships and to these affections, then, we addressed ourselves first of all. The consideration of them gave rise to a number of observations and a number of questions. If we merely confined ourselves to the life of a *child,* we were met with a variety of serious inquiries as to how its affections were to be directed, as to the distortions to which they were liable, as to the influence of the senses upon them, and their influence upon the senses. We seemed to learn a good deal by examining the words which we use to describe these facts, as well as by comparing our experiences of the facts themselves. What the members of my class said to me, and the difficulties which they raised, were very useful to me and helped me to see many things more clearly. If I did not remove their difficulties, I hope I may have shown some of them a way of removing them for themselves, by doing the duty which they are called to do.

Duty? What did that mean? That word introduced us to another series of questions which belonged to the second division of these lessons. At some time there arises in the mind of each of us the sense that he is an individual person, not merely related to certain other people. I pointed out this feeling to you as especially characteristic of a *boy,* as being indicated by certain exhibitions of self-will and independence, and determination to put forth power, such as we had only seen the germs of in the *child.* I tried to show you that if these feelings are left to themselves, he becomes a savage; but that this is not the state that is intended for any one of us. I urged that all the efforts of schoolmasters, where they had been wise, had tended to awaken a sense of responsibility, to make the boy feel that he is subject to laws which must be executed in punishments if they are not obeyed. This dread of punishment may deter from crimes; but it can never lead any one to do a single right action. Till we understand that there is something *due* from us, till the sense of *duty* is awakened, we have no freedom, we are not even in the way to become men. To understand what this sense of duty is, I was driven to speak to you of that mysterious *Conscience,* which all men in some sort confess, which those who deny it in their theories bear witness of in their acts and in their habitual language. Some of you will remember what pains have been devoted to this inquiry during the last term, and how we were driven at last by facts, and in defiance of the speculations of eminent men, men worthy of all reverence, to think that the conscience is not a power of its own, but is a witness to us of some One speaking to us, commanding us, judging us.

Very deep questions indeed started up unawares while we were engaged with this topic, and suggested the third division of our subject, which concerns especially the full-grown *man* after he is loosed from the direct restraints of parents or teachers, questions concerning our Will and our Reason: how the one is only free when it is delivered from self-will; how the other is only in its proper state when it is seeking for truth and does not think that it can make truth; how both together are the very signs of what man is as distinguished from the animals; how both together are proofs that we are members of a race and family, and not a mere collection of individuals; how both together demand a perfect Will and a perfect Reason, that they may not miss the object and fail to fulfil the work for which they exist.

I do not go over this ground which some of us have travelled before, from a notion that no one will profit by these Sunday morning Lectures who has not attended my former courses. I refer to it that both the old and new students may see for what purpose I do use, and for what purpose I do not use the Holy Scriptures. I use them because I think they will show us what is the ground of those affections, of that conscience, of that reason and will, which we have to do with because we are human beings, and which we must have to do with supposing there were no Scriptures at all. I do not use them because I look upon them as substitutes for these affections, or conscience, or reason, or will. I use them because I look upon them as God's revelation to us of ourselves, who are made in His image, and of Himself, who has made us in His image. I do not use them as if they would mean anything to us, or be of any worth to us, supposing we were not made in His image, supposing it were not possible for us to be acquainted with Him. I use them because I conceive they set forth Christ as the Son of God and the Lord of every man. I do not use them because I think they set forth some standard which is good for a set of men called Christians, who are different from other men, and who have not the same God with other men. I use the Scriptures to show us what I believe is the law and the life for all of us, that law and life of which men in the old world had only a partial glimpse. I should not use them if I thought them less universal and more partial than the books of heathens or of later moralists.

Now, then, I have answered the questions with which I began. I am most anxious that you should not think of Christian Ethics, that is to say, of the Christian character, as different from human Ethics, that is to say, from the proper human character. I am anxious that you should not think of Sunday Ethics as different from week-day Ethics. But I am also anxious that you should think of the Ethics which are set forth to us in the Christian Scriptures as being the Ethics for men, of our Sunday lessons as interpreting the experience of the week. That is my reason for wishing to meet you here on these mornings. We form a Working Men's College; that is to say, a college of men not distinguished from other men by any advantages; who want only to be men and to do the work of men. Sunday, the day of rest, is, I believe, given us especially for this end. Work has its ground in rest and its termination in rest. Man is made to work and to rest. In his hours of rest he is preparing for work; in his hours of work he is preparing for rest. One great preparation is to learn what the blessing of rest is, in whom he may rest, that we may learn also what the blessing of work is, and under whose guidance he may work. If the Sunday gives us that wisdom, I believe it does more for us than if it gives us merely animal rest; though I am far from undervaluing that either. At any rate, it is my business to do what I can that those who desire it may obtain the former gift. It is my duty to consider how I may help them most to attain it. And after much consideration, I can find no way in which I can aid them better than by trying to work out with them the meaning of this Epistle of St. John.

As I have told you, generally, why I think the Bible may be our best teacher in Ethics, I will tell you now why I select this book of the Bible as serving that purpose more perfectly than any other. I have been endeavouring, as I said just now, in my evening Lectures, to show you in what sense I regard the Scriptures as a *history*. I should not give them that name if I did not discover in them a gradual unveiling of the divine purpose and divine life to man, a gradual education of men to understand, through their own wants, and weaknesses, and sins, what this purpose and this life is, and how they may be the better for it. Through all the patriarchal period of the Jewish history, through all the legal, through all the prophetical, I trace, and I wish you to trace, this revelation and this education. But if the revelation and the education are good for anything, they must be leading to some result.

I find this result expressed in these words:—"*That which was from the beginning, which we have heard, which we have seen with our eyes, which we have looked upon, and our hands have handled, of the Word of life (for the life was manifested, and we have seen it, and bear witness, and shew unto you that eternal life, which was with the Father, and was manifested to us;) that which we have seen and heard declare we unto you, that ye also may have fellowship with us: and truly our fellowship is with the Father, and with his Son Jesus Christ.*"

Do not suppose that I expect you to take in the meaning of these sentences all at once. If I did, I should not have thought it necessary to examine carefully into this letter. I hope, next Sunday, to go with you into the meaning of the principal words in these sentences, and to consider them in their connexion. But I think you can hardly hear them read to you without feeling that they have something to do with those questions which I said that a Heathen had taught me I must engage in, and those in which I have endeavoured to interest you by recalling to you different portions of your own experience. The very language which perhaps puzzles some persons on first taking up the book, about the Life and the manifestation of the Life, fits in with our previous thoughts and difficulties. Something like this is what we were asking for. The writer clearly means to tell us of a Person whom he has seen and handled, in whom he believes a divine and perfect life was shown forth, with which life, he says, he himself and those to whom he is writing, may have fellowship. I do not care who holds out to me this kind of promise. It so exactly answers to what I am looking for, that I must perforce give heed, I must beg the speaker to tell me what he means; I must look further into the account he gives of this matter, to see whether it is consistent with itself, whether it only seems to meet the demands of my spirit, or does actually meet them. Let the writer be who he will, I have a right to examine his words, not for his sake, but for my own. And if he brings a message to me from God Himself, I believe God will make it evident to me that he does.

I am glad, however, to hear anything I can hear about the speaker and about those to whom he spoke. If he were, as we in England believe him to have been, a fisherman who once mended his nets by the Lake of Galilee, and who was now dwelling, a grey-haired man, in the commercial city of Ephesus, it may be strange that he has anything to tell us who live in this far country of the west—anything to tell refined men and scholars, as well as working men, whose customs and whose language are altogether different from his, who belong to a world which is eighteen hundred years older than it was in his day. But if we shall find that what he spoke to the fathers and young men and children in Ephesus, who had been worshippers of the goddess Diana, or worshippers in the Jewish synagogue, and who had come to think that there was a Person who bound Jews and Gentiles into one; if, I say, we should find that what he told them has some deep interest for us—does make known to us secrets which we need to be acquainted with—we, at least, shall not care less for him because he was a fisherman or a Jewish fisherman. We shall hope that he will not, at all events, speak of accidents that belong to rich and comfortable people, when we want to know of principles which are for all equally. We shall hope that, as he was a Jew, he may be able to explain to us what the law and history of his own people had to do with mankind, and how he himself, being born a Jew, had been led to seek fellowship with men of other tribes. We shall hope that he may tell us how we are bound to our forefathers, and how we shall be bound to those who may dwell upon the earth when we have left it. We shall hope that he may have proved us and our children to be of the same family with the Ephesians to whom he wrote,—not to have a different Father from them or from him.

THE GROUND
OF CHRISTIAN ETHICS*

That which was from the beginning, which we have heard, which we have seen with our eyes, which we have looked upon, and our hands have handled, of the Word of Life; (for the life was manifested, and we have seen it, and bear witness, and show unto you that eternal life, which was with the Father, and was manifested unto us;) that which we have seen and heard declare we unto you, that ye also may have fellowship with us: and truly our fellowship is with the Father, and with His Son Jesus Christ. And these things write we unto you, that your joy may be full. This then is the message which we have heard of Him, and declare unto you, that God is light, and in Him is no darkness at all. If we say that we have fellowship with Him, and walk in darkness, we lie, and do not the truth.

—1 John 1:1–6

We call this book an Epistle, and I do not know that we have any right to say that it is not one. But it does not open like a letter. It is not addressed to any body of men, or to any one man. The author does not speak of himself. He does not introduce any greetings, such as you would expect of one who is at a distance from his friends. In all these respects it differs from the other Epistles in the New Testament, specially differs from those which St. Paul sent to the Gentile Churches which he had founded. The words *"These things we write to you,"* and others of the same kind which occur afterwards, do not permit us to suppose that it was a discourse delivered with the lips. Otherwise we might have fancied an aged man standing up in an assembly of men among whom he had dwelt a long time, to remind them what lessons he had taught them, and for what end he had lived. And that I doubt not was his design. He may have been too feeble to speak what was in his heart, or he may have been away from Ephesus for a while, in his exile at Patmos. Anyhow, it was ordered that his words should be committed to enduring letters, and that we should profit by them as much as those who lived in his day.

The absence of a special superscription has led people to call this Epistle a catholic or universal one. It well deserves the name. Its words, I think we shall find, are as good for London as Ephesus; for the nineteenth century as the first. And we shall understand better how fitly the opening words apply to us, if we consider for a moment what a peculiar fitness they had for the men who had sat by the old Apostle; who remembered that he had talked with our Lord on earth,

*From *The Epistles of St. John* (Cambridge: Macmillan and Co., 1857), Lecture 2, 19–33.

and had been with him at the last supper; who had listened to him while he re-called the words which had fallen from his Master's lips, the acts which had been done by his Master's hand. Do you not think this thought must have often come into their minds?—"Shall we not be terrible losers when he is taken from us?—losers, not merely as all are who part with a dear friend and guide, but in this sense—that henceforth we shall only have the lessons of Christ at second-hand; we shall only have scattered and broken memorials of His works and His life. And will it not be worse for our children than it is for us? Will not the tradition become fainter and fainter in each new generation? Will it not become more mixed with reports that are not true?" To be sure, they may have gone on, "we have books which contain accounts of His words and deeds, which are trustworthy. These we prize now; these we may transmit to the men who come after us and teach them to prize. But will not that be very different from hearing a living voice? Will reading a book be ever a substitute for that? And may there not be false reports which are handed down along with the true ones? Have not lying accounts of our Lord's deeds and words been put together already, which His Apostles have told us not to care for? Who will give these warnings to our descendants? Who will help them to discern between the honest record and the counterfeit one?"

I cannot doubt that such things were said at this time, because, in some form of language or other, people have been saying them ever since. They *have* fancied that each age was less likely to be right than the last, because it was further from the age of the Apostles. They *have* supposed that our knowledge of Christ can only be second-hand, or third-hand, or fourth-hand knowledge. They *have* disputed whether we are dependent on oral traditions or whether a written book is sufficient without them. They *have* asked who is to determine between the false reports and the true reports. They *have* debated these questions backwards and forwards, and are debating them still.

Now, St. John's words, it seems to me, meet these confusions, and answer them as no others can. He begins with speaking of that which he saw and heard and handled. Those who read his letter could have no doubt that he was referring to the time when he saw the face of Jesus Christ, when he heard His discourses, when he grasped His hand, when he leaned upon His breast. There might be some still upon earth who had been in Jerusalem at that time, who had even been disciples of Christ. There would not be any of them upon the earth long. And there was none of them who would have thought he had as much right to use these expressions as the son of Zebedee had. Here, then, he claims for himself the full dignity of an Apostle. Whatever advantage there was in this kind of intercourse with Jesus, he could say, "It was mine."

Yet there is something peculiar in his mode of speaking. Why does he not say *"He* whom we saw and heard and handled?" St. John certainly meant this. Would it not have been more simple and natural to adopt that form of language? Before we decide, let us hear what he does say: *"That which we have seen with our eyes, and our ears have heard, and our hands have handled, of the Word of Life."* The preposition *of,* which our translators have adopted, does not exactly answer to the one which St. John uses. I do not know whether I wish that they had rendered it *"about,"* though that certainly would have been more literal. That would be nearly as unintelligible as *"of,"* if we do not exercise our minds upon the passage; if we do, either may be intelligible. Think of the friend whom you have known best and loved best. Let each ask himself, "What is it that I have known and loved in him?" Suppose he is gone away. You will recollect his look, the tones of his voice, the pressure of his hand. But you would not call these *himself.* You would not say these *were* your friend. You would say these were of him or about him. You would say that what you could not see or hear or handle was much more that which attached you to itself, that which you rested in. You would say— would not you?—"There was a life in him, which took hold of me. It was in that I found the difference between him and other people. It was with that I could converse. It was that which conversed with me. The goodness, the wisdom, the power which I recognised, were in that. The hearing, the seeing, the handling would have been nothing without that. They brought me in contact with the out- side of the man,—an outside that was dear to me because of that which it ex- pressed,—but *he* was within."

Now, St. John says exactly this about that Lord and Master who called him from mending his nets, only he says something more than this. He says that that face of His which he saw, that voice of His which he heard, those hands of His which he handled were "about the WORD *of Life.*" A life was there within that body, just as there is a life within the body of each man whom we converse with. A life revealed itself or was manifested through those outward organs of His, just as a life is manifested through the outward organs of every person who speaks to us, who looks at us, who approaches us. But St. John says that this life which was in Him was not merely *a* life, but *the* Life; the life from which all the life that is in us and in the other creatures is derived. That there must be such a Life, such a central fountain of life as this, we all, I believe, feel more or less strongly. It is what men have been asking for in every country and every age. I showed you last Sunday how one who is seeking a ground for his own moral life is led to perceive the necessity of it. And I observed then how the thought of this life in man asso- ciated itself with the thought of God; how men had dreamed that the true stan- dard and ultimate source of their life must be in Him. To that conviction, also, St. John does justice; the phrase *"Word* of Life" intimates that the life which was in this Person was, in very deed, the expression or utterance of that which is in God. Just as the word I speak contains the thought that is in me and that I put into it; so this life with which St. John had held converse, was, he says, the Word of Life; the expression of the whole Mind and Nature of Him from whom all things have proceeded. We say sometimes of a speech which strikes us as very sin- cere and very powerful, "The speaker threw his whole soul into it." We mean that that speech showed or expressed to us very much of what we think was in the man who delivered it. But we know that no man can tell us *all* that is in him, by a speech. We must compare one thing that he says with another, we must be acquainted with his acts as well as with his sayings; both together help us to understand his mind and purpose. And there is so much in us that is variable and contradictory, that one act or one word may not represent the same mind and purpose with another. You may say to-day, "I fancied that person was one of the gentlest of human beings; now I have seen him in a passion, I find another kind of man in him; I cannot tell what to think of him." But supposing there were a being with nothing variable or contradictory in his nature, whose purpose was always the same, who was himself always the same; the sayings which he spoke and the acts which he did would be always in accordance; each one would tell the truth about him, each one would tell us of himself. And his acts, and his sayings together, would represent one life. Supposing, then, that you could ever say of the life of a man, "This life perfectly expresses the mind and purpose of God, this life perfectly shows the life that is in Him"—then you would say, "This is the Word of God. In him God speaks out Himself. In him God manifests Himself." You would not mean merely that something which he spoke proceeded from God, and declared what He intended or willed. You would mean that he, the whole person, was and is the Word of God.

You will think perhaps that I am in a hurry to put this meaning upon St. John, when perhaps his expressions can be explained in another way. There is nothing that I wish less than that any one should take my interpretation for granted. There is nothing that I wish more than that they should compare St. John's different writings together, and see whether this is not the kind of thing that he is telling us in all of them. I say the *kind of thing;* for I am sure that what he is telling us is much better, and deeper, and larger than I have been able to express in my language. Perhaps one of the first discoveries to which such an examination would lead you, is the feebleness, the poverty, the circumlocution of my phrases, as contrasted with the strength, and the richness, and the directness of his. This, however, you may ascertain for yourselves. The meaning of these expressions *"Word of God," "Word of Life,"* has not been left by the Apostle for other interpreters to bring out. His whole Gospel is an elucidation of it. There is not one narrative in that Gospel which does not help to present it in some new aspect. In doing so, I think—indeed, I have endeavoured elsewhere to prove—that he has made the force of the expression *"Word of God"* in the Old Testament, and so the whole history and purport of the Old Testament, beautifully clear and consistent. And I am also convinced that this language of his is only obscure to us just as the great principles of science are obscure—not from *their* want of simplicity, but from *our* want of simplicity; and that like those principles, we shall at last be led to it by finding that we cannot explain the facts which most need to be explained, without it. Many circumstances in the history of our time, are, it seems to me, tending to this result; none more directly than the conviction, at which we have all arrived, that the deepest knowledge is intended for all classes equally.

The full idea of a Word of God, a Word of Life, a Word who is the Light of men, will come out, I think, as we try to act upon that conviction, and not till then. We shall not see our way through the puzzles of education, till we have taken firm hold of this truth. When we do, we shall find it a very leveling one; we shall find that we are all learners from first to last, and that we have all a perfect Teacher. You will not wonder, therefore, that I should dwell upon this subject in a College of Working Men.

I am advancing but slowly with the passage which I have chosen. But I gave you notice that I should have to dwell upon the separate words of it; and St. John himself stops us when we are over-eager to proceed. Here you will see that he introduces a parenthesis, one, however, which is very necessary for the complete unfolding of his design. *"For the Life,"* he says, *"was manifested, and we have seen and bear witness, and declare to you that eternal life which was with the Father, and has been manifested to us."* Of that thought he is full. He must make the Ephesians understand that this is the beginning and end of all he has been saying to them since he began to dwell among them. *A* life has been manifested; *the* life has been manifested. That which he saw of Christ, while he was with Him upon earth, was to enable him to testify of this life. He had no other business than to tell them that it had been fully revealed. But that he may perform that task properly, he must tell them what kind of life it is. It was the eternal life. Not a life of years, and months, and days, and instants; but a fixed permanent life—the life of a Being in whom is no variableness, nor the shadow of a turning. I am only seeking for expressions that may give you some help in entering for yourselves into the force of this word; I do not want to change it for any other. We all oppose Eternity to Time. Each of us in his heart recognises that distinction as a true and necessary one. The more serious we become—the more we begin to think about what we are—the more real and deep the distinction becomes to us. And yet we are apt to lose ourselves in utter vagueness when we try to contemplate Eternity. It seems to us something not distinct from time, but a very very long time. Unawares, we begin to measure it by our clocks, even while we say it cannot be measured by them. And so by degrees we dismiss the consideration of it as much as we can, because if we put it far from us, it seems to fade into nothing, and if we bring it near to us, it seems too dreadful to endure. May I give you this hint about it? The Bible way of presenting it to us—St. John's way—is the safest and the most rational. He joins *eternal* to *Life;* he joins *Life* to *God.* If the Life is that which was manifested in Christ, in His words and acts, it is a life of gentleness, justice, truth. You cannot measure these by the clocks; you do not wish, or try to measure them. You never did so when you were thinking about the gentleness, or justice, or truth of a friend. And if that is the life of God, surely it is not a terrible thing—though it may be an awful thing—to recollect that He is, and was, and is to come, and that He is not far from any one of us.

But is that what St. John means by *eternal Life* here? Look at the next clause, and you will not doubt it. He speaks of the *"Life which was with the Father and has been manifested to us.*" You will not doubt that when he speaks of the Father, he means the Eternal God. I would not have you satisfied with saying that. The name *Father* is not a name that is ever used carelessly. It is *the* New Testament name. It is that name which we pray to have hallowed. We should ask ourselves, why it is the New Testament name; why every little child may use it now? And I do not think we can get any other answer than this, that He who came into the world, and showed forth that life in it whereof St. John speaks, said, "I come from a Father. My Life is the image of His Life. Therefore it is an eternal life. It did not begin at a certain time; it will not end at a certain time. And as you are partakers of my nature, you are intended to partake of this eternal life; you are the children of Him who has declared me to be His only-begotten Son."

I have thus brought together two names which are never long separated by St. John, the name *"Word of God,"* and the name *"Son of God."* Neither gives forth a complete sense without the other. We might suppose that the *"Word of God"* was only a sentence or decree of God—that it did not point to a person at all. If only the name *"Son of God"* was used, we might mix associations of time with Him who is declared to have an Eternal Life. The two expressions, when they are compared together, discover the full intention of the Apostle. He who shows forth the true life to man is as much one with God as the word is with the thought that it makes known. But that we may understand how personal and perfect the relation is, we must resort to the highest and tenderest of human relations. The union and sympathy between a son and a father, is most imperfect among men. There must be some perfect original of it. It could not be what it is to us if there were not. We are told that the original is where the original of all our life is—in God. The union of the Father with the Son is involved in the very idea of God as it is declared to us in the New Testament. We shall see also that it is involved in the idea of the way in which men are to partake in the life of God.

This is the subject of the third verse, *"What we have seen and heard declare we unto you, that ye also may have fellowship with us; and truly our fellowship is with the Father and with His Son Jesus Christ."* There is nothing, you see, which he claims for himself as an Apostle, that he does not claim for those to whom he writes. The very highest privilege which can belong to him, he affirms to be theirs. His reward is, that he has the delight of announcing to them that it is theirs, and how they may enter into the enjoyment of it. Fellowship or communion with God, he is to tell them, is possible for man. The inferior being may partake the nature of the superior. The creature who has fancied himself limited to threescore years and ten, may enter upon the eternal life of the Creator. The declaration sounds wonderful, the promise incredible. But the Christian revelation means nothing unless this assertion is true—unless this promise can be fulfilled. It professes to be the revelation of a Father through a Son, who has taken the nature of men upon Him—who has entered into our conditions of birth and suffering and death. If it is so, all who have that nature must stand in a direct filial relation to this Father in this Son; there must be some means by which they may acquire His mind, His character, or, to use once again St. John's more comprehensive word, His life.

"These things," says St. John in the next verse, *"write we unto you that your joy may be full or fulfilled."* I supposed that there might be a question among the Ephesian Christians, how they would fare after the Apostle had left the world—how their children would fare after they had left it. Would they be dependent upon a tradition, upon the things which the Apostles had recorded concerning their Master; a tradition that might become more muddy every year? Would they be dependent upon a mere written book? The Apostle answers emphatically "No," to both these demands. He saw and handled Christ; but it was that he might bear witness of a life that was in Him, an eternal life—one which had been in Him before the worlds were—one which would be in Him if all worlds were to come to an end. He had seen and handled that which was about this Word of Life, that he might tell them, because they were men—though they were not Apostles at all, though they had never seen and handled Christ at all—that His life was manifested to them, and that they might participate in it. He now adds, *"And these things we WRITE that your joy may be full."* They are written down, not that you may be satisfied with a set of letters, but that these letters may testify to you and to all generations which shall come after—when Apostles shall have been for centuries in their graves—of a life which cannot cease; of a life which must be the same always because it is in God; of a life which it is God's will to communicate to His creatures, and which it is their highest joy to receive.

One verse more, and I have finished this Lecture. I cannot separate it from those which have gone before, and you will see immediately how it belongs to the subject of my whole course. *"This then is the message which we have heard of Him, and declare unto you, that God is light, and in Him is no darkness at all."* This was the revelation which had been made to men in Him whom St. John had seen and handled—had been made not only with His lips, but in His acts—in the powers which He had exerted for man's benefit—in the death which He had died. If He was the Word of God, if the whole life and purpose of God were manifested in Him, then it was possible to say boldly, "There is not one dark spot in this Being, not one evil malicious thought against any creature whom He has formed. All is clear unbroken light." And this word "Light" is at once the simplest, and the fullest, and the deepest which can be used in human discourse. It is addressed to every man who has eyes, and who has ever looked on the sun, or to whom the sun has discovered the ground at his feet. The more you think of it, the more it satisfies you. It does not only tell you of a Goodness and Truth without flaw, though it does tell you of these; it tells you of a Goodness and Truth that are always seeking to spread themselves abroad, to send forth rays that shall penetrate everywhere, and scatter the darkness which opposes them.

Here, then, is the answer to those terrible conceptions which I said in my last Lecture men had formed of the Divine nature and character; those conceptions which made Aristotle think that it was better and safer to leave what was divine out of his scheme of morals. I did not wonder that he had done so. I could find no fault with him. And yet I could not understand how that which affected men so much, and acted upon their character so much, could be treated as if it had nothing to do with the formation of their characters. In Christian ethics it is the foundation-stone. This proposition. *"God is light, and in Him is no darkness at all,"* is the proposition from which all others start. How it has been demonstrated to men I have tried to show you. That demonstration in a Son leads on to the next proposition, that this divine light is not merely hidden inaccessible light; that it has shone out in a Person Who makes us understand what He is by doing human acts and bearing human sorrows. And so we arrive at the third proposition, that the highest end of man's existence is to have fellowship with this Life and Light. And then a fourth, which we shall have to speak of more hereafter— that fellowship or communion with each other is implied in this fellowship or communion with God and with His Son.

These I regard as the fundamental maxims of Christian ethics. In any true study of them which is grounded upon the teaching of the Apostles, these maxims will precede any considerations respecting the condition of man as an erring and sinful creature. We shall know nothing about that condition unless we understand first what our true and proper state is. We must measure the crooked line by the straight, not the straight by the crooked. But in the next Lecture I hope to show you that these great principles of Christian morals, which St. John has declared to us, are not applicable to some imaginary, perfect world, but to ours—not to some pure and saintly beings, but to you and me.

LIGHT AND DARKNESS: SIN AND PURIFICATION*

If we say that we have fellowship with Him, and walk in darkness, we lie and do not the truth: but if we walk in the light, as He is in the light, we have fellowship one with another, and the blood of Jesus Christ His Son cleanseth us from all sin. If we say that we have no sin, we deceive ourselves, and the truth is not in us. If we confess our sins, He is faithful and just to forgive us our sins, and to cleanse us from all unrighteousness. If we say that we have not sinned, we make Him a liar, and His word is not in us.
—1 John 1:6–10

You will remember the words which immediately precede these. *"This then is the message which we have heard of Him, and declare unto you, that God is light, and in Him is no darkness at all."* I have spoken of that message already, but I must speak of it again, as all the rest of this chapter depends upon it. I can quite imagine a person saying—"Light! Darkness!—What exactly does he mean by these expressions? They are figurative. What is the literal force of them?"

Now I am very glad to hear questions of this kind, and I will answer them as

---

*From *The Epistles of St. John* (Cambridge: Macmillan and Co., 1857), Lecture 3, 34–52.

well as I can; but I must tell you why I do not expect that I shall ever be able to answer them as those who propose them may desire that I should. I have explained to you already that the student of morals does not want letters first and chiefly. He wants a *Life*. He wants letters only as they assist him to the knowledge of a Life. Well, then, if I am bidden to find a *literal* meaning for these phrases, "Light" and "Darkness," I must consider what I am about. They certainly are very living expressions. They belong to the life of us all. Every man who cannot read or write has to do with them, and knows something of what they signify, if he cannot convey his knowledge accurately to another. Nay, sometimes he *can* do that; an ignorant man may tell me something about the effect of darkness or light upon him, which may make me feel what they are more truly, more exactly, than any long descriptions of them which I meet with in a dictionary or encyclopaedia composed by learned men. He may say, "My companion and I walked on pleasantly and cheerily enough as long as the sun was shining upon us. We saw the sky over our heads, and the trees, and the corn-fields, and each other's faces. But night came on. All things were huddled together; we mistook old stumps of trees for houses, we were continually stumbling against each other; it was dreary work enough." If he only said this to me, I should understand him better—he would give me a fuller and more accurate impression of what light is and what darkness is—than if he had been able to supply me with the best definitions of them that were ever invented. Do you not see, then, that to get what are sometimes called literal equivalents for these words, which are just what a dictionary or encyclopaedia affords, might be to lose clearness instead of to gain it? Let us not be deluded with phrases. If what is called figurative language brings us into closer contact with reality than what is called literal language, it must be better for our purpose; and we should resolve to let no one rob us of it under pretence of giving us something more substantial in exchange. If he can prove that it is more substantial, we will take it; if not, we will keep what we have.

Moreover, these expressions were wonderfully suitable for those to whom St. John wrote. The Ephesians had paid an especial worship to Artemis or Diana. They connected her with the moon, the night-ruler. They had paid a worship, in common with the other Greeks, to Apollo; him they connected with the sun, that rules the day. They *connected* them, I say, with these beautiful objects; but they were never satisfied with doing so. The god of light was the god whom they went to consult how they should manage states, conduct wars, make peace. They felt that a higher light than the light which the eyes could see must proceed from him. That could never enable them to choose the right path and avoid the wrong one. That could never keep them in fellowship with each other. But that which could, they were sure must *be* a light. They could not describe it in any language so well. It must be a better, purer, diviner light, than that which they perceived with their eyes. It must be a more human light; the other affected men in common with animals and plants; this must have to do with that in which they were different from animals and plants. So these old Greeks thought. And the more one reads of them, the more one perceives how much all that was great in them and in their deeds was produced by these thoughts. Yet they were perpetually confusing the light which came from the sun and moon—the light which they saw only through their eyes—with that light which they could not see with their eyes at all—which came directly to *them.* They were continually exalting the lower light above the higher light, and supposing the higher to come from the lower. This was their idolatry. They worshipped the visible things from which they thought that the light proceeded. All the time they felt that men were better than these things; therefore, if they worshipped these things, they must also worship men. And men could make wonderful things. They could imitate the works of nature. They could express the thoughts of their own minds in pictures and statues. Why should not these be worshipped too?

St. John had been taught almost from his birth, that he was not to worship things in heaven, or on earth, or under the earth, or the works of his own hands. He had been taught that the Lord his God was one Lord, that He was the Unseen Deliverer, Guide, Teacher, King of Israel. He had clung to this teaching. He had believed that all the institutions of his land were appointed to keep him and his people from forgetting it. He had believed that this was their distinction from the nations that were round about them; that they were a wise, and understanding, and united people, while they trusted in this Deliverer and King, whom they could not see; and that they became a stupid and ignorant and divided people as soon as they began to bow down to things which they could see. *Now* he had believed that this God had revealed Himself to them, not in the sun or in the moon, but in a humble and crucified Man. With this conviction becoming every hour deeper and deeper in his mind, he had settled in the city where Apollo and Diana were worshipped. He saw the mischiefs and dangers of that worship more clearly and fully than he did when people told him about it on the Lake of Galilee. But he did not think that these Ephesians had been wrong because they had dreamt of a God of Light. That was a true dream. Christ had come to fulfil it. The God of Abraham, and Isaac, and Jacob, whom Jesus had revealed, was this God of Light. The sun was His, the moon was His; He had created them for the blessing of all creatures. But that Light which belongs especially to man,—that Light by which he is to guide his steps,—that light which keeps men in fellowship with each other,—that was His own true Light, His own proper nature; that was what He had manifested to men in His Son. For this was the message which they had heard of Him and declared to the Ephesians, that *"God was light, and in Him was no darkness at all."*

If, then, I had told you that "light" meant goodness, wisdom, justice, truth—and that "darkness" meant the opposite of all these—I should have said exactly what St. John will tell us in very distinct words hereafter, and what he has intimated to us already. But I am so afraid of your thinking of these great realities as if they were mere words, that I have taken what may seem to you a roundabout course for the purpose of showing you how both Heathens and Jews were taught in their different ways to feel that Light, which is the great blessing of all in this creation of ours, is the symbol and witness of these, and that He, who is Himself Wisdom and Goodness and Justice and Truth, may be declared in one word to be LIGHT. And I have endeavoured to show you also how there was a perpetual tendency in men to confine this Light by their own notions and imaginations; that is, in better and more intelligible language, by their own darkness; and how this confusion would have multiplied more and more, if He whom St. John saw and handled had not manifested forth this Light in its purity, free from any darkness at all.

But, as I hinted to you last week, there is another reason closely connected with this, why St. John could not abandon the word "light" for any that was more formal and less living. A man may easily fancy that goodness, wisdom, truth, are possessions of his own. Whether he thinks he has got them for himself, or that some god has given them to him, he may still believe that he holds them just as he holds a freehold house or a purse of money. But you can never suppose that you hold light in this way. That I can never boast that I possess. When I go out and walk in the light, my eye receives it, my whole body is the better for it. I shut myself in a room with the blinds and shutters dark, or I close my eyes; the blessing is gone. Now the message which St. John brought to the Ephesians was not concerning a blessing of the first kind, but of this last kind. He did not tell them that God had given them certain possessions here, or had promised them certain possessions hereafter, which they could call theirs. He declared, "God has established a real intercourse between Himself and you. I have no better news for you than this: the fulness of joy lies in this." And he had a right to say so. For it was precisely this which men in all ages, and in all countries, had shown that they were craving for; not this, for the sake of other things, but other things for the sake of this. The religion of every people under heaven had meant a longing for intercourse or fellowship with some superior being; it expressed or indicated a conviction, that that superior being must be actually holding now, or be willing to hold some intercourse with them. The belief was strong, that all the arts of life, everything that made existence upon earth tolerable, as well as everything that had purified or elevated it, was owing to some visitation of mysterious celestial beings, or to some communication from them. The knowledge of the husband-man, as much as the inspiration of the poet, was traced to this source. Then came a terrible conviction that this intercourse had in some way been interrupted; that men had somehow failed in fulfilling their part of the relation. They could not tell exactly how; but it seemed likely that they had withheld from the gods that which they wanted, or had disobliged them as men disobliged their fellow-creatures. These were very natural thoughts; men were certain that there must be a truth at the bottom of them. For intercourse with the gods could not be an imaginary thing; it must be as real at least as intercourse with their fellows; it must have some direct resemblance to that, and connexion with it. Therefore they asked wise men to tell them what the gods wanted which they had not given;

what had offended them; how the quarrel might be made up, and the intercourse renewed. Therefore they paid all respect to the soothsayers who pronounced that this or that was the god they had displeased—that this or that was the wrong they had committed—and to the priests who offered sacrifices to bring the gods into harmony with them.

You see that all these acts and services presume the existence of a being or beings above men, and of an intercourse between that being or those beings and men. It was possible for a teacher to come among them with the message, "There is no such being; there can be no such intercourse." I do not say that such a message would not have found listeners. I do not say that some who had been oppressed with the thought of the enmity which was between them and some power whom they did not see and could not approach, might not have felt that message a relief. But then I am not sure that any one could have received it fully; whether every one would not have had misgivings about it which would have made his life often as terrible as if he were afraid that the gods were always plotting against him. And I am quite sure, that if a man, or a nation, had been able to receive that message completely, it would have led to the death of all hope—ultimately, of all interest in the world—of all struggle to improve it—of all human cultivation. But supposing this message was not brought to men; then the only alternative was, that another should be brought to them. And that was St. John's message: "You are not mistaken. The one living and true God does seek fellowship with you—has created you for fellowship with Him. He has opened the way for a complete fellowship between us and Him in His Son. That Son has made us understand, by His own words and acts, that God is not the suspicious, grudging, covetous being you have taken Him to be; that He has in Him no suspicion, no grudging, no covetousness; that all these have come to you because you were not holding fellowship with Him, because you were not walking in His light."

That is the subject of the next verse. *"If we say that we have fellowship with Him, and walk in darkness, we lie and do not the truth."* I hope what I have said will make you feel what an honest simple expression that *walking in darkness* is, and how impossible it is for us to find some better and more intelligible one. We have only to remember our experiences on a dark night, and then to compare these with the experience we have had in our own minds when we have been playing with some malicious or foul thought, to know exactly what St. John means. Walking in darkness is, alas! the phrase about which we have the least need of an interpreter. Every one interprets it himself. It addresses itself with terrible force to the rich and the poor, the wise and the unwise. Whatever else we have not learnt, we have learnt something of that. That darkness is in us, that it is possible to choose darkness rather than light—this every person can tell for himself. It is just the secret which he *can* tell to himself, and which he can impart very imperfectly to his neighbour. For this darkness comes to each man from his being shut up in himself, from his not seeking to get beyond himself. That is a thick darkness, a darkness which begins to be felt the moment a little light breaks in.

When a man is hiding himself from all but himself, then the light never reaches him; it is to him as though there were none. And yet a man may go on walking in this darkness. Day after day he may become more used to it. Then how startled and shocked is he at even a glimpse of light! How he wishes to quench it, and cannot!

It is possible for a man to be in this dark selfish state, and yet to say that he has fellowship with God. He may repeat prayers, he may offer sacrifices, he may pass for a religious man. But his life, the Apostle says, is a lie. It is not only that he speaks a lie; he acts a lie. He *does* not the truth. This, indeed, he would have us to understand *is* falsehood—the very root of falsehood. If we are made in the image of God, it is a false and unnatural state for a man, not to be looking up to God but only to be looking down upon himself. It is the same sort of falsehood and contradiction as for the earth to be excluding the sun; only there is this more in it—the man *feels* that he cannot shut out God, if he tries to do so ever so much; he is haunted with the thought of Him; the thought of Him mixes with his bad deeds and bad purposes. Then he tries to worship God on purpose that he may persuade Him not to molest him. His prayers and his sacrifices are entreaties to God to go away from him, to leave him to do what he likes, to be as dark as he likes. Surely St. John's words are the only proper description of this state of mind. We cannot make them stronger; we must not try to make them weaker. It is a lying state. The man who is in it is a liar. And yet every one of us has been in it, and may be in it, and may sink into it utterly.

And then comes the next sentence. *"But if we walk in the Light, as He is in the Light, we have fellowship one with another."* The darkness of which St. John speaks is an utterly unsocial condition. A man thinks about himself, dwells in himself; the rest of the universe lies in shadow. It is not that he has not continual transactions with other people; it is not that they do not supply him with things that he wants; it is not that he could dispense with them. But all they do is only contemplated in reference to himself; they work, and suffer, and think for him. It is not that the things which he looks at are indifferent to him; he depends upon them; whether he has less or more of them is his chief concern. But he does not wonder at them or enjoy them; they, too, are only his ministers. Emphatically, then, he has no fellowship with men, no fellowship with Nature. All the world is only a looking-glass which reflects himself. What, then, is the opposite state to this? St. John says, *"If we walk in the Light, as He is in the Light, we have fellowship one with another."* The Light is all around us, while we are most dark. I cannot extinguish the creation because I do not think about it or care about it. Man is living a wonderful life; there is a wonderful life going on in earth, sea, and air; though I am only troubled about what I shall eat, and drink, and put on. But this recollection is not enough to bring me out of my dark pit. My selfishness is too strong for all, however bright, in earth, and sea, and air to overcome. It is not too strong for God to overcome. If I remember that He is in the Light; if I look upon the light which is in these things as coming from Him; if I believe that the light of men—the light in me—is from Him; if I believe that He *is* Light, and that in Him is no darkness at all; then I must believe that I am resisting His will when I am walking in that darkness—when I am acting and thinking as if I had no concern with any being but myself. All those strange intimations which come to me that I am not what I am meant to be, must be flashes of light from the source of light. They are painful flashes. I have often wished and tried to get rid of them. They have discovered me to myself in a way in which I did not wish to be discovered. They are just what men have tried by their false religions—by their insincere professions of fellowship with God—to drive away. But if, instead of doing that, we will hail them; if we will turn to Him from whom they flow; if we will receive them as His messengers, we may enter into His true order. We may walk day by day as if we were in His presence, as if He were looking at us and guiding us, and guiding all our brethren, and all this universe. And then we have fellowship one with another. The proper social life is restored to us, even if we are far away from our brethren. Yes; Alexander Selkirk in a desert island—John Bunyan in a prison—thousands of sick men and women in lonely rooms, may, in this way, have had a fellowship with the human race, such as we, who walk about the streets and talk with a number of people every day, know little of. By walking in light, as God is in the light—by continually recollecting that He was with them, and that He was with those whom they could not see—they may have acquired a habit of fellowship with those in the world now, and with those who had been in it generations before, which might make us covet their island, their prison, or their sick bed, if those could impart to us the same privilege. But they could not, there was no charm in them; St. John tells us the secret: "If we walk in the light, as He is in the light—wherever we are, in lonely rooms or crowded streets, we may have fellowship with each other; we may see each other, not as reflections of ourselves, but as images of Him."

But what are these words which follow? *"And the blood of Jesus Christ His Son cleanseth us from all sin."* They will strike a person who is making out a system of divinity or ethics, as very much out of place. For he will say, "The Apostle has given us no definition of *sin.* He has not even spoken of it in the verses we have read. And though he has spoken of having fellowship with the Father, and with His Son Jesus Christ, he has not unfolded any theory concerning the object or the effects of the death of Jesus Christ. How much, then, must be assumed and explained before this language can have any force or meaning for us?"

I have spoken to you about definitions already. I am convinced that if there is one word of which a definition will tell us nothing, unless we have learnt the signification of it first in some other method that word is "Sin." And I am equally convinced that it is by that method, and not by a theological theory, that we must learn how the blood of Jesus Christ cleanseth away sin. What this method is, St. John, it seems to me, teaches us better than any one ever did. He appeals to our experience. You desire to be true yourself; you desire to have fellowship with other men. The moment that first desire is awakened in me, then arises along with it a sense of falsehood: "I have done false acts. I have been false. I have an inclination to do false acts, and to be false now. I have something in me which violently resists my craving to be true." The moment that second desire is awakened in me, there arises along with it a sense of selfishness: "I have done acts which imply that I have no relation to my fellow-creatures. I have been out of fellowship with them. I have an inclination to do such acts now, to be out of fellowship with them now. I have something in me which violently resists that craving for union with them." About this fact there is no doubt. Each of us can bear testimony of it. We want no doctor to define it or reduce it to a formula. And about the seriousness, the terribleness of this fact there is no doubt. It must be at the bottom of the insincerity of the world. It must be at the bottom of the discord and hatred of the world. But how shall I describe this fact? What name shall I give to that which is contradicting whatever is right in individual men, whatever is for the peace of society? I am at a loss; I cannot find a name. But I discover something more about the strange fact. *"God is Light, and in Him is no darkness,"* I am intended to walk in this light. This inclination not to be true, not to have fellowship with my fellow-men, is an inclination not to walk in this light, not be in that state in which He has intended men to be. Now I am, perhaps, better able to express this inclination of mine, and what has been the fruit of it. One name, however, does not satisfy me. I try several. I call it *transgression;* that is, the passing over a boundary which was marked out for me. I call it *iniquity;* that is, an uneven zigzag course, a departure from the straight even course. I call it *sin;* that is, the missing of an aim; the going aside from the goal which I was intended to reach. All these words imply that there is one who has marked the boundary for me, who has drawn the line for me, who has fixed the goal or aim for me. All imply a disobedience to a Will which I am meant to obey. But the last is the clearest and the most significant, because it implies that the aim or goal which I miss is Himself; that I am meant to set Him before me, and that I set some other end before me; that I am meant to be like Him, and that I prefer to be like something altogether different from Him.

If this be so, the word "Sin" expresses the fact of our disposition to be false, and of our disposition to be at war with our fellow-creatures. Yet we do not feel the power of it, or give to it its full sense, till we believe that GOD is true, and that GOD has created us all to be at one. With that acknowledgment comes the *acknowledgment* of Sin. Now, the message which St. John brought to the Ephesians was, "God has revealed Himself to us in Jesus Christ as the perfect Truth. God has revealed Himself in Jesus Christ as the God who has created men to be one. Therefore it is a revelation to us of our sin; for it shows us how we have fought and do fight against this mind and purpose of God; how, in doing so, we fight against our own proper state, our own proper blessedness."

I do not mean that this sense of sin did not exist before that full revelation of God in Christ. I have shown you already how strong the sense was in men everywhere of having in some way offended an unseen and powerful Ruler; how many efforts men made everywhere to remove the cause of offence, and to establish peace with the gods. And I will add now that everywhere this sense of wrongdoing was connected with a sense of defilement. Besides injuring the *gods,* they had in some way made *themselves* unclean. Purifications or lustrations were necessary for the removal of their own uncleanness, as sacrifices were necessary to appease their rulers. Such testimonies existed among heathens that they had evil in them; that they knew it. The Israelites were unlike these heathens, for they believed that the Lord had declared Himself, at the beginning of their Law, to be their Deliverer out of the house of bondage, and to be their God. They were taught that He was a righteous God, and that He wished them to be righteous. But, for that very reason, the commandments made them tremble; for they showed them what inclinations there were in them to be unrighteous, to break loose from the government of this Deliverer. Their sacrifices, they were taught, were His means of drawing them back to Himself when they had gone astray; their purifications were His way of showing that He was their Purifier. In both parts of the old world, then, there was this feeling of wrong and this feeling that they needed to be set free from the wrong. But how much deeper did each become in those who learnt that God was Light, and in Him was no darkness—that He was seeking to make them dwell in the light—that He had sent His Son to bring them into His Light! What a sense of sin must have been in them! How they must have felt, "It is our own fault, our own *choice* that we have been walking in darkness. We have been striving against a God who has been at every moment plotting for our good!"

If, then, the men in the times of old cried out for a purification—for something to cleanse them—those who heard this revelation must have felt the need of it immeasurably more. But what kind of purification could they have? Outward purification could not avail them in the least. It was in *themselves* they felt the sin. Into the core of each man's heart the poison had entered. What could eject it? What could make each man right? What could make society pure? Such is the question which a man is obliged to ask himself when he seeks to walk in the light as God is in the light, and to have fellowship with his brother. And to such a man, says St. John, the answer comes, *"The blood of Jesus Christ His Son cleanseth us from all sins."* There is a new life-blood put into this nature of ours. God Himself has infused it. The Son of God has taken our flesh and blood. He is the Head of our race. He is the bond of peace between it and the God of Light and Truth. He is the bond of peace between us and all the members of our race. When we seek to rise out of ourselves—to be delivered from our falsehood—to have fellowship with God, and fellowship with our brother; then His blood— the blood which He took for us, the blood which He poured out for us—is an assurance that we have that fellowship. It removes the sense of sin against God which is in us; it removes the sense of sin against men. It gives that atonement and that purification which nothing else in earth and heaven can give.

St. John speaks here of this blood as cleansing or purifying the man. He speaks afterwards of the way in which the death of Christ is a sacrifice offered to God. We must not anticipate any of his lessons, but follow them as carefully as we can. What I have given you this morning is quite enough for one time. As I hope to show you hereafter, it is connected with all that heathen writers have told us about man's blessedness, about habits and virtues, and the choice of good and evil—with all that I have said to you in former lectures about the affections and the conscience and the will. But our Apostle never speaks of the principles of morals apart from the practice of them. He will go out of his way and repeat himself twenty times, rather than let his reader fancy that he has been listening to a disquisition when what he wants is help to live. There is an instance of this at the end of this chapter. St. John had told the Ephesian Christians that the blood of Jesus Christ cleanseth from all sin. He is afraid they should think, as many of them were in fact inclined to do, that by some charm or other, they, as Christians, had been put out of the reach of sin, and were not beset by it like other men. He hastens at once to rid them of such delusion: *"If we say that we have no sin, we deceive ourselves, and the truth is not in us."* Instead of this fancy that you are without sin being a proof how clearly the light is shining into you, it is a proof that you are shutting out the light, for that would reveal to you your own inclination to fly from it and to choose the darkness. The truth makes us aware of our falsehoods; to deny that they are near us and ready to betray us every moment, is to put ourselves out of fellowship with the truth; with the God who is truth. Is that hard doctrine? No; for *"if we confess our sins, He is faithful and just to forgive us our sins, and to cleanse us from all unrighteousness."* His faithfulness and justice are the enemies of our sins; therefore to them we may turn from our sins. They are the refuges from the darkness that is in us. A faithful and righteous Being is *therefore* a forgiving Being. We are unforgiving because we are unfaithful and unrighteous. But His forgiveness is not tolerance of an evil; such tolerance is cruelty. He forgives us that He may cleanse us. The forgiveness is itself a part of the cleansing. He manifests His righteousness to us that we may trust Him. By trusting Him we are delivered from the suspicion which is the very essence of sin.

It is plain simple teaching this; that a man throws off the burden of his sins by confessing them; and that he may confess to God because he knows that God cares for him, that He is true, and hates falsehood, and can understand him, and can set him free. It is simple, but oh, infinitely deep we shall find it to be if we try! This confession, "Against Thee I have sinned," this daring to lay our sin bare; this asking to be made true in the inward parts,—what power, what victory, what peace lies in that! And thus we begin to understand the Apostle's last words which at first may sound very like a commonplace vehemently expressed: *"If we say that we have not sinned, we make Him a liar, and His word is not in us."* If we will not confess the evil in us, we impute that evil to Him. We make Him answerable for that against which He is testifying in our consciences. We thrust away that Word which is shedding abroad His light in us; we bury ourselves in our own darkness. This is the effect of trying to make out a good case for ourselves, when it is our interest, our privilege, our blessedness, to justify God and to condemn ourselves; to say, "Thou hast been true, and we have been liars. Deliver us from our lies! Help us to walk in Thy truth!"

THE TRUE IDEA
OF MAN*

My little children, these things write I unto you, that ye sin not. And if any man sin, we have an Advocate with the Father, Jesus Christ the Righteous: and He is the propitiation for our sins: and not for ours only, but also for the sins of the whole world. And hereby we do know that we know Him, if we keep His commandments.

—1 John 2:1–3

This new chapter in the Epistle is in fact a new chapter in Christian ethics. It is closely connected with the one we were considering before Easter; still it is a step forward in our study, that is to say, a step forward in human experience, and in God's revelations.

You will remember where we stopped. The Apostle had spoken to us of sin. He had told us that *"If we confess our sins, God is faithful and just to forgive us our sins;"* that *"if we say we have no sin, we deceive ourselves, and the truth is not in us."* Now he begins, *"My little children, these things write I unto you, that ye sin not."*

You will be struck with the fatherly tone in which St. John speaks. It belonged to himself—the old man, who had watched over the flock in Ephesus, to whom all the members of it looked up as one to whom they owed more than any child owes to its parent. It belonged to his character as an Apostle. All the Apostles felt themselves to be fathers. Christ had told them that they were not to call any *one* man their father on earth; that would interfere with their faith, that they had one Father in heaven. They gave heed to this precept. St. John did not call himself the father of the Church generally, though he was the last Apostle left. He did not even call himself the father of the different churches in Asia Minor, though they all knew him and reverenced him. He taught them, as you will find in the Apocalypse, that each had a pastor or angel of their own, and that that pastor derived his authority not from him but from Christ. But though no one might usurp this universal fatherhood—though it would have destroyed the very constitution of the Church to do so—each circle or society was to be an image of the great family, each was to have its own father. The Apostles loved and cherished that name, and all that it implied, and all that illustrated it. They much preferred it to any title which merely indicated an office. It was more spiritual; it was more personal; it asserted better the divine order; it did more to preserve the dignity

---

*From *The Epistles of St. John* (Cambridge: Macmillan and Co., 1857), Lecture 4, 53–68.

and sacredness of all domestic relations. It is a sad day for churches, yes, and for nations, when men begin to regard themselves chiefly as officials sent forth by some central government to do its jobs, and not as men who are bound by sacred affinities and actual relations to those whom they preside over.

But St. John had a special reason for using this tender phrase, *"My little children,"* in this place. All sin, we have seen, is connected by the Apostle with the loss of fellowship. A man shuts himself up in himself. He denies that he has anything to do with God; he denies that he has anything to do with his brother. That is what he calls walking in darkness. The inclination to walk in darkness, to choose darkness rather than light, is *sin*. We become aware of this inclination— then arises in our minds a terrible sense of shame for having yielded to it, and for having it so near to us. But as soon as we believe that God is light, and that in Him is no darkness at all—as soon as we understand that He has manifested His light to us that we may see it and may show it forth—with this sense of shame there comes also the pledge of deliverance. We are not bound by that sin to which we have surrendered ourselves in time past, or which is haunting us now. We are not created to be its servants. We may turn to the Light; we may claim our portion in it; we may ask that it may penetrate us. And then, the Apostle says, we *"have fellowship one with another, and the blood of Jesus Christ,"* of Him in whom is life eternal, of Him who has taken the flesh and blood of man, and has poured out His blood for all—that cleanses us from sin. We renounce our selfish life; we claim His life, which belongs to our brother just as much as to ourselves.

If, then, the Apostle wished the Ephesians not to sin;—not to yield to selfishness which was in them, and which was separating them from each other and from God—what could he do better than remind them that they all belonged to one family; that this was their great privilege; that the Son of God had come amongst them to redeem them out of their pride and divisions, and to make them the little children of His Father. These Ephesians might say to the Apostle, "Why, you told us just now not to say that we were without sin; you told us to confess our sins; you told us it was a lie not to confess them. Is not that as good as saying that we cannot help committing sin?" "No!" he answers, "my little children, it is not so at all. You are under no obligation to sin, because you have each of you this selfish tendency, this selfish nature. God has made you one flock, one family. Keep that truth in remembrance, and you will be able to deny yourselves, and forswear that separate nature of yours; to act as if you were bound to each other; to feel other men's sins and selfishness as your own; to feel that you carry their wrong in you; to feel that your Deliverer and Brother is also theirs. I tell you these things; I urge you to confess your sins, on purpose that you may not sin; on purpose that you may enter into fellowship with Him in whom is no sin, who is altogether righteous."

"And," he goes on, *"if any man sin, we have an Advocate with the Father, Jesus Christ the Righteous."* Supposing these words stood alone—supposing there had been no previous words to explain what St. John thought of sin, and no previous

message respecting Jesus Christ the Righteous—we might easily fancy that he meant something of this kind,—"It is no doubt an unfortunate thing to sin; it should be avoided, if possible. But if any man does fall into it, there is one who has such might and influence with God that he can persuade Him to overlook the offence, and not to punish, hereafter at least, the man who has committed it." This, I say, would have been a very plausible interpretation; a heathen of Ephesus would certainly have concluded at once that it must be the right one. He would have said,—"No doubt we all desire to find advocates who can induce our gods to pardon us or to accept some compensation for the punishment they would inflict. You think you have found the Advocate who has influence enough with your God to secure impunity for your misdoings." Many a Jew of Ephesus, perhaps, would have been equally sure that the Apostle must have had this thought, or a thought very like this, in his mind. Such a Jew would have said, "Yes! if you could persuade me that Jesus was the Christ, I, too, might be glad of His advocacy to help me in avoiding the punishments which my transgressions of the law have incurred. But as I see no proof that He is the Christ, I would rather trust to the High Priest of Jerusalem, and to the sacrifices which he offers according to the law." But though both heathens and Jews might have used this language, I am certain that no heathen and no Jew would have found what in his inmost heart he was longing for if he found an advocate who would obtain for him *this* sort of forgiveness. No; the best heathens perceived—every Jew who had been taught by the law and the prophets knew—that it is not a blessing but a misery to escape the punishment of sin. The best heathens perceived—every Jew who was taught by the law and prophets knew—that what a man wants is to be set free from his sin, and that no advocate could serve him in the least unless he could be the instrument of winning for him that emancipation.

But if this is true about heathens and Jews, whose education and whose corrupt practices disposed them to accept this notion of an advocate—if they had the sense of needing help of a kind quite different from any which such an one could afford—think how impossible it was for St. John, after the message which he had just announced to the Ephesians, to tolerate for one moment so immoral a doctrine. He had spoken of Jesus Christ as manifesting the life of God, as declaring to men by His words and acts that God was Light with no darkness at all, as enabling men to have fellowship with that Light. Could he all at once contradict these lessons and say, "Jesus Christ the Righteous does not show forth the mind and purpose of God, but He is one who intercedes with God to alter His mind, to adopt a new and different purpose?" Could he say, "It is not the great blessing of all that God should detect all the darkness that is in us, and scatter it, and bring us into His clear Light? What we want is, to avoid His Light, to find an advocate who will say, Let these poor creatures alone, they cannot bear thy Light. Let them hide themselves in their own darkness; they are so used to it. Do not be hard upon them if they have a preference for it." No; St. John had no such horrible dream as this. He did not so slander the Master upon whose breast he had lain, of whose eternal life he was to testify. He did not blaspheme the God of Light. He did not so hate the men whom God has made in His image.

What he does say is in perfect consistency with his previous lessons, only it is a deepening and an expansion of them. "My little children," he says, "you are not bound to sin. What I have said to you is to remind you that you are brought into a family in Jesus Christ your elder brother, and that His Father is your Father, and that you may have fellowship with them and with each other, and so may rise above your selfish instincts and tempers. And if any of you do sin, if you do fall into low, loose, selfish acts, or low, base, selfish states of mind—then let me tell you how you may be raised out of them—how you may recover your right position again. The effect of those bad acts, of that bad state of mind, will be to make you think that there is a hopeless barrier between you and God; that you have made Him your enemy. The effect of it will be to make you think that you have lost the privileges of a member of this family; that you have nothing more to do with your brethren; that you are shut up in your own evil nature. These thoughts will seem to you true and certain. They must seem so; for you cannot help knowing that you are at war with the God who is all goodness and truth, that you are at war with your brethren. It would be mere mockery and self-deception to tell you the contrary. But understand, you cannot set aside God's order merely because you do not acknowledge it. You cannot change God's countenance, because your eyes are jaundiced. He has made you members of a family in His Son. 'He is Light, and in Him is no darkness at all.' And He looks upon us as we really are—one body in Jesus Christ the Righteous, though we choose to act as if we were a set of separate creatures. And He wishes us to act upon a true belief, and not upon a lying fancy. Remember, then, that Jesus Christ the Righteous is ever with God, the sharer of His counsels. Remember that He represents us as one family, one race before God. Remember that He is the same, though we change; and then you will feel that there is always a way open for you to return to Him from whom you have wandered, always a passage out of your darkness into His light; one which is for all; one which no evil act, no evil state of mind can close up; for it is the way out of these evil acts, out of that evil state; it is the way which God Himself has prepared for us."

This, I think you will see, is a different notion of an advocate from the other, and one that is considerably more helpful to struggling and sinful men. The word "advocate," which our translators have used, is in itself a very good one. The word signifies etymologically, "one who may be called to us; a helper and counsellor." Here it describes Him whom St. John speaks of as God and with God; one in whom we may read and understand His mind; one in whom God can look upon men, and in whom men may look up to God. The belief that there is such a one is, I think, the most elevating, most comforting that it is possible for human creature to cherish. We are apt to look out upon the world and count heads, and then say to ourselves, "What a hopeless mass of misery and crime is here! Perhaps Paris is better than Constantinople; perhaps London is better than Paris. But if so, how wretched are the prospects of mankind! For what is this London, if one considers it in the aggregate, if one thinks of it in any of its portions?" So we reason, and then we too often go on—Pharisees as we are—to wrap ourselves in our own righteousness and wisdom, and to thank God that, at all events, we are not as the great majority are. A man is stopped in the midst of that self-congratulation. The question is asked him straightly and roughly, by one who means to have an answer, "Is not that very thought of thine a proof that thou *art* as the great majority are? What else is destroying them but the very selfishness, the very want of understanding that they are members of a kind, which you are now indulging? And do not you see that they are members of a kind in spite of all this selfishness in them and in you? Don't you see that they have affections one for another, however sunken and fallen they may be? Do not you see that they are related to each other as husbands and wives, brothers and sisters, even when they are quarrelling most and tearing one another in pieces most? Do not you see that there is an order in the world, and that God is upholding it, in spite—yes, in spite of you and your narrowness and pride, and your wish to be a solitary creature?" Then one begins to say to oneself, "An order? Where is it? What is it? Who can tell me anything about it? How is God upholding it? Will it triumph at last over all this disorder? And what have I to do with it? If I have been living as if I did not belong to it, how may I begin to live as if I did belong to it?" Then it is that these words, "We have an Advocate or Representative with the Father," acquire such a meaning and power. We need not be separate from our kind. *He* is not separate from it. *He* cares for it, watches over it; holds all the different elements of it together. We need not learn what man is in Constantinople, or Paris, or London. He is the Man. It is in Him that we know what we are, and why we were created. In Him each man may draw nigh to the Father of all and say, *"Father, I have sinned against Heaven, and before Thee."* In Him we may confess other men's sins and crimes as well as our own, and may learn that their crimes and sins have not destroyed them yet, because Christ is on their side; because Christ is the advocate and supporter of that in them which He has himself created; because it is not His will or His Father's will that that shall perish.

Perhaps you will say, "It is all very well to use these fine words about London, and Paris, and Constantinople, but St. John was acquainted with none of these cities; one of them at least was little more than a collection of mud cabins in his day. And the people he was thinking of was a very small circle indeed, which was surrounding him in the city of Ephesus, or at most a set of men called Christians who were scattered up and down the Roman Empire, separated from the rest of the world, denouncing its customs and its worship." Wait a moment till we have read the next verse, and then let us consider whether they were all that St. John was thinking of; whether it was possible for him to think only of them when he spoke of the Advocate with the Father, *"And he is the Propitiation for our sins: and not for ours only, but for the whole world."* Our translators have introduced the word *"sins"* into the second clause, supposing it ought to be repeated from the first. Perhaps they are right; I am not sure; and I believe, when we have examined the principal word in the passage, we shall find that it makes no great difference whether we say that He was a Propitiation for the whole world, or for the sins of the whole world.

That principal word is *"Propitiation."* What does it signify? I must refer you back to what I have been saying about the word *"Advocate."* Those heathens and Jews who looked for an Advocate who should induce some Divine Ruler not to punish them, also looked for something which that Advocate should offer to the Divine Ruler, in order that He might be moved to compassion. They expected that He should give the God some adequate or sufficient motive not to execute the vengeance which it seemed to them that He was executing, or was likely to execute, upon them. No more natural notion could come into the minds of people who had done wrong, and who knew they had done it. If some fellow-creature had displeased them, this was the course they were inclined to adopt; the more inclined the harder and crueler their feelings towards him were. *"Pay me that thou owest,"* as our Lord says in His parable, is the language which one fellow-servant is apt to use to another. He does not care to make his fellow-servant better; he cares only to get an amends for some injury which he thinks he has suffered at his hands. And he supposes that the Lord of all acts upon the same principle; that He, too, wants compensation for some injury He has suffered; that He, too, is spiteful and vengeful; that He, too, cares that His servants should pay Him what they owe, not that they should become right and gracious men. How, indeed, could a Being desire them to be that which He is not himself?

But I must repeat what I said in the other case. Though this was the natural notion of both Jews and heathens, one which they could justify to themselves by arguments, one that they became strengthened in by a series of religious acts which were grounded upon it—no Jew and no heathen was satisfied with it. The conscience in each of them acknowledged a wrong which no such compensation could clear away. The conscience in them confessed that they had grieved some Being who could be content with nothing else but that they should be right and true men. The best heathens said that the Being they worshipped must be right and true Himself, and that it was dangerous and wicked to attribute any acts to Him that would be base and evil in them. The Jew, taught by the law and the prophets, believed that the God and Judge of all the earth was a righteous being, and could only do right; and that the whole scheme and purpose of His government was to make men right. Whatever sacrifices and offerings He appointed, such a Jew was sure, were appointed for this end. They were, as I said in a former lecture, God's way of bringing back those who had wandered from fellowship with Him and with each other into that fellowship. They brought an animal which God had prescribed to the door of the tabernacle of the congregation. They confessed their sins over it; the priest presented it; it was declared to be the sign and pledge of an atonement and reconciliation between God and the worshipper.

These Jewish offerings, then, were no compensations to an offended Prince. They were indications and expressions of the will of a gracious Ruler. They were acts of submission on the part of the Israelite to that Ruler. They were witnesses of a union between Him and them which could not be broken. And there was in that tabernacle in which those sacrifices were offered, a mercy seat, where God declared that He would meet the worshippers. It was the most conspicuous object in the building; the cherubims covered it with their wings. The High Priest who offered the sacrifices died; this sign of God's presence with the people lasted on from generation to generation. It said to all Jews, young and old, "Though you have erred and strayed, though you are stiffnecked and rebellious, God is still claiming you as His people; God is inviting you to claim Him as your God."

St. John had been used to gaze on this mercy seat when he was a boy in the Temple at Jerusalem, when he went yearly to the feasts. He had seen it as a man. He had seen it when he walked with Jesus in the Temple; he had seen it after Jesus had died and had gone away from the world. He was far away from Jerusalem. The Temple was perhaps still in existence; but if it was, it was desecrated; it was surrounded with armies; it was soon to be burnt with fire. What had become of the sacrifices, and the priests, and the mercy seat? St. John says, Jesus Christ the Righteous, our Advocate, is the Mercy Seat. In Him God meets us; in Him we may meet God. In Him God is satisfied with us; in Him we can be satisfied with God. Why did he say so? Because he believed that the only sacrifice with which God can be pleased is the voluntary sacrifice of a self; is the sacrifice of one who delights to do His will, and to suffer it. Because he believed that Christ had offered this sacrifice. Because he believed that God had signified His delight in it, by raising Jesus from the dead. Because he believed that that act declared Him to be the Son of God—the Mediator and High Priest who had always united God to man, from whom all other mediators and priests derived their worth and meaning; without whom they were nothing. Because he believed that, being this, Jesus Christ the Righteous fulfilled the idea of the Mercy Seat, in whom God and His creatures can have fellowship, in whom the children who have wandered from their home may find it again.

But was this all? No; the Jewish sacrifice, high priest, and mercy seat were gone. Was this, then, a *Jewish* high priest, sacrifice, mercy seat? If He was that (and He was that) He must be more. The Lord had taken the nature of man; He had died the death of man. Was He not then, a high priest, a sacrifice, a mercy seat for man? Could St. John dare to say He is a mercy seat for our sins only? Must he not say, "He also accomplishes what the Gentiles have been dreaming of in their miserable propitiations? He is the mercy seat for the whole world. The world is atoned or reconciled in Him. All have a right to draw nigh to God as their Father in Him. All have a right to cast away the fetters by which they were bound, seeing that He has triumphed over sin and death and the grave, seeing that He is at the right hand of God." Therefore we have a right to say, "Our race, our manhood is glorified in Him. Whether we live in London, or Paris, or

Constantinople, we are no longer separated. There is a common Lord of us all. There is a common life for us all. Confessing that common Lord, renouncing by the strength of this common life our selfish divided life, we become men indeed; we obtain the rights, the stature, the freedom, the dignity of men."

This, then, is the second part of our Christian ethics. The groundwork is laid in the revelation of God to man, as the Light in whom is no darkness. That revelation was made to creatures who had sinned and walked in darkness. It told them that they were meant to rise out of their sins and to walk in the light. To-day we have heard of the elevation of men into union with God. Jesus Christ the Righteous is the Person through whom the revelation of God is made. Jesus Christ the Righteous is the Person in whom mankind recovers its true position and glory. Therefore our ethics are in the strictest sense Christian; but they are also in the strictest sense human. They adapt themselves to the wants of individual men. They concern societies of men. They prove that there is a fellowship for the whole race of men.

Next Sunday we are to enter, if God permit, upon another subject:—the worth of commandments—the nature of obedience. That subject is wholly unintelligible, so long as we fancy that an advocate or a propitiation is necessary that we may escape from our obligations or from the penalties of neglecting them. But there is another practical topic of which I must say one word before I conclude.

The longing of men for fellowship with God—the sense in men of a separation from God—had both found their expression in prayers or litanies; some of these had been general, offered up by the priest for a whole congregation or society; some had been special, the utterance of an individual's cry for help under his own misery, the acknowledgment of his own evil. These prayers were, I may say, the very signs of humanity, the proof that man does not and cannot reckon himself among the beasts that perish. They point to the past: they look on to the future; they are connected with all the needs of the present. And yet these prayers might become most inhuman. They might be struggles in one man to get something which his neighbour had; they might be cries to a divine power to aid a strong man in crushing a weak one; they might be coverings for deceit and violence, and encouragements to persevere in them. Prayers and sacrifices have served these vile ends. As long as men think meanly of God—as long as they forget their relation to each other—they must serve such ends.

Christian ethics rescue prayers from these vile applications, and vindicate the strong conviction of human beings that without prayers they cannot live. When we believe that there is an Advocate or Representative of mankind, who ever lives to make intercession, that we may not sink but rise, that we may be delivered from our own darkness, that we may know the God who is Light—our prayers become cries against a common enemy—the pursuit of a common blessing. When we believe that Jesus Christ the Righteous is the Propitiation or Mercy Seat for us and for the whole world, that He has made the sacrifice of Himself which is well pleasing to God, our confession of our individual sins increases our confidence in the purposes of God for the universe; our most earnest petition being that He will make us true and loving sacrifices to accomplish His good will to us and to mankind.

DOING AND KNOWING*

And hereby we do know that we know Him, if we keep His commandments. He that saith, I know Him, and keepeth not His commandments, is a liar, and the truth is not in him. But whoso keepeth His word, in him verily is the love of God perfected: hereby know we that we are in Him. He that saith he abideth in Him ought himself also so to walk, even as He walked. Brethren, I write no new commandment unto you, but an old commandment which ye had from the beginning. The old commandment is the word which ye have heard from the beginning.

—1 John 2:3–7

I am speaking to those who attend the Sunday evening class on the relation of the Law to the Gospel. *Speaking* is not the word I ought to use, if it conveys to any one the notion that I am giving lectures on this subject, or laying down certain maxims upon it. Our plan is, to read alternately the Pentateuch (what are called the five books of the Law) and the Evangelists (what we call the four Gospels). By considering them together we try to ascertain what are the characteristics of each, how they are related to each other.

For instance, it happened a Sunday or two ago that we read the fifth chapter of Deuteronomy, which contains the repetition of the Ten Commandments. Either just before or just after, I forget which, we read of our Lord's conversation with the young ruler, who came asking Him, *"What good thing shall I do that I may inherit eternal life?"* To his surprise, the young man who had fancied he was to do some great thing, which other people could not do, that he might attain some great prize which other people could not attain—who fancied that he certainly could and should do this great thing, if he only was told what it was—heard that the way to enter into life was to keep those commandments which had been addressed to all Israelites as well as himself, and which he said he had kept from his youth up. Such a doctrine, coming from such lips, forced us to ask—how heeding the commandments which bore upon such ordinary works, which prohibited such ordinary crimes, could have anything to do with the eternal life which God is said to bestow, and to bestow freely? The question offered itself to us, in one shape or another, in all our readings; we could not avoid it if we tried; and as we wanted light upon it, of course we did not try. But I refer to this one example, because the very words which occupied us when we were considering the passage about the young ruler, in the Gospel according to St. Matthew, are

*From *The Epistles of St. John* (Cambridge: Macmillan and Co., 1857), Lecture 5, 69–86.

those which present themselves to us in this Epistle of St. John. We have been hearing of life—of an eternal life— that was manifested in Jesus Christ. Of this life the Apostle says he and his disciples at Ephesus may partake; they may have fellowship with it. That is the highest blessing, the greatest reward he can hold out to them; if they had that, their joy would be full. And now he comes to speak of commandments. *"And hereby we do know that we know Him, if we keep His commandments."*

It is a curious phrase, *"we do know that we know Him."* But it is a familiar one to us in other applications. I say to a friend, "Are you sure that you *know* that man? I am aware that you meet him often. You see him, perhaps, every day; you work with him; you talk with him. But do you know that you know him? Have you got any real insight into his character? Have you any confidence that you are not thinking of him better or worse than he deserves?" These are questions which we often ask, and to which we get various answers. Sometimes the answer is quite confident. "I am certain that he is, or that he is not, an honest, or a kind, or a wise man." And yet it may inspire us with confidence. We may say, or we may think, "You are deceived in that man. You have been flattered or in some way taken in by him. In due time the mask will fall off, and you will find out your mistake." Or we may say, "You are not just to that man. You have distorted his acts. You have misinterpreted his purposes. There is a far truer mind in him than you give him credit for." But now and then one has a strong conviction that a friend does understand the man we are asking him about, does appreciate him. I cannot tell you how we arrive at the belief; I think it is generally because he helps us to understand and to appreciate that person. He throws light upon our own experiences of him; he corrects some wrong impressions we had formed. And when it is so, his report, especially if it is a favorable one, never satisfies us. We are determined to verify it. We must try to know him whom he praises for ourselves. We must be able to say, "We know that we know him."

I have supposed the case of two men who are equals, and who associate on equal terms. But let us suppose the case of a youth and an old man; and to be more exact, let us suppose the one to be the son of the other. How does a child come to *know* his father? It has been my misfortune, I dare to say it has been yours, to meet with many sons who did not know their fathers, who did not the least understand what they were aiming at, either in the general work of their lives, or in the particular discipline of their families. I have also heard sons say, and sometimes I fear they spoke truly, that their fathers did not know them. They did not always mean that their fathers crossed them, or contradicted them, or laid heavy burdens upon them. That may be the complaint of many; but very indulgent fathers, who take little notice of the offences of their children, who easily pass them by, may exhibit what strikes them as want of comprehension. They do not perceive what their sons need, or what is leading them wrong. Their commands are seldom severe, but they appear as if they were arbitrary. They are not enforced with any consistency; a punishment sometimes follows the breach of them, sometimes not; the offender has a good chance of begging himself off; when he does suffer, he is apt to think that it was by accident, and not by law.

On the other hand, I have met, and I doubt not you have met, persons who could say honestly, "The rules which our father laid down for us often cut very disagreeably against our inclinations; but we had always a feeling that he was just, and that he cared for us as much when he punished us as when he commended us. And then, by degrees, we found that he was wise as well as just in his management of us. At last we are beginning to see what the principles of his conduct are; what he is in himself. We know that we know him."

Now St. John assumes that the knowledge of God is as possible, is as real for human beings, as any knowledge they can have of each other. Nay, he goes farther than this. There are impediments to our knowledge of each other, which he says do not exist with reference to that higher knowledge. There is an uncertainty, a capriciousness, a mixture of darkness with light, in every human being, which make us hesitate a little, even when we think he has given us the clearest evidence of what he is. We dismiss the suspicion; we say we are sure that he is substantially right—right in intention—though he has done some things which puzzle us, and which appear wrong. But still there is something that bewilders us, in him as well as in our own perceptions. And sometimes we are utterly at fault: we say such and such a person has entirely disappointed us. I think that on the whole this happens most rarely with those that have been under the government of a person, as their commanding officer, their schoolmaster—above all, their father. When you hear a person say, "I can speak to the temper and character of that man, for I have been a long time under him," you rely more upon his word than if his acquaintance had been of another kind; because you reflect that the superior had continual opportunities for exhibiting tyranny, vacillation, incapacity for guidance; and that if he did exhibit those qualities, the inferior was sure to take notice of them, and to smart under them. The testimony that he did not—the assurance of his subaltern that the service was a free and honourable service, one in which there was no favouritism, one which acted upon his own life, and made him wiser and better—is the highest testimony and assurance that we can demand or receive.

And it is just this test which St. John says we may have in its highest perfection in our relations with Him whom we cannot see. We may know that we know Him if we keep His commandments. I sometimes suspect that we give too loose a sense to that word "keep." No doubt it means to "obey"; it does not mean *more* than that; for obedience is very comprehensive, a little too comprehensive for slow and narrow creatures such as we are. The word "keep," if we consider it, may help us to know what obedience is, and what it is not. A friend gives me a token to keep for him; he wishes that it should remind me of him, that it should recall days which we have spent together. Perhaps it may be only a flower or a weed that was gathered in a certain place where we were walking or botanizing; perhaps it is something precious in itself. If instead of giving me anything, he enjoins me to do a certain act, or not to do a certain act, I may be said as truly to keep that injunction as to keep the flower. To fulfil it is to remember him; it is a token of my fellowship to him, of my relation with him. The injunction may be one which is in itself indifferent. We are told by the prophet Jeremiah that Jonadab, the son of Rechab, had desired his sons to drink no wine. His descendants kept the tradition; it was a homage to their ancestor's memory. The prophet set before them flagons of wine. He did not count it a criminal act to taste the liquor; but when they refused, he commended and admired them, for they were keeping their father's commandment; it was a holy pledge and token of their reverence for one whom they could not see; it kept them as a family together. But the knowledge you obtain of the person who gives the commandment depends upon the nature of the commandment. Jonadab's descendants might get a certain knowledge of their ancestor from this precept about wine. They might fairly conclude that he was a self-restraining man, who had preserved himself, and wished to preserve them, from temptations. Those commandments of which St. John speaks, are not of this limited or arbitrary kind; they are not mere signs or tokens. Still if they are *kept,* if they are watched over and thought about, and cherished as the commandments of a friend; if they are done as His commandments, they will give us an acquaintance with Him which we can obtain in no other way.

Let us consider this point a little more. Let us take the Ten Commandments; for St. John was an Israelite, a hearty Israelite, and of course would think first about the commands which were given to his nation, whatever else he connected with them. Some of you may have gone over this ground with me before; but I am less afraid of repeating myself than of passing lightly over a topic which is connected with the most practical part of Christian ethics.

The commandments open with the words, *"I am the Lord thy God which brought thee out of the land of Egypt, out of the house of bondage. Thou shalt have none other gods but me."* How could a Jew keep this commandment? He must break it—he must acknowledge another lord than the one who was speaking to him—if he did not think within himself, *"My* God is a Deliverer, a deliverer of slaves from the hand of a tyrant. That is the name by which He wishes me to remember Him; that must denote what His character is."

Next he is told, *"Thou shalt not make to thyself any graven image, nor the likeness of any thing that is in heaven above, or in the earth beneath, or in the waters under the earth. For I the Lord thy God am a jealous God, visiting the sins of the fathers upon the children unto the third and fourth generation of them that hate me, and showing mercy unto thousands in them that love me and keep my commandments."* How could this commandment be kept? The words *the* Lord *thy* God which were used in the former, here acquire a more distinct signification. "I am not to worship things that I make, for He is *the* Lord. He has created me in His image. I cannot create Him in my image, or in the image of any of these things I see. No! I must not fancy Him like the most glorious of them. He is the Lord *my* God. He has more to do with me than with them. He is nearer to me than to them.

He cares for me more than for them. He says He is jealous over me. He keeps hold of my heart; He will not let me give it away to some meaner thing. And as it is with me, it will be with my children and my children's children; He will be the Lord their God, as He is the Lord my God. He will love us from generation to generation; and each generation will be worse than the last, if it sets up some visible thing in place of Him; and each generation will be better than the last, so far as it remembers that He, the Deliverer, our God, is the Lord."

Next comes, *"Thou shalt not take the Name of the Lord thy God in vain: for the Lord will not hold him guiltless that taketh His Name in vain."* How could a Jew keep this commandment? He would have learnt from the first two commandments, that he was in the presence of a Deliverer, an unseen Being who was watching over him, whom he must not imagine to be like even the best of the things which his eyes saw and his hands handled. The *Name* of this Being was that which denoted Him to be a real Person, that by which one could tell another of Him. To fear the Name was to fear the presence, the Person; to recollect, "A true God, a living God is taking account of my acts, and of my words." To take the name in vain, was to act and speak as if there were no such presence, no such Person; as if a man's words were his own, and there was no lord over him. He who did this would not be held guiltless; he would have the sense of guilt in him; he would feel as if the friend whom he had trifled with was pursuing him. To keep the *Name* in the heart as its special treasure, would be to keep this commandment.

The fourth says, *"Remember the Sabbath day to keep it holy. Six days shalt thou labour, and do all that thou hast to do. But the seventh day is the Sabbath of the Lord thy God. In it thou shalt do no manner of work, thou, nor thy man-servant, nor thy maid-servant, nor thy cattle, nor the stranger that is within thy gates. For in six days the Lord made the heaven and the earth, and all that therein is, and rested the seventh day; wherefore, the Lord blessed the seventh day and hallowed it."* How was an Israelite to keep this commandment? According to the very terms of it, remembrance or recollection was involved in the act of observing it; there could be no sanctification of the Sabbath without this. Merely to do certain things on the Sabbath, or to leave certain things undone, would not be keeping it. Unless the Jew said to himself, "God has appointed the six days, God has appointed the seventh day; I am to work because He works, I am to rest because He rests"—he would in vain strive to obey even the letter of the precept. The command is nothing apart from the divine reason for it. The man who thought most of that, who considered most why the Lord his God had ordained rest for him, and work for him; what one had to do with the other; why the man-servant and the maid-servant and the cattle were to share in both; why the ground of both was said to be in the creation of heaven and earth—he would be most filled with delight and wonder at the order in which he found himself placed; he would most devoutly ask God to teach him so to behave himself, that he might not follow his own pleasure and his own foolish notions, either about working or resting, but might conform himself to the divine purpose in each; he would be most afraid of judging his neighbours.

Next comes, *"Honour thy father and thy mother, that thy days may be long in the land, which the Lord thy God giveth thee."* How was an Israelite to keep this commandment? The very word "honour" indicates a certain temper or habit of mind. I do not honour a person to whom I make certain presents—on whom I bestow some customary ceremonious respect. The command to honour involves, therefore, a recollection of this father and mother; a recollection of them in this character; a recollection of the bond which unites me to them. It involves too, as the latter part of it shows, a recollection of God as the giver of the soil on which my home is placed; a recollection of Him as the preserver of families on that soil; a recollection of Him as the cause of their continuance upon it from age to age; of my continuance on it from day to day; a recollection of this continuance as in some way inseparable from the reverence to parents.

"Thou shalt not kill." How might a Jew keep this commandment? No doubt he might abstain from taking the life of his neighbour, having either no strong temptation to do it, or being hindered from yielding to the temptation by the terror of the punishment which the avenger of blood would inflict upon him. But how might he keep it as if it were not man's commandment, but God's; as if it were not enforced by man's terrors, but by the thunder and lightning which are in His hand? Only while he thought of God as the author and preserver of life, only while he remembered "He watches over the life of me and of every one of these my fellows. I may take their life at His bidding. I am not to gratify any instinct of mine."

"Thou shalt not commit adultery." How was a Jew to keep this commandment? Perhaps, he might never be tempted to pollute the marriage bed; perhaps, he might overcome the impulse by thinking of exposure and disgrace and probable punishment. But, to keep it as God's commandment, to say, as Joseph did, "How can I do this great wickedness and sin against God!" he must surely recollect that God is the author of wedlock; that He binds man and wife together; that He protects this union; that it expresses some truth in His own nature which I am to be acquainted with. And so obedience to this precept serves the same purpose as obedience to all the others serves; that purpose of which St. John speaks, when he says, *"We do know that we know Him, if we keep His commandments."*

Again, *"Thou shalt not steal."* How might a Jew keep this commandment? He might be a rich man like the young ruler. The motive to rob might be as far as possible from him; or he might be poor, and the fear of the prison might deter him from meddling with that which is not his. But how might it be God's commandment to him? How might it be God's presence which held back his hand? If he thought of God as fixing what was his and what was another's; if he looked up to God to set right what man's fraud or violence had made wrong; if he committed his cause and the cause of all people to Him as the just God, and the upholder of order; then he would delight in this law in his inner man, however

strong might be the inclination of his bad nature to break it. And every observance of it and victory over that inclination would be a step in the knowledge of
God.

"Thou shalt not bear false witness against thy neighbour." How could an Israelite
keep this commandment? Outward and open perjury was dangerous—it might
be detected—a righteous recompense awaited the offender. The lies which pass
from mouth to mouth in companies of men, slanders and private whispers, are
not so easily found out. They may circulate further and further, and each new ut-
terer may keep the last and the original forger in countenance. Still, a man may,
through prudence or good nature, abstain even from this kind of false witness.
But to abstain, because God has commanded it, how may he do that? Only if he
thinks of God continually, as a God of Truth, as the hater of every false way and
false word, as pledged to destroy lies as well as to lay them bare. Must not those
who kept this in their mind, who turned it into act, grow in the knowledge of Him, who was keeping them from that which He hated?

Once more, *"Thou shalt not covet thy neighbour's house; thou shalt not covet thy
neighbour's wife; nor his man-servant, nor his maid-servant, nor his ox, nor his ass,
nor anything that is his."* How may an Israelite keep this commandment? Think
what it is! Not to covet! What law can take hold of me there? What public or private accuser, what quick-sighted judge, can bring that charge home to me? Surely
not one. And, therefore, if it *is* brought home to me, if my inmost heart does confess it, I know who must be saying this to me, *"Thou shalt not covet."* I know it
must be an unselfish and uncovetous Being. I know it must be one who desires
that I should not covet: who is willing to deliver me from my covetousness; who
can impart to me that unselfish, uncovetous life of His. So then, I have to interpret, "Thou shalt not," to mean, "If thou trustest thyself to me, I will not let thee
do the things which I hate." So then I come to know by that which He would
not have me do and be, what He himself is.

But here a question arises, which I must treat before I go further. St. Paul appears to speak of these commandments very differently from St. John. It would
seem not from a few passages in his Epistles, but from the whole tenor of them,
as if the commandments had been to him great burdens, as if he had turned to
the Gospel of Christ that he might find deliverance from them. Especially he says
of this last commandment, *"Thou shalt not covet,"* that it wrought in him all
manner of concupiscence; that he was alive before he heard it; that with the commandment sin came to life, and he died. What is the reason of this diversity of
language? Were these apostles in very deed at issue with each other? They both
taught the Ephesians. Did they bring to them contradictory tidings?

I am certain that they did not preach opposing doctrines; that their lessons are
essentially harmonious; that we cannot enter into the one unless we enter also
into the other. Saul of Tarsus had reverenced these commandments as the peculiar treasure of his nation; he had considered all other nations accursed, for not
possessing them. Saul of Tarsus believed, as the young ruler who came to our

Lord believed, that he had kept these commandments from his youth up. Had he kept them as treasures committed to him by a Friend? Had he learnt the nature and character of that Friend by means of them? Had he learnt from the very first of them, that he was to worship a Deliverer, and none else? No such thing. He had read the commandments as letters written in stone, laid up in the Temple; he had read them as the decrees of an arbitrary Being who was determined that they should be obeyed, and who would have his satisfaction in punishing to the death those who did not obey them. And the discovery came to him, with dreadful power, that he himself, the pure Israelite, the strict Pharisee, was at war with the Being who made these laws. He says, "Thou shalt not covet. And I do covet! Yes! I covet more since I have been told not to do it than I did before." What did this mean? These commandments were not condemning others, but him; they were not cursing the Heathen; they were cursing him who had believed himself to be separated from the Heathen, to be the object of God's especial favour. There was no escaping from this conviction. The more he tried to obey the law, the more it forced itself upon him. There was a deep covetousness down in the very depths of his nature; it seemed as if it was a part of his very self. And God was proclaiming this to be evil; this to be hateful in His sight. How did he arise out of this misery, which seemed to draw all the past and the present and the future into it? "It pleased God," he says, "to reveal His Son in me, that is, it pleased God to show me the Lord of my spirit, the Lord of all men; to show me that though in myself there dwelt this deep, radical covetousness,—though in myself there dwelt no good thing,—yet that in Him I might claim God as my Father; in Him I might claim men as my brethren." Yes, claim men as his brethren; for this discovery made him no longer a mere Israelite, though he could thank God more than ever for being an Israelite; though he could feel more than ever the responsibility of his calling and his education. But he was raised to be a Man; he had been taught what is the condition and glory of a man; and his calling and responsibility as an Israelite were, to tell all people—to tell those Heathens whom he had hated—that this condition and this glory were theirs as well as his. He could preach to them the Gospel, or good news, that Christ was revealed as their Lord, as the root of their life; that in Him they might call God their Father; that in Him they might renounce their selfish, covetous nature. Therefore, St. Paul having had this terrible experience himself, having this commission to mankind, could say once for all, "The law shows us our sins; the law makes us aware of the evil nature that is in us. It is not something to boast of; if we look at it as separate creatures, whether we be Jews or not, it simply curses us, it simply drives us to despair. But if it is our schoolmaster to teach us of one true Lord, of Him in whom we are created, of Him in whom we have a new and true life, then indeed it is a blessing to us; for then we give up boasting altogether of ourselves; then we can surrender ourselves freely and heartily to God as our Friend and our Deliverer; then we can become His ministers to carry the news of Him to those whom He knows, though they know not Him."

Well; St. John, we saw, *began* with this revelation of God to men in His Son. It was the ground of all his teaching. He had told the Ephesians already that there was that darkness, that covetousness, in them which St. Paul had found in himself, which had caused him so much horror. But he had told them also, as St. Paul had also told them, that they were not created to walk in this darkness; that they might walk in the light which Christ had revealed, and have fellowship with it. So now, taking this for granted, he can tell them that these commandments might be kept as the commandments of a God who was at one with them in His Son, and that the more they kept them the more they would know of Him.

I have been speaking to you of one of the most difficult of all questions in Christian ethics; one with which some of the greatest troubles in the lives of individuals and in the history of Christianity have been connected. But the confusion is not in the doctrine; it is in us; and it is a confusion out of which we can be delivered, I think, only in the way St. John speaks of here. He says in the next verse, *"He that saith, I know Him, and keepeth not His commandments, is a liar, and the truth is not in him."* The Apostle uses strong language, for this lie was spreading in the church of his own day, and would spread, he knew, further and further in the times that were coming. There were many in that time who used this very phrase, "We know God," and used it for the purpose of self-exaltation; therefore for an immoral, destructive purpose. "There are a set of common Christians," they said, "vulgar people, who may learn certain lower lessons; they are capable of nothing better. The law is very good for them. But we can enter into the divine mysteries; we can have the most magnificent conceptions about the spiritual world which Christ has opened; we can talk about angels, and emanations, and divine essences and properties; we can give them names, and trace their relations to each other. What are the commandments—what is common earthly morality—to us?" "I tell you," says St. John, broadly and simply, "that if they are nothing to you, *God* is nothing to you. You may use what fine language you will; you may have what fine speculations you like; but it is in practice, in that daily vulgar practice of life, in the struggle with the temptations to cheat and slander, to be unchaste and to be covetous, which beset us all in different ways and forms; it is in revering parents, and the name of God; it is in heeding God's rest and God's work; it is in keeping ourselves from idols; it is in worshipping Him as the common Deliverer, that we come to know Him; thus, and only thus." And he adds words which, if understood rightly, were even more crushing to the pride of these haughty men than those which were aimed at themselves. *"But whoso keepeth His word, in him verily the love of God is perfected; hereby know we that we are in Him."* As if he had said, "You talk about the perfect, the initiated man, and the mere beginners or novices. I will tell you who is the perfect or initiated man. Look at that poor creature who is studying hard in the midst of all opposition from his own ignorance, to be right and to do right; who is trying to hold fast that Word which is speaking to him in his heart, though he can form no high notions at all about things in earth or heaven. There is the initiated man; he is the one who is learning the perfect love; for God's own love is working in him; God's own love is perfecting itself in him. He is keeping the commandments, and they are teaching him that in himself he is nothing; that in God he has everything that he wants."

It was so then; it is so now. I have seen hard fighters among poor men and rich men; some on sick beds and some in the world, in whom I am sure the love of God was perfecting itself. One longed to sit at their feet and learn their wisdom. But it was the wisdom of life, not the wisdom of letters; and in life it must be learnt. They were striving according to St. John's precept to walk even as Christ walked; to live, by daily trust and daily self-renunciation, as He lived. And since they could not do this by any efforts of their own—since all their efforts only showed them their own weakness—they learned to abide in Him; they learned the deepest of all secrets, by learning more than others of their own shallowness; they came to know God by finding that they could not be honest men without knowing Him.

RELATION OF LOVE TO RIGHTEOUSNESS*

For this is the message that ye heard from the beginning, that we should love one another. Not as Cain, who was of that wicked one, and slew his brother. And wherefore slew he him? Because his own works were evil, and his brother's righteous. Marvel not, my brethren, if the world hate you. We know that we have passed from death unto life, because we love the brethren. He that loveth not his brother abideth in death. Whosoever hateth his brother is a murderer: and ye know that no murderer hath eternal life abiding in him. Hereby perceive we the love of God, because He laid down His life for us: and we ought to lay down our lives for the brethren. But whoso hath this world's good, and seeth his brother have need, and shutteth up his bowels of compassion from him, how dwelleth the love of God in him? My little children, let us not love in word, neither in tongue; but in deed and in truth. And hereby we know that we are of the truth, and shall assure our hearts before him. For if our heart condemn us, God is greater than our heart, and knoweth all things. Beloved, if our heart condemn us not, then have we confidence toward God. And whatsoever we ask, we receive of Him, because we keep His commandments, and do those things that are pleasing in His sight. And this is His commandment, That we should believe on the name of His Son Jesus Christ, and love one another, as He gave us commandment.

—1 John 3:11–23

I have taken more verses to-day than I am wont to take for the subject of a single Lecture, not certainly because I think any of them unimportant, but because I do not know how to separate them without injuring their sense. The passage

*From *The Epistles of St. John* (Cambridge: Macmillan and Co., 1857), Lecture 13, 200–214.

may seem at first sight to include many different topics which might be easily considered apart. But when we have carefully examined it, we perceive one principle unfolding itself gradually through the different clauses, which we might fail to apprehend, if we did not observe how each contributes to the illustration of it.

What that principle is, I hinted at the close of my last Lecture. St. John had joined together two signs of the birth which is not from above, but from beneath; of the birth that is not of God, but of the devil. Not doing righteousness, was one sign; not loving the brethren, was another. We often set these two signs in opposition. That man, we say, is rigidly just; he holds to the law; but he is not affectionate, not loving. *That* man, we say, is one of the kindest, most charitable, most tender-hearted creatures in the world; but he is sadly wanting in justice; he will always overlook evil rather than punish it. There may be a plea for such language; there are men, doubtless, who have cultivated the sterner virtues, and who have crushed what they think interferes with them; there are men who have been driven by the sight and experience of this severity into the temper which is most directly the reverse of it. But the contradiction is solely the effect of our imperfection; it has no existence in the nature of things. The proof that it has not, is that it does not last, even in those who appear to present the most remarkable specimens of it. The just man becomes unjust from the want of that sympathy which enables him to understand the degrees of criminality in different men; the merciful man becomes unmerciful, because he is without a standard to which he can refer his own acts, and to which he can raise those whom he spares. So it is shown that there is and must be a radical union between these two great human characteristics. And so it becomes a most important question in ethics to ascertain the ground of this union, and how it may bear upon our practice.

I spoke to you in my sixth Lecture of the contempt which some had thrown upon the Old Testament, as if it were set aside by the New, and of St. John's assertion, that the word which they had heard from the beginning was that which he was declaring to them. I showed you, at the same time, how he justified the reverence for the New Testament as a higher revelation than the Old, on the ground that the true Brother of men had appeared; that the commandment that each man should love his neighbour as himself had become *true in Him and in us;* a law actually fulfilled; a law which could be obeyed. The question presents itself here under a new aspect. It is not whether the New Testament has superseded the Old; but whether, if the New Testament sets forth Love as the principle of human action, it does not contradict the Old, in which Righteousness and Law are so prominent. You shall hear St. John's answer. He does not now speak of the commandments which were given on Sinai. He goes back to an earlier record still. *"This,"* he says, *"is the message which ye heard from the beginning, that we should love one another. Not as Cain, who was of that wicked one, and slew his brother."*

Here is the oldest story almost in the Bible. You call it the story of a great transgression. A transgression implies something to be transgressed. What was that?

There were no decrees then; no tables of stone. But there was God's message to men in the very fact of these two men being brothers. *"Ye shall love one another"* is involved in the very constitution of the universe, in the very existence of a family. Cain proved himself to be *"of that wicked one,"*—to be the servant of the rebel against Right and God,—by this act against his brother. Are Righteousness and Love, then, hostile principles? Is one the mitigation or softening of the other? Is not Love presupposed in Righteousness? Is not an outrage upon Love an outrage upon Righteousness?

He enforces his argument in the second clause of the verse, *"And wherefore slew he him? Because his own works were evil, and his brother's righteous."* The story represents the dislike of Cain to Abel as originating in anger against God, because his sacrifice had not been accepted. The Epistle to the Hebrews affirms the sacrifice of Abel to have been good, because it was offered in faith; the sacrifice of Cain to have been evil, because it was offered in unbelief or distrust. St. John asserts the same doctrine in different language. The righteous man of the Old and New Testament equally is the man who trusted in a righteous God; the unrighteous man is the distrustful man. The story represents God as arguing the case with Cain's conscience, as saying, *"If thou doest well, shalt thou not be accepted?"* He refuses to listen to that voice. He turns from the righteous Lord; he hates Him; then he begins to hate his brother, *for* his faith, *for* his righteousness. What was the Gospel doctrine but the expansion of this primary history? What was it but the unfolding of a LAW which that History had indicated? What were the experiences of those who accepted it, but this first experience multiplied?

But here was the perplexity. If there were only an Adam and an Eve, a Cain and Abel, it might be easy enough to say that the loving man was the rule, and the unloving man the exception. How could this be said in an age when the majority—the world at large—was full of hatreds and murders, when there were only a few protestants on behalf of unity? St. John does not blink this difficulty. *"Marvel not, my brethren,"* he says, *"if the world hate you."* Do not let this fact stagger your faith, that the proportion of haters to lovers seems so enormous. *"We know that we have passed from death unto life, because we love the brethren."* It is not a question to be decided by a poll. It is a question which each man may decide for himself. Is it not the state of Death to hate? Is it not the state of Life to love? Did we not hate because we had been separated from the life of God? Are we not able to love, because we are in communion with the life of God? What then if a frightful number are hating each other? *"Whosoever hateth his brother, abideth in death."* He is cutting himself off from the universe; he is at war with its law; at war with its Creator and Lawgiver. He goes on: *"Every one that hateth his brother is a murderer; and ye know that no murderer hath eternal life abiding in him."* The thought of the "primal eldest curse" is still present to him. Murder, he says, as that story indicates, is hatred developed into act. Hatred is murder in the heart. But he has been occupied through his whole letter, with telling us that the life of God, the Eternal Life, which was implied in the divine code, but which no divine code could adequately express or make effectual, had been manifested in Jesus Christ. As the code fights with the act, this life fights with the principle. As the code deals out vengeance on the crime which is perpetrated by the murderer's hand, this life is the contradiction of the hatred in the murderer's heart. With that it cannot abide. What, then, must this life, this Eternal life, be?

Last week the question was raised, What does he mean by the Love of which he discourses so much? I said I felt sure that he would not cheat us of an answer, though I doubted whether it would take the form of a definition. In the first verse he produces the answer even in a more direct and formal manner than you would perhaps imagine from our version.

"Hereby perceive we Love," (the words *of God* are added): *"Because He laid down His life for us; and we ought to lay down our lives for the brethren."* He has been tracing the operation of the law of love, and the transgression of the law of love in former ages. He has fully vindicated the Old Testament from those who say that this law of love is not the one which it recognises. But he agrees with those who exalted the New Testament above the Old, to this extent: he admits that the love which was involved in every true set that had ever been done, which had been the hidden principle of every true life, which was seen in Joseph's tenderness for the brethren who had sold him, in the care of Moses for the people who were ready to stone him, in the burning patriotism of every prophet whom his countrymen put in the stocks or the prison, or doomed to death,—had not yet fully revealed itself. A man of the old time could not say "I know it." He longed to know it; he looked forward to a time when it should be known. The time, says St. John, has come. The blessing is ours. The Son of God *"has laid down His life for us."* By this we know Love. This is the Divine interpretation of it: for Divine interpretations come in acts, not words. I might call it a Divine *definition.* So far as a definition *excludes* all that does not belong to the nature of that which it explains, Christ's death is a definition of Love; for it shows what love is *not;* how unlike it is to that tolerance of evil which men have confounded with it. So far as a definition *includes* all that belongs to the nature of the thing which it explains, Christ's death is a definition of Love. For there is no possible element of Love which men in their right minds have felt that they have need of, which they have recognised in the most heroic and the most sympathizing acts of their fellow men, that is not found in this act. Why, then, do I shrink from using that phrase, *definition?* Why would you feel it to be inappropriate? Because you must attach some notion of what is finite to definition. Because your conscience tells you that the Love which you see here is infinite. There can be no measure found for it in earth or Heaven. I am sorry that our translators inserted any words that are not in the original. It was both wrong and weak to do so. They left room for the thought, that we may learn what Love *itself* is somewhere else than at the Cross of Christ. They anticipated what St. John will tell us in better and fuller language

hereafter. But I do not admit for an instant that they introduced any false doctrine. *The* Love, the infinite Love, must be God's Love. If the death of Christ showed us what the infinite Love is, it showed us what God's Love is.

He goes on— *"And we ought to lay down our lives for the brethren."* The taking away the life of a brother was proved, by the earliest experience of the world, to be the result of departure from the law on which God had formed His world. The laying down a life for others is proved, by the latest experience in the history of the world, to be the principle, the essence, of that law. The life of the Lawgiver—the life eternal—which had never been manifested till Christ was born, which had never been completely manifested till Christ died, was now shown to be the life of self-sacrifice. Love cannot exist apart from sacrifice; therefore he says, *"We ought to lay down our lives for the brethren."* It is startling language. We are wont to say, that one who lays down his life for another performs a transcendant deed of virtue, for which he may give himself credit. The Apostle says, "This is our ordinary duty." We are not to count it heroic at all; but simply obedience to the law under which we exist. And surely the conscience of mankind confirms his judgment, however the pride of men may rebel against it. The action in the heathen world, which has always inspired most of admiration in true minds, is the death of the 300 Spartans who guarded the pass of Thermopylae against the army of Xerxes; and it was recorded on the graves of these 300, that they died in obedience to the laws of their country. They felt that it was their business to be there; that was all. They did not choose the post for themselves; they only did not desert the posts which it behoved them to occupy. Our countrymen heartily respond to this doctrine. The notion of dying for glory is an altogether feeble one for them. They had rather stay by their comfortable or uncomfortable firesides, than suffer from what seems to them a fiction. But the words, "England expects every man to do his duty," are felt to be true and not fictitious words. There is power in them. The soldier or sailor who hears them ringing through his heart will meet a charge, or go down in his ship, without dreaming that he shall be ever spoken of or remembered, except by a mother or child or an old friend. So it is in private experience. Women are found sacrificing their lives, not under a sudden impulse of feeling, but through a long course of years, to children and their husbands, who often requite them very ill; whose words are surly; who spend what affection they have on other objects. The silent devotion goes on; only one here and there knows anything of it; it is quite as likely that the world in general spends its compassion upon those to whom they are ministering; none count their ministries so entirely matters of course as themselves. Christian ethics explain these facts by which so many are puzzled. There is a law of sacrifice throughout the universe. Some submit to it reluctantly. They try to set up another law, the law of self-pleasing. They try to accommodate all things to that. They cannot succeed. They do *not* please themselves. Earth and Heaven are at war with them. For the mind of the Ruler of Heaven and Earth is a mind of self sacrifice; it is revealed in the Cross of Christ. Some submit to the law of sacrifice cheerfully. They feel it to be a good law. They allow it to shape their acts. These are consciously or unconsciously yielding to Christ, confessing Him as their king, bearing His Cross. It is the privilege of those who live in Christian countries to yield to Him consciously. So they are freed from self-consciousness. Their acts may be perfectly simple. They need not be proud of their humility, for their humility is His. They need not glorify themselves upon the giving up of themselves, for they look upon no sacrifice as satisfactory but His; every other only derives its virtue from His.

St. John might have good reason to fear that his words, carefully as they were guarded, would still suggest some notions of a special martyrdom, such as many were permitted to undergo in that day for the name of Christ. An Ephesian might say, "Oh, yes, of course, I must lay down my life for the Church, if a persecution should arise, and I should be called either to renounce my profession, or endure the axe, the cross, or the fire. But I hope I may escape that alternative."

The next verse shows that the principle he had asserted had no such limited application, and was reserved for no extreme case. *"If any man hath this world's goods, and seeth his brother have need, and shutteth up his bowels of compassion against him, how dwelleth the love of God in him?"* As if he had said, "The law of sacrifice is not a law for moments and crises of our existence; it is the law for the whole of it. The pettiest events and occasions will be tests whether you are subject to it or at war with it. You may have very ecstatic feelings about the Christian brotherhood at large; but are you ready to help that particular brother, who is lying destitute there, not with feelings, but with a little of the actual food and raiment that he is in need of?"

This would be a searching question. I do not know which of us might not sometimes quail at it. But what does St. John mean by putting it in this form: *"How dwelleth the love of God in you?"* Does he wish us to understand that the very love which is in God, is communicated to us, is to dwell in us? Does he blame us for not allowing this love to dwell in us? That must be what he is saying. It is impossible to explain his words in any other sense. You will see as we proceed, that he repudiates the other sense which is sometimes given to them, as if by the love *of* God he signified the love we bear *to* God. And without anticipating future passages of his discourse, I think we have read enough already to see that his whole method would be changed if he taught that we climb to Heaven by acts of love, and not Heaven comes down and declares itself to us in acts of love.

"My little children, let us not love in word, neither in tongue; but in deed and in truth." That easy way of loving, by talking about love, was a way into which Christians might fall in Ephesus as well as in London, in the days of the Roman emperors as well as in the days of Queen Victoria. St. John warns his children of it with fatherly gentleness; but there is a sting in that very gentleness. He would not tell them not to commit this hypocrisy if he did not know that they were likely to commit it. No; nor would he tell them of it, if he could not also tell them how they might avoid it. If they had no love to draw upon but their own, I do

not see how it could fail to run dry very soon, or what would be left but a sedi-
ment of word love and tongue love, which never clothed any human body or
comforted any human soul yet. But if he could assure them that they were under a law of love, that God's love was burning clearly and brightly always, and
that it was their fault if it did not burn in them,—he might well add, "Why
should we cheat ourselves of the greatest of all blessings by not yielding to the
power of this love, by not allowing it to express itself in our acts?"

"And hereby," he adds, *"we know that we are of the truth, and shall assure our
hearts before Him."* This verse, like the last, seems to break down the barrier
which separates the Apostle's world from ours. How often we hear persons say,
"Well, I hope I believe as I ought to believe. I hope I am holding the truth. But
there is great uncertainty. Some people think one thing, some another. I should
like to have some security. I wish I knew some one who could tell me, That is the
opinion you should hold, that is the opinion you should reject; that is the thing
you should do, that is the thing you should not do." Those who speak thus generally ask for some external dictator who shall relieve them of their responsibility. There are others who are craving for an inward assurance. They want to be
able, as the hymn says, "to read their title clear to mansions in the skies"; to have
some authentic token that they shall be blessed hereafter.

These anxieties which are at work now, have been at work always, though they
may have presented themselves in different aspects. St. John addresses himself to
them, and turns them to the most practical account. You want to know that you
are of the truth? Ask the God of truth to keep you from loving in word and
tongue, and not in deed and in truth. You want to assure your hearts respecting
your relation to God? Ask the God of love Himself to dwell in you, and to direct
your thoughts and acts according to His will. You will not need dictators to tell
you what the truth is, if the Source of all truth is leading you into it. You will not
need assurances about a future heaven, if you have heaven within you now.

*"For if our heart condemn us, God is greater than our heart, and knoweth all
things."* What tricks that we have all practised upon ourselves does this sentence
lay bare! What webs of theological and ethical sophistry does it cut through! A
man wants some comfortable assurance that he is right with God. And yet his
heart is not right with itself. There is uneasiness and bitterness in his conscience.
He feels that he has not been loving in deed and truth, but only in word and
tongue. His heart tells him so. "Well," says the Apostle, "you must be right with
that heart, if you wish to be right with God. You are not at peace with yourself,
because you know that you are wrong. Do you really think God does not know
you are wrong? What is this verdict of your heart but His verdict? Can you get
Him to reverse it, if it is, as you feel it is, a true verdict?"

The argument is very plain, the doctrine indisputable. And yet by practically
admitting it, by accepting it as the rule of our lives, what trouble, what a multitude of complicated calculations, what infinite distress, we shall save ourselves!
At first, perhaps, it begets a kind of despair. "Whatever my heart says, God says

first, and with greater emphasis. He knows more against me than I know against myself. How terrible to encounter His scrutiny! Hills and mountains, fall on me, and hide me from Him!" But look again. *"God is greater than my heart, and knoweth all things.* He knows what has set me wrong, as I do not know it. He can set me right, though I cannot set myself right." This is the comfort of not merely believing in a conscience, but in a God who speaks through my conscience; this is the comfort of not thinking that *it* is my lawgiver, but that *He* is my lawgiver; this is the comfort of being able to say to Him who is my Judge, Search me, and see if there is any wicked way in me, and lead me in the way everlasting.

And so we are brought to peace with the adversary who is within us. When we turn round to the light from which we have been turning away, our heart no longer condemns us; it tells us we are right. *"And if our heart condemn us not, then have we confidence towards God."* We can look cheerfully up to Him who has reconciled us to Himself, and wishes us to be at one with Him. We can be sure that His will is the right will, the blessed will, and that to be in subjection to it is our right and our blessedness. Or, as St. John expresses it more fully and satisfactorily, *"And whatever we ask, we receive of Him, because we keep His commandments, and do the things that are pleasing in His sight."* I have endeavoured before to explain that phrase, *"keep His commandments."* What we have heard to-day has thrown further light upon it. To keep God's commandments is to remember what that law is which He has established for the universe; what the law of His own mind, of His own life, is. When we submit to that law, His life acts upon our life. As St. John says, "He dwells in us, and so we are able to do the things that He would have us to do, *'the things that are pleasing in His sight.'* "

But a question might still occur to some person who had been used to hear the doing or keeping of the commandments set in opposition to faith in Christ, "All you want us, then, is to *do* right. You do not care so much what we *believe.*" Nay, he says, "If you ask me what God's first commandment is, I should say, *that we should believe in the name of His Son Jesus Christ.* For have not I told you that the perfect law of God, because the perfect life of God, is set forth in Him; specially in His death? Have I not said that there we see Love, and how inseparable it is from the giving up of self? How, then, can we keep God's commandment, how can we come under His law so completely, as by acknowledging this Son as the brightness of His glory, the express image of His person; by trusting in Him as our elder brother and Mediator and Advocate? For by doing so we are able to keep that commandment which He Himself gave us, which He gave us because He had fulfilled it and embodied it in His life, *that we should love one another.*"

Thus we arrive at the two counter-signs to those of the devilish birth with which we began. Doing righteousness and loving the brethren are the signs of the heavenly birth. They denote the adopted child of God; because they denote the only-begotten Son of God. He was perfectly righteous, for He perfectly trusted His Father, and would not glorify Himself. He perfectly loved men. That love came forth in the sacrifice of Himself. But this sacrifice set forth, as nothing else could, the character, the righteousness of God. When we come into this region, all the seeming contradiction between Righteousness and Love disappears. They must be one if the Father is one with the Son; they must be one if the Son is the perfect image of the Father; they must be one if the Son is He in whose image Man is created. . . .

CHAPTER 3

The Conscience:
Lectures on Casuistry

ON THE WORD "I"*

You may wonder at the title which I have chosen for my first lecture. I have taken it because I can find none which explains so well what will be the subject of all my lectures; what kind of facts will be considered in them, what claim they have to be practical.

There are grave doubts among men of the world whether the student of morals has any real subject to treat of. He can talk much about the blessings of virtue and the mischiefs of vice. But Lord Macaulay, who spent a great part of his life in dealing with virtues and vices as a legislator, or in recording the effects of them as a historian, said, you may remember, that the most brilliant writer upon them did not deserve half the gratitude from mankind which is due to the maker of a substantial pair of shoes. Again, the moralist may dwell upon different opinions which have descended upon us from other times, or have been produced in our own. He may speak of Sensualists and Utilitarians and Transcendentalists. Grand names assuredly; but how do they or the doctrines which they represent concern the business of life? Who that is occupied with facts can care about them? Who that is seeking for amusement will not find elsewhere what is much more lively and stimulating?

Or if the moral teacher adopts the distinction which is sanctioned by one of the ablest and most accomplished of his class—if he says that his business is with what ought to be, that of other students with what is—can there be a clearer or fuller confession that he means to leave the actual world for some other world which he has imagined? . . .

---

*From *The Conscience: Lectures on Casuistry Delivered in the University of Cambridge,* 2d ed. (London: Macmillan and Co., 1872), Lecture 1, 1–23 (abridged).

Beginning then with that objector who especially boasts the title of the practical man, I venture to ask, "Does the word *I* seem to you an unpractical word, one which only concerns shadows? You do not act as if this were so. You do not speak as if this were so. You are rather angry if reverence is withdrawn from this word, if there is a hint that any can be equally dear to him who utters it. In making your calculations about the doings of other men or your own, is it not your maxim that this I is entitled to a primary consideration? Well! it is this which the Moralist claims for his investigation. He agrees with you in your estimate of its importance. He thinks as you seem to think, that whatever may be the value or interest of the things which are seen and handled or tasted or smelt, I who see and handle and taste and smell am at least as interesting to myself as they can be.". . .

Wherever any language is cultivated, the I cannot be thus forgotten. If you take up Homer you will find that when he wants to express the distinction not between Trojans and Greeks but between both and the horses which they tame, the dogs which look up to them as masters, he calls them *meropes*. Articulate speech is the characteristic of *men*. How does the speech become articulate and human? What is the difference between the cries of beasts or the songs of birds which Homer must have known intimately, and the winged words which went forth from the mouths of his heroes? Each of them called himself I. There is the difference, there is the articulation. Ascribe that word to a cat or an elephant, and you are sure that you are in the region of fable, that the man is imputing to a lower race that which is the necessary condition of his own. . . .

It is to this question [the meaning of the "I"], which is left with such testimonies to its significance, as a waif or estray by all those who are not afraid to face other questions, that I believe the student of Morals must address himself. He ought to explain why this I is so troublesome to the physical student, why it casts its shadow over all his enquiries into the order of the outward world. He ought to show why it has struck its roots so deeply into language. He ought to assist the historian in casting off some of those vague generalities which obscure the facts that he is describing, and yet offer themselves to him as such convenient modes of accounting for them. I do not think that the moralist can advance a step, can make out any reason for his existence, unless he girds himself to this task. And yet no one has more opportunities for evading it, more hints from illustrious practitioners of his art how he may evade it. Instead of using the word I, which men use in their common speech, he may talk about Individuality or Personality. And though, if he is rudely asked "what is your personality, what is your individuality?" he may be obliged rather ignominiously to reply that it is a more philosophical way of saying "I myself;" he will find so much comfort in this phraseology—such a graceful plea for it as being a refuge from egotism—such an apparent justification for it in the necessity of alluding to the mass of human creatures and not to a single unit of the mass—that the word "I" will vanish out of his school dialect, whilst he is resorting to it every hour, almost every minute, if he is speaking not as a school-man but as a man. So the link between the two characters is broken; his talk is of men, but that which characterises a man is gone; you have killed him that you may dissect him.

At whatever risk of appearing egotistical—even of being so,—at whatever risk of exchanging grand technical words for common words, such as men speak in the market-place—we must make an effort to show that morality means the life and practice of each person who walks this earth and calls himself I, that it is not wrapped up in theories and speculations about some general human nature which is no man's particular nature. . . .

There is no attraction in general formulas and propositions; there is an immense charm in one, however uncouth in his appearance, who can enter into desires and perplexities which he has first realized in his own life, and through which he has fought his way. There is no terror in mere propositions and formulas; there is great terror in one who arouses us to remember that which we had rather forget; he would take from us the Lethe cup; we may be willing that he should drain the cup of hemlock.

The geniality of Socrates, his hearty humour, his appreciation of all the forms of common life, his habit . . . of showing his thought, not formed, but in the process of formation,—were nearly wanting in his accomplished panegyrists of the 18th century. And, therefore, all their talent and all their desire to be useful could never obtain for them the influence which was exerted by men whom they could often despise for want of taste, by men whom they could often condemn for more grievous faults than any against taste, but who had the courage or the audacity to reveal that which had passed in the inmost sanctuary of their being. Amongst us the disciples of Wesley announced, often in grotesque phrases, often with a mixture of wild and morbid fancies, facts of which they had become aware, not in the world without, the world which they saw, but in their own very selves. The grotesque phrases might be ridiculed, the morbid fancies might be detected and exposed by those who were acquainted with diseases of the body or the mind. But the facts were recognised by men whose circumstances and education had been altogether different from those of the persons who disclosed them; chords which had been silent in the hearts of refined men and women responded to the touch sometimes of very coarse fingers; general moralities were rejected as feeble; he who used the Ego was hailed, for there was an Ego in the hearer.

There was a man who spoke in altogether different accents from those of the Methodists to the people of France. Amidst the voices of philosophers who were listened to with wonder and delight in the salons of Paris, because they struck at hypocrisies which were becoming intolerable, and did *not* strike at vices which were fashionable, there echoed from the hills of Switzerland the Confessions of Jean Jacques Rousseau. They were the utterances of a disturbed, even of a deranged mind; were outrageous in their display of the writer's evil acts and thoughts; did not spare the polite society of the day, or the notions which were popular in it. But in spite of their strangeness and madness, in spite of the disgust which they often excited, they had, for Rousseau's countrymen and strangers, a fascination which was found in no dogmas however destructive, in no jests however keen and brilliant. In the most superficial of all societies there was still a craving to look below the surface; where men were most crushed by conventions, there was still a welcome for any one who could prove that he maintained an existence, though it might be a very incoherent existence, under the pressure of them.

I quite admit that there is in the English character something which shrinks from both these forms of egotism, even whilst it gives them entertainment. The silent self-contained man who avoids such exhibitions commands our respect; we have a certain dislike, even contempt, for the man who relieves himself by whispering his confessions into the ear of the public, though we are not unwilling to use our privilege of listening. The reserve of such writers as Butler often tells us more of their characters than any discoveries which they could make respecting their history. They hide, under language which concerns the world, many a struggle which they have gone through in themselves; slowly we become as much convinced that a man is speaking to us in these books as if he admitted us into his closest privacy. If such reticence were lost from our literature we should lose much that is most precious in it, much that has been ultimately very powerful. If we banished it from our own characters they would suffer a more serious injury; the most sacred treasures would be profaned. That danger should always be remembered when we commend Egotism. There must be . . . some way of uttering ourselves without talking about ourselves, some way of carrying on living communications with each other, even when we dwell least on our idiosyncrasies—when our dialect is even less moulded by our own habits and prepossessions than that of the philosophers in the last century was.

Such a method I have wished to indicate by taking for the title of my Lecture "The *word* I." "If you must have that I for your subject," some one may say, "why not tell us of the *thing,* why give us the mere name of the thing?" I answer, I cannot call this I a thing; you would all be scandalized by such language. If the I were a thing I should have nothing to do with it; you would get your knowledge of it in the rooms where things are treated of. But, if not a thing, what shall I say of it? Am I to allow that it is a mere abstraction, that it points to no substance? Every man who is most busy in the affairs of the world would raise his voice against me if I did that. "What! you put this slight upon number one! You say that I am a nonentity. What then, pray, is not a nonentity?" A question which I should find much trouble in answering. If in this perplexity I resort to the phrases Personality or Individuality, I have told you already what consequences I foresee must follow from that proceeding; how, after all, I should be driven to the shame of giving I in exchange for those splendid polysyllables. In despair then of getting a substitute for this word, I content myself with drawing your attention to the fact that you do use it, that you must use it whenever you speak the speech of men. And so I would lead you to reflect a little on the grandeur and power of words;

of those words which we repeat most frequently, which we trifle with most. Not the words which are appropriated to the service of Art and Philosophy, which are withdrawn from daily usage, but those which are passing from hand to hand, those which are the current coin of every realm, those which are continually liable to lose their image and superscription from the friction of society, are the truly sacred words; in them lies a wealth of meaning which each age has helped to extract, but which will contain something for every fresh digger. The word *I*, with its property of being demanded by a whole community, and yet being only capable of denoting a single unit, is a key to that mystery in words which makes them interpreters of the life of individuals, of nations, of ages; the discoverers of that which we have in common, the witnesses of that in each man which he cannot impart, which his fellows may guess at, but which they will never know. . . .

There is one class of words which especially rebels against arbitrary definition, and which may be especially profitable for the end that Socrates proposed to himself. I mean such words as "Consciousness" and "Conscience." There are a multitude more which we discover by degrees to be of the same kind and to point in the same direction as these; but these are centres from which light falls upon the rest. They are inseparably connected with that pronoun of which I have been speaking in this lecture. Take away the I from language, and they must disappear also. There is no demand for them in any of the things which I see or taste or handle. They come into existence only because there is an I who sees, tastes, handles. . . .

They are full of difficulty, full of apparent contradiction. Yet I must grapple with them at once if I pursue the course which I have marked out for myself. I have proposed to treat of Casuistry. Now *the* subject of Casuistry is the Conscience. . . . I have told you in this lecture that I dread the temptation to lay down a general scheme of morals or of human nature. The examples of eminent men in former days who have adopted that course—the craving for facts, the impatience of mere opinion, which I welcome as some of the most hopeful signs of our time,—alike lead me to desire . . . a more egotistical kind of study. Casuistry, it seems to me, is such a study. It brings us face to face with the internal life of each one of us. The world without, it leaves to the examination of other enquirers. The Casuist's business is with him who looks into that world, who receives impressions from it, and compels it to receive impressions from him. . . .

I have pleaded for egotism. It is that each of us may reverence his own life and the life of his fellow-man above all theories that any have formed about him or them. It is that we may study the problems of life seriously and truthfully, whether we can make out a theory about them or no. It is that in studying these problems we may profit by the lessons of those with whose dogmas or conclusions we may the least agree. . . . Think of the word I, and you will be able to enter upon the study of the word Conscience with some hope of a satisfactory result. . . .

Dr. Whewell, . . . in the second of his lectures on Systematic Morality, asserts with great force and eloquence the maxims which I have been trying to maintain this morning, that the moral student is as much occupied with realities as the physical student, and that he has as wide a field to examine. "He has" (I must quote his words, for I would gladly take them as the motto for this Course of Lectures) "for his region of thought everything about which other men think most eagerly, all that occupies the mind of the historian, the poet, the tragedian, the comedian, the advocate, the statesman, the poor, the rich, the recluse, the man of the world; he has to consider not only all the means which they have to gain their purposes; but he has also to weigh their purposes against each other; to compare the ends of life according to each view; to decide how far each lies in the road to the far end, the true aim of human life. . . . For the *microcosm,* the little world of man, is really not less than the *macrocosm,* the great world of Nature."*

ON THE WORD "CONSCIENCE"†

Many definitions of the Conscience are to be found in books of Philosophers, many accounts of its operations. We may consider some of these in due time. I should be sorry to neglect them, for each thoughtful man will supply some hint which may make our thoughts clearer. But, as I said in my last Lecture, we must begin with asking ourselves what meaning we have given to the word and do give it in our ordinary discourse. We are using it on the most vulgar occasions. We say that a tradesman who sends in an extravagant bill, or adulterates the food which he sells, has no conscience. And yet we do not really admit that he or any man is without a conscience. We appeal to it as if we thought it was in him, and could respond to the demand we make upon it.

I observed in my last lecture that the adjective Conscious is inseparably connected with the word I. Nothing, I said, which we taste or smell or handle would suggest it to us. I am conscious of the taste of the orange or the smell of the rose. I never dream that the orange or the rose is conscious. I *know with myself* what impression I have received from the rose or the orange. The difference of the effect of sights or scents on different men or women, as on different classes of animals, may depend on peculiarities of their bodily structure; but when you have taken all account of these, if you understand them ever so perfectly, you will have to say at last, "It is I to whom the pleasure or the pain comes which is brought to me through any sense." If I were not there the words pain and pleasure would carry no signification with them. I can only tell anything about either, because I am conscious of it. . . .

But there are some cases in which we cannot dispense with the word [consciousness], in which none other would serve us so well. Oedipus meets Laius on

---

*Whewell on Systematic Morality, p. 48.
†From *The Conscience,* 2d ed. (London: Macmillan and Co., 1872), Lecture 2, 24–36 (abridged).

a cross-road going to Thebes. There is an encounter. Laius is slain. Is Oedipus conscious of what he has done? Of course he knows that he has killed a man who would have killed him. He meant to do that. But is he conscious—does he know with himself—what sort of act he has done: is he aware that he is a parricide? The story which the genius of Sophocles has so wonderfully unfolded is the story of the awakening of this Consciousness, of the discovery to Oedipus of what he has done, of what he is. And this Consciousness is fresh and alive years after, when he himself is a father and a king. The act done so long ago is with him then. It has become a part of his own existence.

The moment I pass from the consideration of the things with which I have to do to the consideration of that which I am, this problem confronts me; it is this conscience which binds the different parts of my existence together, which assures me that the past still belongs to me. It seems very terrible. But banish it, and there is no drama, no biography, no history: human existence becomes the dreariest blank; men only brutal. . . .

We do not always use the epithet "conscientious" as one of strong commendation. We may not like the person on whom we bestow it. There may be something like a sneer or a curl of the lip when we observe "That man is always thinking what he ought to do or ought not to do." Such surly judgments, hastily thrown off, are often of great value. They indicate, better than formal explanations, what force we give to the words which we utter most frequently and familiarly. I am not sure that if we sought long we should find a more exact account of a conscientious man than this, He is one who is always considering what he ought or ought not to do; or whether there is a more exact description of the Conscience than this, It is that in me which says, I ought or I ought not. . . .

However we may account for it each of us does say "I ought" and "I ought not." We cannot weed those expressions out of our dialect or out of the dialect of any civilised nation. Like the word I they have established themselves in language; it could not exist without them. How is that? Do you think it would be so if *we* could exist without them, if the I and the *ought* had not some very close affinity? . . .

[T]he I and the ought are twin words. Like the *Siamese twins,* they are not without violence or risk of death to be severed from each other. I impress that remark upon you because it will save you many confusions hereafter if you thoroughly take it in. I said that you complained of the want of conscience in the shopkeeper who charged you more than you thought was reasonable for articles you had purchased of him. You ascribe a conscience to him because he calls himself I, just as you do. And you cannot suppose that he is like you in that respect without supposing that like you he says to himself "I ought and I ought not." But I am only *conscious* of that which passes in myself; as he is only conscious of that which passes in himself. There is no doubt in some persons a very wonderful apprehension and divination of that which others are thinking, imagining, purposing. Those who really have that gift,—who do not merely fancy they have it and make all kinds of false, suspicious, and ill-natured guesses about their neighbours—we call men and women of genius. Sympathy has much to do with genius, perhaps is the essence of it. But it cannot exist, I apprehend, except in a person who has a lively consciousness of what is passing in *him*. He is awake to that, and so can make more than a guess at which is passing in me. This divination therefore does not interfere with my maxim or even offer an exception to it. The act of conscience is an act in me. It means "I ought or I ought not." I may pass judgment on other men's acts; but that is another process; I am abusing terms and what the terms represent if I identify it with the Conscience.

Perhaps you will say to me "What! if I see my friend pursuing a course of conduct which I am sure will ruin him, is it not my conscience which bids me warn him of his danger, though I know he may quarrel with me, even hate me for doing so?" Yes, I fully admit that it is your conscience which bids you warn your friend. What I affirm is, that the conscience does bid *you,* and no one else. When you speak to him you try to arouse *his* conscience. You will effect nothing for him unless you arouse it. And therefore it is of great practical importance to remember the distinction which I have drawn. Many hard pharisaical censures, which lead to no result, are the consequences of our forgetting it, as well as the omission of many counsels which would benefit our neighbours because they would be the fruit of our experience of ourselves.

And thus another perplexity may be taken out of our way. "What must we call the Conscience? Is it a special faculty? Is it a faculty in all men or only in some men?" Butler describes it as a faculty of human nature. Dr. Whewell demurs; it is according to him only an exercise of the Reason. Which opinion are we to adopt?

Just because I hold the fact of the existence of a conscience to be one in which each of us is deeply and practically interested, I decline to enter into these controversies between learned men. . . .

But we may thankfully accept their joint testimony in support of a fact which each of them had realized in himself, and which each of us may realize in himself.

I am not the least afraid of bringing the question whether there is a conscience to this test. I am only afraid lest our decision about it should be embarrassed by the introduction of other questions to which the test cannot be applied. If I am told there is a Conscience in Human Nature, I begin to ask whether there are not the widest conceivable differences between the persons to whom this Nature is attributed, and whether what is true about one may not be untrue about another. Especially when this Conscience is credited as it is by Butler with the grandest functions, when it is appealed to as the highest of all authorities, the question will suggest itself, Do you say that of every man's Conscience, or of some particularly exalted Conscience? Dr. Whewell was aware that Butler had laid himself open to cavils of this kind. He tried to avoid them. "We cannot," he said, "properly refer to our Consciences as to an ultimate and supreme authority. It has only a subordinate and intermediate authority standing between the supreme law to which it is bound to conform, and our own actions which must conform to it, in order to be moral." He adds a little further on, "As the object of reason is to determine what is true, so the object of Conscience is to determine what is right. As each man's reason may err, and so lead himself to a false opinion, so each man's conscience may err, and lead him to a false moral standard. As false opinion does not disprove the reality of truth, so the false moral standards of men do not disprove the reality of a supreme law or rule of human action."*

This language is moderate and cautious; yet it has provoked a criticism which I will read to you from the 15th chapter of Mr. Bain's volume on the Emotions and Will.

"What then," asks Mr. Bain, "is this standard? Where is it to be found? Until it is produced we have nothing to discuss, affirm, or deny. Is it some model conscience like Aristotle's serious man (*ho spoudaios*), or is it the decision of a public body authorised to decide for the rest of the community? We have no difficulty in deciding what is the standard of truth in most other matters, but what is the standard conscience? That *must* be got at, or morality is not a subject to be reasoned or written about." . . .

[N]ow supposing that "I ought and I ought not," are the formulas of the Conscience, does it strike you that we must produce a model Conscience before we can affirm that each of us so far as he is an I uses those formulas? Of course Mr. Bain is at full liberty to say "I decline to reason or write about your doctrine of a Conscience, unless you do that." No British subject is compelled to write or reason about a subject except on his own terms. But if the point to be ascertained is whether that which I call a fact is a fact or a fiction, one would fancy that the vulgarest specimen of our race would supply a much better test than some person of rare excellence. After thinking much who might serve the purpose of an experiment most effectually, I can remember no one whom on the whole I should prefer to Mr. Tennyson's *Northern Farmer*.

You will not complain, I hope, that he is a fictitious character. He is real enough. He is very strictly an individual. Yet he could not have been described to us by any writer who had not taken a careful observation of his class. We at once recognise him as a member of our own tribe; an Englishman to the very bone; one whose brutality we cannot put at a distance from us and ascribe to any people as being more characteristic of them than of us; one who has a manliness breaking through the brutality, which as patriots we may think is also not uncongenial to our soil. . . .The strength which we disguise under flattering phrases about Anglo-Saxon muscle and toughness lies in the "owt." That rises out of the coarse nature of the farmer as out of a prison-house or a grave. But it is the same which spoke forth clearly, musically, effectually in Christopher Columbus, when he determined that he ought to cling to his belief in a new Continent if all the

---

*Elements of Morality, vol. 1, p. 161, 2d ed.

wise heads in Europe derided him, if all the crowned heads trifled with him; in Martin Luther, when he said that he ought to go forward to the Diet though there were as many devils in Worms as there were tiles on the houses; in John Hampden, when he said that he ought not to pay the forty shilling tax of ship-money, if the resistance to it involved him in ruin, even if it ended in a civil war for his country. How different the standard of any one of these men was from that of the Northern farmer, I need not stop to explain; how different the sense in each of the power which could enable him to follow that standard. But the Conscience of an obligation, involving some effort, endurance, sacrifice, dwelt in them all; the presence of this light is most conspicuous in the farmer from the darkness of the ground which throws it back. . . .

THE CONSCIENCE AND
ITS MASTERS*

The conscience in me says I ought and I ought not. . . . The ought does not belong to things—it does not suggest some vague possibility for their improvement—it is linked inseparably to me. It may be that when I use it most emphatically I am least inclined to imagine some different condition from that in which I find myself. Perhaps I ought to be acting more in conformity with this state than I do act; perhaps I ought not to be doing so many things which are inconsistent with this state.

This was unquestionably the doctrine of . . . Bishop Butler. I have already referred to those discourses of his on Human Nature. I have spoken of them as especially bearing of this question of the Conscience. If you would understand them you should be aware of the intense dislike which Butler felt for all schemes by which an Order made out of our fancies is substituted for the one in which we are placed. His other great work, the *Analogy,* is full of vehement even scornful expressions towards those who fashion worlds for themselves, and are not content patiently to examine the characteristics and indications of that wherein they are sent to live and work. He exhibits precisely the same temper in these discourses. He seeks to find out what human nature is, not what it might be or ought to be. Though a preacher, he is anxious to exclude all notions of divinity which would interfere with this design. And therefore the office which he assigns to the Conscience is primarily that of warning us that we should not do acts which disturb the harmony of this Nature,—what Shakespeare calls "unproportioned acts."

That is Butler's principle. He demands a Conscience to exercise a control over our thoughts and acts, to declare which are and which are not consistent with the Order or Constitution of our Nature. But then Mr. Bentham tells us that ac-

*From *The Conscience,* 2d ed. (London: Macmillan and Co., 1872), Lecture 3, 44–63 (abridged).

cording to this Order or Constitution of Nature, Pleasure and Pain are our Sovereign Masters. And though we may not understand this lofty phraseology, we are wont to say in plain prose that we find it natural to take what we like and to reject what we dislike. If that is what Mr. Bentham means, I should be afraid to oppose to him some general theory of what is natural, even if there were ever so much to urge in favour of it. I would rather at once give up the dispute with him so far as it is a verbal one, and admit that if my Conscience tells me I ought not to take what I like and to reject what I dislike, my Conscience is bidding me not stoop to my nature, but resist it.

Do I then give up what I take to be Butler's meaning in these statements respecting human Nature, because I find myself puzzled and entangled by the terms which he has chosen? No; for I recur to my old question, "What am I?" There are a few simple answers to that question which shew me that there is an Order in which I am placed, a real order, not an imaginary one—not an order which might be desirable but which exists. I *am* certainly a son, I *am* a brother, I *am* a citizen. Perhaps I *am* a husband, perhaps I *am* a father. And if the enjoyment of any pleasure or the avoidance of any pains leads me to acts which are inconsistent with any of these positions, my Conscience says "I ought not to enjoy that pleasure, I ought not to avoid that pain." Let the enjoyment or the avoidance be as natural as it may, it involves a departure from the order in which I am placed. I care nothing about ideals or possibilities. It is a violation of my actual state; a disturbance and interruption of that.

Let me see then to what we have come. Bentham tells us that we are under certain obligations. So far we are agreed. In using the words "I ought," I confess that I am under an obligation. Next, he says the obligation is not one of mere force. I am not moved as a stone is moved, by external violence. So far also we are agreed. Thirdly, he says that there are certain influences of pleasure and pain acting upon me, and that it is natural for me to yield myself to these influences. Once more, there is no difference. I confess these influences. I feel the force of them; I am not angry that they should be called natural; it does seem to me natural to bow before them. But here our strife begins. You tell me that I must yield to these motives; that when I use the word *ought* I only mean, if I mean anything, that I do what they tell me. I say I mean something when I use the word ought, and that I never did mean that; I say no one has meant that by the word; no one less than Mr. Bentham. The word signified to him what it signifies to me, what it signifies to every one, precisely the reverse of this; it is a self assertion, a denial of the claim of external powers to rule me. Pleasure and Pain are not things which I can see or touch or taste; they are secret influences which come to me through my sight or touch or taste. I cannot find them by dissecting or analysing the things through which I receive them. If I were not, they would not be. They have no business therefore to set themselves above me. Every time any man or woman or child says "I ought," it says "I am under an obligation which is not to you."

To what then? If we said to Nature, we should retract our previous concession. Moreover we should incur the peril of Mr. Bain's denunciation against "those who set up abstract, unseen, unproducible powers." But if I shew by broad patent facts that I am in a certain order—an order which affects me at every moment—an order into one part of which I entered at my birth, parts of which I have deliberately adopted,—it is not a great assumption to say, In this order I ought to abide; its influences, like those of Pleasure and Pain, are invisible, but they are just as real. And if they come into conflict, as we know that they do continually, my obligation to the one may be an obligation to resist the other.

Obligation to an Order or a Constitution may not sound very practical language. Translate it as quickly as you please into obligation to fathers and mothers, to brothers and sisters, to a wife, to your Queen and country. Change as soon as you will the long word Obligation into the shorter homelier word Duty. I shall never object to such alterations; the mother tongue is always sweeter, often more distinct and definite, than the tongue of philosophers. But happily when we speak of persons we cannot forget the affections which we have for them. How precious these are, how closely they are intertwined with the roots of our social existence, I hope to shew you when we come in a future Course of Lectures— that on Moral Philosophy—to speak of the Family and the Nation. But there is a danger of treating those affections as if they created the Order which calls for them. If we fall into that mistake, the affection will become merely a part of our pleasures or pains. As long as we like a person we shall suppose we are bound to him; our dislike will dissolve the tie. We shall live in a circle of what are called in the cant of our day *elective affinities;* the grand old name of Relations will be treated as obsolete. That you may escape this danger, I dwell upon this fact—that we are in an order; that relations abide whether we are faithful to them or neglect them; and that the Conscience in each of us affirms "I am in this order, I ought to act consistently with it, let my fancies say what they please." The necessity for such firm and distinct language becomes more evident to us the older we grow and the more we notice the habits and doctrines which are prevalent amongst us. The reverence for parents, the sanctity of the marriage vow, the permanence of friendships, are all in peril from the confusion between likings and affections. Those who resolutely draw a distinction between them will have their reward. They will find that the conscience protests not against the fervency, but against the coldness, feebleness, uncertainty of our affections. . . .

[N]o one I suppose would dispute the assertion that the parent or teacher of a child exercises an authority over it which is external to it. Nor should I, or any one I know, say that punishment is not one of the instruments of this authority, or that it may not be used for the purpose of awakening or cultivating the Conscience. That the community of which a parent or a teacher is a member is deeply concerned in the question, *how* he exercises this authority, *how* and to what end he wields this punishment, is a belief which I think we should all entertain. . . . But in that "how" and "to what end" lies a tremendous controversy. The distinction of the civilized man from the savage is, as it seems to me, that he is not to the same extent the victim of external influences, that he rises above them and tries to rule them. The external authority of the parent or teacher I maintain is useless unless he appeals to that which is within the child, is mischievous unless it is exerted to call that forth. The external authority must become an internal authority, not co-operating with the forces which are seeking to crush the I in the child but working against those forces, working to deliver the child from their dominion. The punishments therefore which are the weapons of this authority but never can be confounded with it, must be directed expressly to *this* purpose. If the child stoops, as it will stoop continually, to the attraction of outward things which it has been forbidden to touch or taste because they will do it harm, punishments will remind it that to obey its teachers is better than to obey its inclinations. The teacher will endeavour so to contrive his punishment that "the sentiment of the forbidden" may always be accompanied with the sentiment of trust in the person who has forbidden. If the child is taught to have a dread of him as one who is an inflicter of pain, not to have a reverence for him as one who cares for it and is seeking to save it from its own folly—if the child is instructed carefully to separate the pain which rises out of its own acts from the pain which the parent inflicts so that it may associate the pain with him rather than with them—then all has been done which human art can do to make it grow up a contemptible coward, crouching to every majority which threatens it with the punishments that it has learnt to regard as the greatest and only evils; one who may at last, "in the maturity of a well-disposed mind," become the spontaneous agent of a majority in trampling out in others the freedom which has been so assiduously trampled out in itself. A parent or a teacher who pursues this object is of all the ministers of a community the one whom it should regard with the greatest abhorrence, seeing that he is bringing up for it, not citizens, but slaves. . . .

Inquisitors and persecutors of all ages . . . have thoroughly understood [the] identification of authority with punishment. . . . By punishment to bring a reluctant minority into conformity with the will of a majority has been their expressed and deliberate purpose. To cultivate a Conscience in the young which should begin with a dread of transgressing the decrees of the majority, which should at last acquiesce in them naturally and enforce them upon other men, has been the aim of their policy. And having had great and wonderful success in putting down recusants by force, and in reducing nations to servility, they have looked forward with a certain dim anticipation to a period when the higher grade of the prudential motive shall be attained, when no man who has thoughts unlike those of the majority shall utter them, when very few indeed will have any thoughts to utter.

These inquisitors and persecutors of old times . . . appealed to "an abstract, unseen, unproducible power." . . . No power that I ever heard of is so "abstract, unseen, unproducible" as the Society which is put forth to terrify and crush each man who dares to claim a distinct existence. Where is it, what is it, who brought it forth? Parents, Schoolmasters, Legislators, are its agents. It remains full of ghostly dread, gathering into itself all that is most tremendous in the phantoms which we boast that modern enlightenment has driven from our nurseries. When Mr. Bentham speaks of a Community he says that "it is a fictitious body composed of the individuals who are *considered* as constituting *as it were* its members." A man who abhorred fictions and figures of speech falls into these strange expressions, because he cannot quite divest himself of the old belief that a community is a body, real and not fictitious, consisting of individuals who are its actual members. There is in his phraseology the after-glow of a sun which has set. . . .

And therefore it may be quite necessary, in order to avoid the terror of these "abstract, unproducible powers," that we should face the question whether the Conscience bears witness of any actual living superhuman power to which it owes homage. . . .

CASES OF CONSCIENCE*

I have found myself already in conflict with two eminent philosophers of this century on the subject of the Conscience. I should not have plunged into such disputes if they had only concerned certain Moral Systems. But the assertion of Mr. Bentham that Pleasure and Pain are the Sovereigns of mankind, the doctrine of Mr. Bain that the Conscience is to be trained by punishment till it bows before the decrees of a majority, involve questions which affect every act of our lives. A number of those cases of Conscience with which the Casuist professes to deal, and which, whether he deals with them or not, perplex our conduct and distract our thoughts, take their rise in the demands: Ought I or ought I not to obey the commands of this Pleasure or this Pain, or of this Nature which appears to be their Mistress? Ought I or ought I not to obey the commands of this Society, this Majority, which is able to enforce its decrees by terrible penalties, and which has various bribes for bringing me into sympathy with it? I cannot, as I said last week, avoid entering on a third enquiry, Ought I or ought I not to perform certain services, to offer certain sacrifices, at the bidding of some *invisible* divinity? I might comprehend this enquiry in the other two, for Pleasure and Pain, Nature and Society, as Mr. Bentham and Mr. Bain set them forth to us, *are* invisible powers, whatever visible forms they may assume. Still we shall find that for practical purposes it is convenient to speak of Cases of Conscience under each of these three heads.

I. I begin with those which concern Pleasure and Pain. Mr. Bentham appears to have thought that there are but two ways in which this subject can be contemplated. He himself, the champion of the principle of *Utility*, maintains that it behooves us to seek the greatest amount of pleasure which it is possible for us, being such creatures as we are, to enjoy, the least amount of pain which, being

---

*From *The Conscience*, 2d ed. (London: Macmillan and Co., 1872), Lecture 4, 65–84 (abridged).

such creatures as we are, it is possible for us to suffer. Another set of men are champions of what he calls the principle of *Asceticism*. These, he says, "approve of actions so far as they tend to *diminish* the happiness of the persons whose interest is in question, disapprove of actions so far as they tend to augment it." . . .

(2) The Stoical *theory* was deduced from an observation how much power a man possesses who is not the victim of pleasures or of pains. The endurance of pain, the contempt of it, seemed to the Stoic the signs of a man. He exaggerated the notion, till pain itself acquired a glory in his eyes, till he thought himself grand for hating pleasure. Such pride involved contradiction. Pleasure was not his master, what was? To be simply his own master, to be alone in the world, was a poor result of his victory. Men might say with great reason, "It is better to eat, drink, and be merry, than merely to dwell in this magnificent self-sufficiency." The Asceticism of the Monk had a different ground. It was associated with the belief that the best man is he who can bear pain for his fellows. But it often passed, like the Stoical doctrine, into a notion that pain had some virtue or excellence of its own. Out of this arose a greater contradiction than in the former case. He who was to be a sacrifice for others began to think how much glory his pain could bring to him.

(3) This is the second form of Asceticism; that form under which it presented itself to Mr. Bentham as the direct antagonist of his principle of Utility. There is a third form which is, as it seems to me, not opposed to that principle, but a development of it. A man believes that by enduring pain he may save himself from pain in a future state, may even perhaps obtain pleasure in a future state. He calculates, as Mr. Bentham would teach him to calculate, how he may secure the least amount of pain, the greatest amount of pleasure, possible. His calculation may take in elements which Mr. Bentham would exclude; their fundamental axiom is the same.

(*a*) In each of us there will arise cases of conscience into which one or another or all three of these ascetical notions may enter. Every one has some work to do. Every one has inducements to forsake that work for things which, whether pleasant to others or not, are pleasant to him, which no sophistry can persuade him are not pleasant. Mr. Bentham's assumption that what is pleasant is natural, that Nature has appointed it for us, commends itself to his judgment. Only there is something in him which says I ought not. The agreeable thing will hinder me from doing the thing which I am occupied with. The agreeable thing accepted to-day will make me weaker to-morrow, less capable of determining my course, more the victim of the impulses and impressions that come to me from without.

Some men get rid of this troublesome remonstrance easily; "I like it" drives away "I ought not" speedily. Some at once . . . take the ascetical course. They have a distinct object before them, nothing shall tempt them to forget it. A great number, perhaps the greatest number of men, touch neither of these extremes. They hover between Nature and Conscience. They cannot silence the "ought not." But they ask themselves *why* they should pay heed to it, *why* they should not take this or that pleasure which it seems to prohibit, undergo this or that painful effort which it seems to enjoin? "What is this restraining, tormenting voice? From what cavern does it issue? Do I clearly catch its messages? Are they indeed saying, Avoid this and this? Do this and this?" Here begin cases of Conscience. The man consults himself or consults some friend or some professional Casuist about these points. "May I indulge my own taste or fancy? If not, why not? If it is not bad for that man, why is it for me?" What answers the Casuist may make to these enquiries I am not now considering. I am only tracing the cases which come before him to their sources, and showing you that they are not imaginary, but such as enter into the transactions of every day, and are mingled with the threads of each man's existence. One remark I would make in reference to them here. You may have thought me pedantical or fanciful for insisting that the Conscience should be contemplated in each particular man, that it should never be treated as something general or belonging to a number of men. But when these cases present themselves to us, the danger of departing from that maxim becomes apparent, even if adherence to it is troublesome. The habit of measuring ourselves by others is one into which we slide most easily, and which involves continual unfairness to them, still greater to ourselves. I ask why I may not indulge in extravagances in which a man of twice or thrice my means indulges freely; why I may not eat or drink what a man with twice or thrice my strength or my labour perhaps needs. I cling therefore to the "*I* ought" and the "*I* ought not," that will not interfere with the discovery and acknowledgement of laws by which we are all bound; it will prevent me from assuming the practice of this man or that as the standard of mine, or my practice as the standard of his.

(*b*) The first form of Asceticism, that which Mr. Bentham . . . practised, may then be very needful for you and me; we may not be safe if we discard it. Shall I tell you how we become involved in the second? in that kind of Asceticism I mean which treats pain as a positive good, pleasure as a positive evil? We do not drop into Stoicism naturally. A few may have some bias to it from education; in general when it is enforced in childhood there is a reaction against it in later years. A few may be drawn into it by the arguments or the example of others; more attractive arguments and examples will probably in a little time break the force of those; the Stoic may soon be turned into an Epicurean. The doctrine is much more commonly embraced by one who has for a long time acted on the maxim that pleasure is the supreme power which he must obey. He has had some stern and clear intimations of the effects which come from subjection to this ruler. A violent quarrel with himself is the consequence; with himself or with the tendencies to which he has passively yielded. He gnashes his teeth at the things which have been the occasion of his distress and humiliation; he calls them by hard names; he denounces pleasure as pleasure; he greedily seizes upon pain as if by enduring it he could take some revenge upon himself for that avoidance of it in times past which now seems to him feeble and cowardly. Cases of Conscience involving this kind of Asceticism are very numerous. The symptoms which they disclose are hard for the patient himself to deal with; they may be much aggravated by the prescriptions of quacks. Mere abusive epithets, such as Mr. Bentham indulges in, or the solemn announcement that we ought to seek the greatest amount of pleasure and the least amount of pain possible, will not touch even the surface of such cases.

(c) Still more embarrassing are those cases into which the third notion of Asceticism enters. Suppose a man rich and comfortable, who has never for a moment dreamed that there could be any maxim of life but that which Mr. Bentham enunciates, who has habitually sought as much pleasure as he could get and avoided pain of every kind,—Or suppose an Irish labourer with dilapidated trousers and straw peeping through his hat, who yet to the extent of his means has wooed pleasure at wakes and fairs, sometimes inflicting a little pain with a shillelagh as a way of diversifying the pleasure. Either of these awakens on a certain day to the feeling that there is something which he ought to have done, or ought not to have done. The past which he seemed to have left far behind him comes strangely back to him. His yesterdays claim to be part of him as much as the present moment: they may continue to put forth that claim for ages. He may *never* be able to shake them off. That would be dreadful. How can he banish the apparition? What can he do that it may not give him much more pain, and greater pain, than it is giving him now? Some one is tormenting him: seems to like tormenting him. Could he not make terms with the enemy? Could he not agree to suffer something now that he may have less weight of suffering hereafter? Could he not find, or could not some one find for him, a scheme of arrangements, compromises, compensations, by which he might be excused from part of the punishment which he dreads, and might also retain a certain tolerable share of the present pleasure which he is loath to part with? How many cases have occurred, and are occurring every day, of this kind, no words can tell; or what schemes of Casuistry have been devised to meet them. The precepts of Mr. Bentham, diffused ever so widely, embraced ever so cordially, can have no effect in settling them. For as I said before, his precepts have to all intents and purposes been adopted already by these troubled spirits. They are turning to the religious Casuist for help, because their Utilitarian adviser has failed to take account of a disturbing force in them which makes his medicines ineffectual. "You can of course call me an Ascetic if I resort to plans plausibly and skillfully devised for supplying the defect in your system: for avoiding a pain which I actually feel, and which, upon your own showing, I ought to account the great and only evil, for obtaining as much pleasure as I can under the conditions in which I find myself. Some may call my calculations ignominious; you cannot. I learnt the need of them in your school."

II. I pass to that class of Cases which has reference to Society. Whether the Education which Mr. Bain speaks of—the education which shapes each man's wishes, purposes, convictions, according to the wishes, purposes, convictions of a majority—is desirable or not, there can be no question that such an education exists, that it is working very extensively and with great power. The philosopher has here also generalised from the practice which he sees around him; his doctrine is certain to meet with favour for precisely the same reason which secures favour to Mr. Bentham's doctrine respecting Pleasure and Pain; it represents accurately what a number of men in various quarters are actually doing or striving to do.

To appreciate their work or their endeavour we must recollect that the grand word *Society* or *Community* really represents a number of different Societies or Communities, each of which is acting upon a certain number of individuals. For instance, in every trade there is a community aiming to train the notions of those who belong to it in accordance with the notions which it has inherited or which it has adopted. The Conscience of the individual who engages in the trade is formed, Mr. Bain would say, by the majority of those who have entered into it already; punishments, such as exclusion from the intercourse or sympathy of his fellows, make him feel the great inconvenience of adopting any maxims or practices unlike those of the majority. The younger members by degrees rise to their share of government and enforce the same rules upon their pupils and successors. A great number attain that "high grade of the prudential motive," at which conformity becomes no longer a difficult effort, the result of terror at a rod continually suspended over them, but means the ready submission to a rule which they feel to be convenient, and which they have the pleasure of making others feel to be inevitable. All that is, no doubt, true. Mr. Bain himself allows for occasional exceptions; a few men like to be independent, to choose a way of their own. He does not deny that there is a certain amount of benefit to be derived from these anomalous individuals. He does not encourage their growth; all the processes of his discipline tend to discourage it. But if they start up in spite of the discipline they may perhaps be turned to some account. However dangerous, an optimist will hope that their existence may at last turn to the benefit, not the mischief, of the Community.

Now when I speak of Cases of Conscience in respect to Society, I mean this; that every man whatsoever who has been brought under this kind of discipline not only feels tempted to rebel against it, for the reason which Mr. Bain supposes,—because it thwarts his inclination, because it restrains some of his enjoyments,—but for another very different reason; because it prescribes acts to him which, though they are agreeable to him, though the punishment for not doing them is very severe, yet something tells him that he ought not to do. I say that there are moments when such qualms come over every one; and further that those individual men in whom they become most strong are not those who find their luxury in arrogant independence, but are those who have the liveliest sense of their obligations to their fellow-men, the greatest desire that the laws of the Nation to which they belong may be not violated, but maintained.

Consider that instance of trades to which I referred just now. A man finds a custom established in the trade to which he has been bred, the trade by which he is to get his living, which directly interferes with the observance of a contract recognised by the law of the land between the tradesman and his customers, at all events interferes with what he knows to be the understanding of the customer when the article is bought. There is the smallest possible fear of his ever coming within the reach of the law; there are a hundred ways of evading that, a hundred reasons why any person who discovers himself to be injured, if he does discover it, may not wish to trouble himself with a lawsuit. The reputation he might get with the customer, if he knew—which is unlikely—that a maxim of the trade had been broken through in his favour, would not be the weight of a feather against the loss of credit and caste with those who surround him. Those for whom he has most respect—men much better than he counts himself—have gone on in these practices for years; they will be grieved if he adopts any other. It will seem to them, it seems to himself, a pharisaical exaltation of his own opinion against theirs. And yet the voice in him says, I ought not to do it. Here is a case of Conscience. A whole world of Casuistry rises out of that struggle between the opinion of the majority and the "I ought not" of the single man. But the "I ought not" is not working against an Order, but with an Order. It is protesting against a disorder, which however long it has been sanctioned, however many votes concur in the support of it, is a disorder still, and will prove itself to be so more and more, the longer it exists.

I dwell upon this instance of Contracts which have reference to Property, because we are told again and again that these depend for their security simply upon the punishments which enforce the observance of them, or upon the opinion of their usefulness which those punishments create, or upon a general experience of the disadvantages arising from the violation of them. No country furnishes so good a test of this principle as the England of the present day. We are a commercial people. Punishments have been especially devised to support the fidelity of pecuniary engagements. They have been suggested by mercantile men. They have passed under the revision of lawyers. They have been accepted by parliaments. They have been enforced by the strongest public opinion. Seldom is there much compassion felt for a fraudulent debtor; still less for one who has been a trustee of others' money and has converted it to his own purposes. The newspaper press strengthens and supports the severest judgment of onlookers and sufferers. It would seem as if commercial crimes in this country were prohibited by every motive which could act upon reasonable beings. And yet which of us has not heard complaints that they are on the increase? And which of us has not heard those who dwell most on the force of punishments and of public opinion—who laugh the bitterest laugh when a moralist speaks of any other—yet appealing in despair to the conscience of individuals, trying whether they cannot arouse that to sustain the weakness of the power which, according to their theory, should be invincible? To be sure when they explain themselves they affirm that it is Opinion which gives effect to Conscience, that all they want is to create an Opinion against certain acts that are mischievous to Society. Wearisome and endless see-saw! From Opinion to Conscience; from Conscience to Opinion. You want Opinion to produce the effects of Conscience; the Conscience must itself create the Opinion. Oh learn to bear the scorn of the philosophers who talk to you in this fashion! The scorn is not for you, but for themselves. There is a Conscience in each of them, whether he owns it or not. Give him credit for it; appeal to it; let him keep his theory along with it, if he likes, and if he can.

The cases which arise in the Conscience of a Tradesman or Merchant, and which often set him at variance with the customs and maxims of his class, are not more numerous than those which occur in the Conscience of the Lawyer, the Physician, the Clergyman. A man asks himself if he ought to do this, if he ought not to do that. Why? That he may have a way of his own? No! precisely because he fears that he has been following a way of his own which was not consistent with his position as Lawyer, Physician, Clergyman, with that which was due from him to his clients, his patients, his flock. A Conscience of Duty wholly apart from any punishments which may be inflicted on him for the neglect of it is awakened in him; he asks whether this duty has been done. Suppose some opinion or censure or even punishment has brought out that Conscience; still it is there. The opinion, the censure, the punishment has only called it forth—availed nothing till it was called forth. So here again is a multitude of cases, various as the circumstances and as the characters of individuals are various, but all of the same kind; all beginning with the discovery in each man that he has responsibilities which no class, no majority of men, has imposed upon him, and from which no class, no majority of men, can release him.

The treatment of such cases—the methods which may or may not be effectual for settling them—I am not concerned with in this Lecture. But I may perhaps assist you in understanding better the cases themselves, if I wander for a moment beyond the limits of our own country. Suppose an American, living in one of what were then Slave States thirty years ago. He is brought up under that discipline which Mr. Bain recommends for the formation of a Conscience. He is taught to consider the slave as a chattel. He has acquired all the habits which naturally and necessarily develop themselves out of such a belief, when it has become a belief. He perceives the absurdity—the intense absurdity—of treating a *thing,* a chattel, as capable of rights, as able to form contracts. Perhaps some religious notion about the doom of a race helps to strengthen what would else have been merely the tradition of a Society. Suddenly the question presents itself to him, "Is the premiss, from which the conclusions I have accepted logically follow, a correct one? Is this creature a chattel? Do I stand in no relation to him? If not, clearly I have no duties to him; he has none to me. If there is a relation that must involve duties." Out of this doubt cases of Conscience have proceeded, which cannot be treated with indifference, for they have produced a revolution in an immense Continent. What I want you to notice is the turning-point in these cases. A Society has organised itself on the ground of *Property.* We are *possessors;* as such we are bound to each other. These creatures are simply *possessions.* The

Society has taught its members to look upon each other in this light, to fraternise on this ground. The discovery of which I have just spoken does not merely affect the Negro. Are there not *relations* between those who have called themselves the superior race? Are not these Relations a deeper ground of Society than Property can ever be? By acknowledging the manhood of the black they obtain a new conception of their own.

You will perceive that the question when it takes this form may lead to cases of Conscience affecting many beside the slave owners in North America; it may issue in a different belief respecting the foundation of Society in all countries. . . .

III. I come to the last class of cases of which I proposed to speak. I can illustrate it best by a familiar instance. The Greek fleet is stayed at Aulis by contrary winds. An acknowledged prophet declares that nothing will change the wind but a Sacrifice. No Sacrifice will avail but the daughter of Agamemnon. A power which is declared to be divine, which the opinion of the Greeks holds to be divine, imposes the command. It is obeyed. . . .

Whether the story is true or not, even if it and the whole Trojan war are to be consigned to the region of fable, it bears witness of facts that were characteristic of the age to which it was referred, and of many later ages; of facts which belong to Greek history, to Hindu history, to the history of modern Europe. The poet who recorded the tale of Iphigenia so brilliantly felt as you know that it concerned his own nation and his own time. . . . He believed that the religion of Rome in his own civilised period might persuade men, if not to such a sacrifice as that of Iphigenia, yet to very monstrous crimes. From a religion of this kind—from the worship of capricious and cruel gods—he fled to such notions of physics as Epicurus could supply him with; he thought he could discern the vestiges of an order in the world which these notions of a divine government could not disturb.

This poet, then, who counted himself an Atheist was demanding an Order; he was solemnly protesting against that which seemed to him the transgression of an Order. Powers which persuaded to evil deeds he could not recognise, let the claims which they put forth, let the terrors of public opinion which enforced these claims, be what they might.

This I hold to be a protest of the Conscience, one which the poet would never have made if there had not been a Conscience in him. Because there was that Conscience in him, I believe he could never have been satisfied with those hints of an outward Order which his Greek teacher offered him; no not if those hints could have ripened for him into the actual discoveries of modern science. Still there would have been the question, "Is there not somewhere that which ought to rule me?" still there would have been the answer, "These things ought *not* to rule me." As long as there is that terrible "I," there will be the "ought" linked to it; there will be the demand, What am I? what therefore ought I to do? And in that is implied, as Mr. Bentham and Mr. Bain no less than any other philosophers teach us, the further demand, "What must I obey?"

Vainly, therefore, are we told that if there is a Conscience in each man that Conscience must be its own standard, that the only escape is to suppose a Conscience created by a Social Opinion. All such propositions look very plausible upon paper; bring them to the test of living experience and they melt away. There is that in me which asks for the Right, for that which ought to have dominion over me; there is that in me which says emphatically, "This is not that Right, this ought not to have dominion over me." I may be long in learning what the Right is; I may make a thousand confused efforts to grasp it; I may try to make it for myself; I may let others make it for me. But always there will be a witness in me that what I have made or any one has made, is not what I ought to serve; that is not the right, not what I am seeking for, not what is seeking me.

This class of Cases then lies beneath both the others; they are derived from it; they enter into it. The demands of Pleasure or of Nature upon me, the demands of Society upon me, both suggest cases of their own. But *the* case is that which the Roman poet has raised. There are powers which demand *evil* things of me. Ought I to acknowledge their demand? Very numerous are the cases which fall under this head, complicated in various ways, taking different forms in different times and places. But no one who speaks of Casuistry at all can dare to evade them, or must be hindered from handling them through fear of the censures which he may incur from one set of philosophers or another. . . .

THE RULES OF CONSCIENCE*

I have spoken to you of cases of Conscience. From these the Casuist derives his name. I come now to the Rules by which Casuists have tried to determine these cases.

What has suggested these rules? A man who is troubled with the questions, "Ought I to do this? Ought I not to do that?" has just the same impulse to seek for advice as the man who is engaged in any controversy about property, or who is suffering from some bodily complaint. As I ask a Lawyer who has studied books of cases the judgments which have been delivered upon them the general maxims or the particular statutes which bear upon them, to tell me what is his opinion of the particular case which I submit to him—cannot I find one who will explain to me this debate which is going on within me, who will say what is the proper decision upon it? As I try to explain the pains I have suffered the symptoms which I have observed in myself, to a physician, trusting that his learning will suggest questions which may draw out clearer statements from me than I have been able to make, and that the same learning will suggest remedies for what he has discovered to be my disorder—cannot I, in like manner, make some one understand the influences which sway me to the right or to the left; cannot he

*From *The Conscience,* 2d ed. (London: Macmillan and Co., 1872), Lecture 5, 87–101 (abridged).

make me understand them better than I do; cannot he put me on some method of dealing with them, so that I may not continue in restless embarrassment, or escape from it by some rash determination which I may lament hereafter?

The demand for such counsellors and prescribers has been great in all ages; the supply has answered to the demand. Some of them have been suggested to us by the circumstances of our birth, by the accident of our position. A parent who does not identify authority with punishment wins the confidence of his child in his wisdom and in his affection. The less he tries to worm any secrets from him the more frankly they are told; the utterance of them is a relief for the present, the reproof and the warning which follow a help for the future. The friend, judicious or injudicious, to whom we ascribe great discernment or experience, is resorted to next; he may give us hints which will shew us the way out of a confusion, or he may make the confusion worse confounded; the knots of the conscience may be untied or cut by his hands, or may be entangled hopelessly. And then comes the professional director of the Conscience, to whom is attributed in most countries of Christendom, by not a few men and women in our own, a divine capacity of penetrating into the sources of the derangements from which the Conscience is suffering, and of administering the medicines which it requires.

Are such advisers to be trusted in virtue of their personal sagacity or their official illumination? The Lawyer points to the Statute book, to maxims which have been established for ages, to a series of judgments the result of careful investigations by able men. The Physician appeals to experiments upon the actual frame of man, to a science ever expanding which rests on those experiments. Has the director his books to which we may turn for the correction of his own private instincts? Can he make us aware of the laws and principles by which his opinions on special cases are guided?

The necessity for such books began to be very loudly proclaimed in that very bookish century, the 17th. It was affirmed that nothing could be more dangerous than to trust particular persons with the authority which they claimed to settle questions affecting the life of states as well as of individual men. He who could tell men what they ought or ought not to do, what should be their purposes as well as their acts, was exercising a dominion which no king or parliament could exercise, which might greatly interfere with the dominion that kings and parliaments had a right to exercise. It was found as a matter of fact that the influence of Confessors and Directors over the consciences of monarchs and statesmen, was such as affected in a number of ways the condition of nations; there was a complaint deep, sometimes loud, that it did not cultivate in them any special reverence for veracity and honourable dealing. Let us know what the maxims of these directors of the Conscience are, was the cry, what rules they lay down for the acts and life of men. There was, it must be owned, no tardiness in answering this cry. The volumes recording Cases of Conscience as well as solutions of the Cases and rules for the guidance of the Conscience which that age accumulated, would alarm you if I only enumerated the titles of a few, more still if you looked into them, far more if you were fairly to examine their contents. I do not enjoin any such task upon you, or recommend it. I do not think that would be a fair way of testing the question, whether Rules of the Conscience are ever likely to be found which will settle Cases of the Conscience. . . .[W]ere not these rules of Conscience drawn up expressly because these guides of souls had "made the cases of conscience and the actions of men's lives as unstable as the water and immeasurable as the dimensions of the moon"? Can it be the ultimate resource to fall back upon them, to confess that the rules are impotent without them, and that the final appeal must be to their wisdom? And yet if the comparison is between rules and the very lowest kind of human sympathy, the man who is in any difficulty will choose the latter. If he is not able to find the amount of illumination which he craves for, he will suppose that there must be some one in whom it dwells and to whose guidance he can fully trust himself. . . .

If what I have said to you before about the Conscience is true, the failure of such rules was inevitable. Try them by any of the cases of which I spoke in my last lecture. A man is disposed to indulge in certain pleasures, say of the appetite. He doubts whether he ought to indulge them, whether they will not interfere with his health or his work. The physician may give him some hints about the first; about the second he knows better himself than any one can tell him. General rules will only lead him to that comparison of his own case with others which issued, as I observed, in so many bewilderments, in such insincerity of practice. The rules prescribe for a multitude; what he wants is a prescription for himself. He will therefore do as Taylor bids him. He will ask the spiritual guide to interpret the rules, to apply them to his circumstances. And then he may be involved in all that system of alternate severities and indulgences, the perils of which induced Taylor to undertake his treatise. The passage from sound Asceticism to the Asceticism which glorifies pain for its own sake, to the Asceticism which reckons how much pleasure or exemption from pain can be secured by the relinquishment of pleasure or the endurance of pain, will be promoted not hindered by the formal rule as well as by the special expounders of it.

So in those cases which regard Society. Taylor proposed to lay down rules which may help us to conduct all our relations. I said that a man often finds himself in circumstances which lead him to ask, "Ought I to do what the Corporation of which I am a member commands? Can I fulfil my relations to this man or that set of men if I do?" Of all the abuses to which the Casuistry of spiritual doctors had led, and which Taylor desired to correct, there were none so great and scandalous as those which concerned this subject. The ecclesiastical Corporation of Christendom had taught with pertinacity the lesson which had a Jewish origin. "*If a man shall say to his father and mother, It is Corban, that is to say, a gift,* (to some ecclesiastical treasury) *he need no more do aught for his father and mother.*" The maxim of the Society had been used to disparage the relation in which the man found himself at his birth. So again the maxim that no faith is to be kept with heretics, is just as legitimate a deduction from the principle that the heretic stands in no relation to those who have excommunicated him, as the doctrine that there can be no contract with a slave is from the principle that the slave is a chattel. But could any *rules* about men's relations counteract, even in the smallest degree, theories of this kind or the acts and habits which were justified by them? The relations must be closer to the man than the rules can ever be; if he makes them dependent upon rules he renounces them. He will ask what acts or gifts will compensate the neglect of care for the father or mother; pecuniary compensations will occur to him as the most natural, since the money scales will be those in which he has learned to weigh all affections. And the Society which he has been taught to regard as that which adjusts compensations and as more sacred than all others will be the one to receive the offerings. The rules will be found inoperative, the man with the doubtful conscience will go to the guide of souls to interpret them, and that will be the result.

So again in those more tremendous cases, of which the sacrifice of Iphigenia furnished us with an instance, no one knew better than Taylor how little directors of the Conscience were to be trusted; no one would have tried more zealously to find some rules which might avert the tragedies they had caused. But it is just in these very cases that the force of rules is scattered to the winds. How can they be alleged against a claim which is said to have proceeded from a superhuman authority? That must override all rules devised by men; it comes forth with the boast that it can. It is to a power which owns no rules that the father surrenders his daughter.

Why then do men who strive to be practical, as Taylor strove in the best sense of the word—why do men who claim to be practical in a much lower sense than his—agree in liking rules which, on this shewing, are not practical, but the reverse of practical? The explanation is this. Rules have a use of their own which it would be absurd and ungrateful to deny. There are many points in a man's demeanour towards his fellow-men which without any evil intention on his part, nay, when his intentions are full of kindness, may irritate and wound them. There are many influences which he may receive from them, through the very frankness and openness of his disposition, which may do him harm. The maxims and rules of experience are directed most beneficially to these particulars of conduct. They are often effectual when we meet with them in books applied to persons, real or imaginary, whose blemishes and awkwardnesses remind us of our own. They are more likely to be effectual when they come from the lips of some parent or judicious friend; then they bear upon us with the momentum of affection and prudence combined; the Conscience recognises them in recognising the voice which utters them. But the parent or friend if he is wise as well as prudent,—if he is not a stranger to inward struggles,—will not apply such admonitions to any of those great debates of the man with himself which give the force and interpretation to the word Conscience. He will understand that these affect the resolution to act, not the mode or shape which the action shall take when it has been resolved on. . . .

LIBERTY OF CONSCIENCE*

We are very familiar with the phrase "Liberty of Conscience.". . . . Be sure that Liberty of Conscience is a sacred expression, however much it may have been profaned. But is it not a political expression? Does it not point to the policy of statesmen, and of the nations which they direct? It may have much to do with their policy. *What* it has to do with that I believe we shall not understand unless we first understand what it has to do with you and me. I have treated the Conscience, its cases and its rules, in reference to each of us, distinctly. Unless each of us called himself an I, the Conscience I have said would signify nothing. Only by remembering that position have I been able to get any glimpse of light respecting the Liberty of Conscience.

But if I adhere strictly to my method, I must begin by changing this form of speech; by inverting it. I have never allowed myself to lose sight of the origin of the word Conscience. Though I have distinguished it from Consciousness, and shewn you how utterly unlike the Self-conscious man is to the Conscientious man, I have always treated them as kindred words. . . . The Conscience of Liberty is therefore for me a more intelligible phrase than Liberty of Conscience. I would not part with that. We cannot safely part with any form of speech which has been accepted as a veritable utterance of their thoughts by our ancestors and our contemporaries. I shall hope to enter more thoroughly into their meaning if you allow me for a little while to pursue my own course.

The advantage which I gain by the change is this. I do not wish to assume that the Conscience is something good in itself. . . . The words "Liberty of Conscience," taken by themselves, still more when taken with their ordinary associations, seem to intimate that the Conscience left to itself is always grand and glorious, incapable of debasement or degradation. No such impression is conveyed by the words Conscience of Liberty. They do not import that there may not be also a Conscience of Slavery. The very first remark which I shall have to make in considering them is, that there *always* will be a Conscience of Slavery where there is a Conscience of Liberty.

(1) Mr. Bentham has taught us to despise the Stoics, calling them Ascetics, and saying that they preferred Pain to Pleasure. I have admitted that there were Stoics who deserved his censures, who did learn to regard Pain with a certain complacency, as if it were a good in and for itself; who glorified themselves on the endurance of it. I did *not* admit that either Asceticism or Stoicism necessarily involved this honour to pain, or this vanity in the choice of it. . . .

I am going to speak to you of one of the [practisers of Stoicism]. He belongs to the period of the Roman Empire. He cannot be called a Greek though he spoke and wrote in Greek. He cannot be called a Roman, for he was a slave, the slave of a freedman of Nero. You are familiar with the name of Epictetus. . . .

---

*From *The Conscience*, 2d ed. (London: Macmillan and Co., 1872), Lecture 6, 106–23 (abridged).

Unquestionably he had all the Conscience of Slavery which a man in his condition could have. He was born in that condition. Could he rise out of it? What a chasm separated him even from his master Epaphroditus! who could measure that which separated him from the Emperor of whom that master was the freedman? Shall he fill the world with his groans that he cannot be like Nero; that an irresistible fate has made one the king over all kings, and the other not even a citizen? Epictetus has sent down to us not his groans but his thanksgivings, that he was not bound to be a slave such as he perceived Nero was; that, being Epictetus, he might enjoy freedom if he did not cast it away. For this he said was slavery, to be the victim of the representations made to the senses,—of the impressions which we receive from without. To this ignominious state of bondage Nero was reduced. Able to command all pleasures, able to decline all pains, the poor man was the passive victim of the things about him; he was sinking lower and lower under their dominion; he was less and less able to assert himself. If Epictetus was a slave, submission to these impressions, not the power of a master to send him to the metals or to inflict chastisement on him, was the cause of his slavery. If he did not fasten the chains upon himself, no one else could put them on him; he had the key of the prison-doors.

That is the Stoicism of Epictetus. It is the Stoicism of a man with an intense conscience of slavery, with an intense conscience of freedom. . . . If one moment he maintained that the key of his prison was in his own keeping—in other words, that he could not be a slave unless he yielded to the impressions which made him one—he asserted as strongly the next that he must turn for deliverance to a god who was near him, and watching over him. If he could not trust his impressions, he could not trust himself. He must have a helper, who was higher than himself, who cared more for him than he cared for himself, who knew him better than he knew himself. Epictetus the Heathen did not worship Pain or Pleasure or Nature or any modification of these, however he might be confused by the notions which he had been taught respecting Gods of Pleasure and Pain, or Gods that were merely Powers of Nature. He confessed amidst all perplexities a God over himself, who would set him free from the tyranny of Pain and Pleasure. I wish that all of us who are called Christians had as strong a faith in such a God as he had. Here is an instance of the Conscience of Liberty existing beside the Conscience of Slavery; an instance which encourages us to believe that the most outwardly unpropitious circumstances may be the means of leading a man to know what his state is and to claim it. . . . The recollection of liberty, the hope of liberty, may come to any, as Epictetus said, who find that there is a stronger force within than the likings and impressions which fasten them to outward things. The Conscience is bidding each of us seek for that liberty; we cannot be content till we have found it.

(2) It is exceedingly difficult in practice, as [this example] may shew, to separate the tyranny of Pleasure from the tyranny of Society. They weave together silken chains, which mere strength will never rend asunder. It may be as hard for

the Roman slave or the English slave to defy the fashion and the contempt of the Society in which he dwells, as to overcome his own inclinations. I hinted when I was speaking of Cases of Conscience, that the Conscience of Obligation, which is only another word for the Conscience of Relations, was the great antagonist power to this Social oppression. The victim feels, "I cannot be a member of Society unless I set at nought the maxims and decrees of Society." A very remarkable example of this rebellion is afforded by a man, not far removed in time from Epictetus, sharing many of his habits of thought, in a position more unfavourable, as Epictetus deemed, to freedom than his own; for instead of being the slave of an Emperor's freedman, he was himself an Emperor.

I speak of Marcus Aurelius Antoninus. He wrote in Greek; he dwelt in all the effeminacy of a Court. But he desired above all things, he says, to be a male and a Roman. What he meant by that we can understand from his acts, and also from his thoughts; for he is one of those who has let us look into the secrets of his life; who has told us what he was striving to be, and what helps and hindrances he met with in his strivings. He had evidently taken account of the causes which had made the Roman a ruler of the world. He had seen that self-restraint had been one main secret of his power; that reverence for the relations in which he found himself had been another. Out of both had come the habit of obedience; that obedience was involved in the oath of the soldier; that obedience was the only security for the fidelity of the citizen. . . .

Marcus Aurelius . . . aimed at freedom through self-government, through that triumph over external influences and over his own tendencies which Mr. Bentham would have called Asceticism, though no one deprecated more than Marcus any useless or affected Asceticism. Specially he aimed at it by the cultivation of reverence for all those to whom he was united by ties of blood, or ties of service. Under that last name he included those who had served him and those whom he was appointed to serve. Nothing that I know is more touching than his enumeration of the debts which he owed to his mother, to his predecessor who had adopted him, to his instructors in every department, to the friends who had preserved him from any flattery, who had given him hints for the fulfilment of any duty. For Duty meant to him exactly the reverse of that which it means in the philosophy of Mr. Bain. It was literally that which, under no dread of punishment but with great thankfulness, he confessed to be *due* from him. He was aware of the temptation to neglect it; that was the slavish impulse; freedom to perform it was what he sought with all earnestness. To aid his purpose of being a Roman he would avail himself of the helps which Greek professors of philosophy could afford him, admiring those who frequented his court far more than they deserved, humbly using the books which they or their predecessors had compiled, always shunning the display for which so many of them were eager, not caring to decide between the claims of their different schools, but ready to learn from any of them if they warned him of any insincerity into which he was likely to fall, or showed him a better way than he knew of improving his character and shaping his actions. Philosophy was never an excuse to him for avoiding troublesome business; he denounces in words that make many of us quiver the disposition which private men, as much as Emperors, feel not to answer letters, or to keep suitors waiting. He had a conscience of the bondage into which we bring ourselves by the neglect of little things; he would have accepted those grand words of our poet in his ode to Duty, which recognise all freedom and all joy as springing from submission to its commands.

And of Marcus Aurelius it is as true as of Epictetus, that he did not depend upon himself for protection against the slavery of which he was conscious, or for attainment of the freedom of which he was conscious. He spoke as Epictetus had spoken, of a God near him, a God within him, who was watching over him, and to whom he must have recourse if he wished to live a true life. He might sometimes call the true life, a life according to Nature, as Butler does, but it was this Lord and teacher of himself, not some external power, in whom he trusted to make such a life possible for him. Marcus, however, it must be remembered, was not merely the ruler of himself. He was the ruler of a people in whom faith and reverence were fast disappearing, on whom the traditions of their land were losing their hold, whom he saw no way of imbuing with his higher convictions. What should he do to keep the people straight, to prevent them from sinking lower? How could he sustain that which was perishing in them? Must he not use the powers which had been committed to him to punish any who induced them to distrust their old divinity? These reflections led Marcus to acts of which I may speak presently, acts in which he has had many imitators among those who have not generally taken him as a model.

(3) There is another kind of slavery to which men are liable, besides that to Pleasure or to Society, one which may be combined with either or both of these. They may dread the caprice and cruelty of unseen powers which demand such sacrifices as those of Iphigenia. The Conscience of liberty which comes from trust in a Being who is not capricious and cruel, who is emphatically a Deliverer, was that which gave all the emphasis to the "I ought" and the "I ought not" of the Christian witness under the Roman Empire. "I ought not to bow before this demon. I ought not to sacrifice to the image of the Divus Imperator"—that was his formula. The formula became real for him, it issued in martyrdom, when he could say, "I do not reject a faith, but an unbelief. I do not set up a God for myself. I cling to the God who is the Deliverer of my race." When the Christian's profession was merely the assertion of an opinion—formed after weighing the probabilities for or against it—there was no strength in him for any martyrdom. What did ignorant men and weak women understand about probabilities? Wiser men could overthrow any probabilities with their scorn or their stakes. But if there had come to the Conscience the certainty of an actual Deliverer, then the threefold cord of immediate punishment, of loathing by Society, of threatened vengeance hereafter, could be rent in pieces by the feeblest. If you read Opinion for Conscience, you change the history of that age and of all subsequent ages.

At this point I may pass without effort, from the inverted phrase which I have adopted, to the old phrase Liberty of Conscience, which I said I should be most sorry to lose. What I hope you will have learnt is, that this last phrase *cannot* bear some senses which loose thinkers attach to it. (1) Liberty of Conscience cannot mean liberty to *do* what I like. That we have seen, in the judgment of the wisest men, of those who speak most from experience, is bondage. It is from my likings that I must be emancipated if I would be a freeman. (2) It cannot mean liberty to *think* what I choose. Such men as Marcus Aurelius discovered the slavery which came from thinking what they chose, the necessity of bringing their thoughts under government lest they should become their oppressors. Every teacher of physical Science, here or elsewhere, repeats the same lesson. The scientific man bids us seek the thing as it is. He tells us that we are always in danger of putting our thoughts or conceptions of the thing between us and that which is. He gives us a discipline for our thoughts that they may not pervert the facts which we are examining. From not heeding this discipline men assumed that the Sun must travel round the Earth, because it appeared the most natural thing to them that it should, the most strange thing that it should not. If Galileo (according to the old tradition) said, "And yet the earth does move," he said, "Neither my thoughts nor the thoughts of all the doctors and priests that live now or ever have lived can the least alter facts. You have no right, I have no right, to determine what is. All our determinations must fall before the truth when that is discovered to us." (3) So again Liberty of Conscience cannot be a gift which men are to ask of Senates or Sanhedrins or Assemblies of the People. They have it not to bestow; if they had, no one could receive it from them. Those who groan because any of these bodies withhold it from them have not yet learnt what it is. The slave Epictetus would shew them that it could not be kept by mere external force from any one.

But when we have got rid of these confused notions which have fastened themselves to the cry for Liberty of Conscience, there remains a most wholesome and indispensable protest in it to which no Statesmen or Churchmen or Philosophers can be indifferent, except at their great peril. The opinion has prevailed among all three, that the Conscience is a troublesome disturber of the peace, which it may be necessary to endure but which it would be very desirable to silence. So long as that doctrine prevails, so long as any fragment or shred of it remains in our minds, we may talk about persecution as much as we please; we may boast of our age for having discovered the inutility of persecution; but we shall, under one pretext or other, persecute. The most ingenious political, ecclesiastical, philosophical excuses will always be ready to prove that the particular persecution we are practising deserves another name and belongs to a class of acts altogether different from that which we denounce in other countries, or in former days. What satisfactory demonstrations there will be that we are really vindicating toleration when we are most intolerant, that we are not interfering with a man's belief, but only with his desire to crush ours! Therefore I deem it needful to proclaim that in every instance to which we can point, a Society which has succeeded in choking or weakening the Conscience of any of its members has undermined its own existence, and that the defeat of such experiments has been the preservation and security of the Society that has attempted them. . . .

But I would warn you that the Liberty we have been speaking of to-day, the liberty which Epictetus and Marcus Aurelius sought, is far remote from eccentricity. They did not care to be different in their ways from other men; they would rather be like their fellows. They refused to be the slaves of the fashions and habits of their time, or of any time; but since there must be fashions and habits they would rather take what they found than change them for others which in themselves were equally unimportant. A man may make himself a slave by adopting the modes of some other time and country, or by devising new modes of his own, as well as by copying all that he sees about him. . . .

"Marcus Aurelius, the gentlest and most amiable of philosophers and rulers, under a solemn sense of duty, authorised the persecution of Christians. To my mind," adds Mr. Mill, "this is one of the most tragical facts in all history. It is a bitter thought how different the Christianity of the world might have been if it had been adopted as the religion of the Empire, under the auspices of Marcus Aurelius, instead of those of Constantine." To the lamentation and the wish contained in these last sentences I do not in the least subscribe. I believe that Christianity would not have been the least better for being taken under the patronage of this good Prince. I believe it proved its vital strength much more by evoking his hostility. I do not imagine that its professors should have been free from any of the sins into which they fell, or would have been more faithful to their principles, if they had passed through the trial of alliance with a doomed Empire—a far greater trial than any persecution—in his days rather than in the days of Constantine. But the other part of the paragraph belongs to facts and not to speculation. There is no doubt that the gentlest of philosophers and rulers authorised the persecution of Christians, and authorised it from a solemn sense of duty. He believed that he was doing his duty as a ruler by keeping alive the reverence of his subjects. He believed he was doing his duty as a philosopher by putting down men who, as he thought, mimicked the endurance of pain which belonged to philosophy without entering into its principles. And when Mr. Mill goes on to press the moral upon Christians that they cannot be sure they are doing right in persecuting any form of infidelity, if they hold Marcus to have been utterly wrong in persecuting that which he deemed infidelity, I should only complain of the charge for its inadequacy and feebleness. I am not the judge either of him or of the Christians who have followed in his steps. But there were excuses for him which it would be impossible to plead for them. If we believe that the Redeemer of the Conscience has come, what is any attempt to corrupt it or stifle it but an act of direct treason against Him?

THE SUPREMACY OF
CONSCIENCE*

I have spoken to you about the Liberty of Conscience. Butler appears to demand for it much more than Liberty. He claims for it Supremacy. . . .

You may remember that in my last Lecture I proposed a change in a customary form of speech. For "Liberty of Conscience," I read "Conscience of Liberty." I explained my reasons for the inversion. . . . "The Conscience of Supremacy" may seem to be no substitute for the "Supremacy of Conscience," but the very opposite of it. Nevertheless it may show us *what* "judgment, direction, superintendency is involved in the very idea of the conscience," in *what* sense "it may have a right to govern the world." . . .

May not this Conscience, which has been regarded with so much suspicion by Lawgivers, be in truth the great bulwark of Law? Need its strength be abated that the strength of the Law may be increased? Will not the strength of one be greatest when the strength of the other is greatest? Do not Laws call forth the Conscience; when that has acquired the utmost superiority which can be claimed for it, is there not the greatest, the only, security that Law will be reverenced? . . .

1. I would appeal first to your own experience. Schoolmasters, says an old poet, deliver us to Laws. In the nursery we are acquiring among other sentiments "the sentiment of the forbidden," either according to Mr. Bain's plan, by trembling at the rod which will descend on us if we do what we are told not to do, and so contracting a dread of the person who wields the rod; or, as I have maintained, by discovering that the forbidder is wiser than we are and cares to save us from the injuries that we should do to ourselves by following our own likings. Of course there are irregularities and caprices in all mortal discipline. The two maxims may be often mixed together. He who most tries to act on the one may drop through passion into the other. But I believe many a man can say, "Whatever true sentiment of the forbidden I have, whatever in me is not crouching but manly and erect, was nurtured by this fatherly treatment. God be thanked for that." Still this was not Law. The apprehension of *that* arises when we are introduced into a Society consisting of boys each with a desire for independence, each with a sense of bodily energies corresponding to this desire, each with tendencies which may lead to mere savagery; yet each capable of understanding that he has relations to his fellows, each capable of saying, I ought to do this, I ought not to do that. To bring forth this conviction in its full force is the function of the Schoolmaster. Many in our day have clearly understood that it is their function. The difference between them and some of their predecessors is, not that they enforce laws less strictly, not that they tolerate the breaking of them under any circumstances, but that they appeal to something in the boy which recognises the worth of laws; to that in him which confesses punishment to be directed against

---

*From *The Conscience*, 2d ed. (London: Macmillan and Co., 1872), Lecture 7, 124– (abridged).

acts of his which are wrong. The Schoolmaster of this age owes his nobleness not to his invention of new Canons, but to his vindication of those old simple maxims which had been exchanged in the practice of the last generation for the more refined principles of conduct that Mr. Bain has so ably illustrated and defended.

2. All School discipline points in the same direction. We learn the rules of grammar. They are learnt out of a book. There is a list of exceptions to them. But they remind us of laws to which speech must conform itself, laws that must somehow account for the exceptions. They say to each of us, Thou, if thou speakest, and wouldest make thyself intelligible, must speak according to a Law. And we are taught this lesson not that we may be hindered from uttering ourselves freely, distinctly, each saying what he has to say, but that we may do this. We are shewn by exercises in writing how the words must follow each other to make sense. If we do not care to speak or write, the laws will never explain themselves to us. It is always the same. The Law demands individual energy to fulfill it. The more the individual energy is awakened, the more it recognises its need of a Law. . . .

4. So we are prepared for the study of the most obvious and striking facts in the history of the peoples whose languages have occupied us. Why should you read about Greeks or Romans more than about any barbarous tribes? Find distinct men among the barbarous tribes, men who can express themselves, and they become as interesting to us as any of their conquerors. A Caractacus or a Galgacus is more dear to us than a Suetonius Paullinus, perhaps than an Agricola. But we must get a Tacitus to tell us of a Caractacus or a Galgacus. They stand out clear and brilliant figures before us, because the Roman historian has recognised them as such. And how does he differ from the countrymen of Caractacus or Galgacus? He has learnt the worth of Laws, he belongs to a law-governed people. The Savages form a horde, out of which a living form, an actual I, starts up ever and anon to remind us what the horde consists of, what each element in it ought to be. But of nations which recognise Laws, it is the characteristic that they are composed of I's; that is to say, the Laws have awakened the Conscience, and the Conscience being awakened owns the majesty of Laws. So we are reconciled to the triumph of Romans over Britons. We do not give up our reverence for national life; we do not worship the force of arms. But we perceive that a true national life could only be called forth, could only be sustained, by Laws; we are sure that when it has been called forth, the Laws will be respected more than the force which has been the instrument of establishing them. . . .

Law carries with it for the Conscience a witness of divinity even when those who administer it have become devilish. Those lawgivers therefore who would weaken the Conscience cut away from under them the ground on which security for Law must rest, just as the ecclesiastics who would crush it deliberately destroy the greatest witness for the direction, superintendency, judgment of a righteous God. I accept the testimony of Butler to the supremacy of the Conscience, notwithstanding what I take to be the imperfection of his language, as a grand recantation and repudiation, from an illustrious divine of the English Church who was to become one of its Bishops, of all those apologies for restraints upon the Conscience which members of his Communion had put forward in former days; a protest against all similar apologies which should be devised in the times to come. . . .

Do not suppose that by the Conscience of . . . [S]upremacy I mean the general recognition of a Supreme Power existing somewhere to whom the world is subject, and therefore to whom I as one of its inhabitants am subject. The Conscience has nothing to do with such vague and distant propositions. It is emphatically the witness of a supremacy over me directly, not over me as one of the atoms of which the world is composed. I do not proceed from the world to myself; but from myself to the world; I know of its governor only so far as I know of mine. Nor do I begin from the acknowledgment of a Power who *as a Power* governs me. In Butler's bold language I own only one who has a *Right* to govern. The Conscience takes no account of Power except as it is joined to Right, except as it has its ground in Right. The very business and function of the Conscience is to disclaim and repudiate any other, to say that it will serve no other. . . . [I]f we hold that in every man there is a Conscience of judgment, direction, superintendency, and that in every man the Conscience, so far as it testifies of this, testifies truly—we avoid any such difficulties; the Conscience in itself has no authority; its authority begins when it goes out of itself, its supremacy consists in its abdication of supremacy. . . .

The more there is of Conscience in me—the more I confess a higher law—the greater will be my degradation and the sense of it. And as the depth of this degradation is measured by the elevation of which I have the Conscience, so all those pettier and more ignominious forms of self-consciousness to which I adverted in my first lecture,—all the tricks of vanity which may make us laugh or weep when we recollect them in ourselves or others,—are accounted for in the same way. This self-consciousness attests the grandeur of which the man is capable, it shews that he cannot be satisfied with looking at mere things which are outside of him. But it verifies the two assertions of the poet, which often sound contradictory, that the man who is occupied with himself is occupied with the meanest of all objects in creation and yet that he is wise

> Who still suspects and still reveres himself
> In lowliness of heart.

11. I have touched upon the subject of the Laws of Nations solely as it bears upon the question of the Supremacy of the Conscience. Any direct treatment of that subject must be reserved for Lectures on Social Morality. But I cannot omit to notice a phrase which you will often hear from the wisest men and find in the best books; "The Conscience of a Nation." Can I accept that form of speech after taking so much pains to connect the Conscience with each man, with the word I? Most heartily do I accept it; I should regard the loss of it as an unspeakable calamity. It reminds us that the Nation is composed of I's; that therein con-

sists its preciousness; that a Society such as Mr. Bentham describes, which is "a fictitious body composed of the individual persons who are considered as constituting, as it were, its members," is not a Nation at all. Men are not wont to live and die for an "as it were." The Nation for which men are content to live and die must have a Conscience; a Conscience to which each of its citizens feels that an appeal can be made, a Conscience which makes it capable of evil acts; a Conscience which gives it a permanence from age to age. . . .

THE OFFICE OF CASUIST IN THE
MODERN WORLD*

I have been now lecturing for some weeks on Casuistry. . . because I think Casuistry is even more wanted for the England of our days than for the England of any previous day.

Am I then using the word Casuistry in some unwonted sense? There is an excuse for the suspicion, since I have told you that I entirely disclaim an office which many Casuists have deemed their principal one. I do not undertake to lay down any rules for the Conscience. I have tried to show you why I think no rules can be of use to the Conscience. If you say, "Then you are deluding us by the use of an ancient phrase; you still call your instrument the same knife though it has a new blade and a new handle;" my answer is, "No! I adhere strictly to the original sense of the word. It always meant the study of Cases of Conscience. That is what I mean by it." The reason I gave for not liking rules of Conscience, even when they are recommended by such eloquence as Taylor's, was that they do not settle the Cases of Conscience which they undertake to settle; that they leave those cases more unsettled than ever. Cases of Conscience want, I think, a different treatment. The Conscience asks for Laws, not rules; for freedom, not chains; for Education, not suppression. It is the Casuist's business to give it aid in seeking for these blessings. What special calls there are for his occupation in this present time it is proper that I should tell you before I conclude my Course. Then you will perhaps see more clearly why I refuse to confound his work with that of the Moral Philosopher, properly so called, why I suppose Casuistry is the right introduction to Moral Philosophy.

First, then, I do not think there is any kind of writing in our day which is so popular as what is called "the Analysis of human feelings and motives." I am not speaking of philosophical books. I may allude to them by-and-bye. I am thinking of newspapers, magazines, novels. The greatest talent, so far as I know, which is to be found in any of these, is exhibited not in the invention of plots, not in that which is properly the dramatist's art, the shewing forth persons in action, but in the careful dissection of their acts, and of the influences which contributed

---

*From *The Conscience,* 2d ed. (London: Macmillan and Co., 1872), Lecture 9, 163–75 (abridged).

to the formation of their acts. When such a craft is much pursued, there will of course be a number of bunglers in it; operators who give themselves credit for the skilful and delicate use of the knife when they have really no skill at all and are never likely to acquire any, though they may inflict considerable pain and do some permanent mischief whilst they are trying to acquire it. But if there are many of these, there are also many, both men and women, who display a degree of cleverness in these processes which would have caused our ancestors great admiration. Though there is much delicacy of observation in all the more eminent Essayists of the last century, in the best of them a calmness which I am afraid we have almost lost—though a novelist like Fielding had a very remarkable insight into many of the deceptions which men practise on themselves, as well as into some of their better impulses—yet in the peculiar kind of observations and criticisms to which I am referring, I doubt if they could bear comparison with several of our contemporaries who in mere artistical gifts may be far inferior to them. Criticism is that of which our age boasts, and in which no doubt it excels. We are nothing if not critical. Much of this faculty may be directed towards books; but the books are treated as indexes to the character of the person who has composed them. He is brought out of his hiding-place, even if the critic prefers to remain within his own. I do not regret that it is so. We ought to look upon books not as a collection of written letters, but as the utterances of living men; if they are not, they are nothing. There may be much cruelty, often much baseness, in the exposures which are made of the ways and habits of authors who have not been the least anxious to obtrude them upon the world, who have only wished to say something which they thought they had to say. But on the whole it is good that a man should be recognised as a being, and not merely as a speaker; as having spoken out something of his own very self. At all events, for good or for evil it has come to pass that our discourses of every kind tend to assume a personal character. Our statesmen, soldiers, preachers, must either be photographed, or sketched by an artist who thinks he understands their features better than the sun does.

To complain of that which one finds so much the habit of our time as this is useless and not very wise. We are a part of our time; its ways are our ways; in finding fault with them we are sure to be unconsciously finding fault with ourselves. That is just the account to which I would turn these remarks. I think a critical age wants to be reminded that it is criticising itself; and critical men that they are criticising themselves. We are apt to forget that there is a critic within us, a sterner, fairer judge than we are, who is taking account of what we do and speak and think; who is now and then saying to me when I am pouring out my righteous indignation against the robber of the ewe lamb—much more distinctly than any prophet could say it—"Thou art the man." The Casuist is called to remind us of this fact. He must say to the critic, "Yes, this analysis of other men's acts and motives is wonderfully clever and acute. It may do those much good whom you desire to improve. But then am not I, are not you—conscious of something which is nearer than that man's acts and motives? You pronounce what he ought to have done and ought not to have done. Is not that 'ought' and 'ought not' derived from a Conscience to which thou canst appeal in him because it is in thee?" . . .

As a Sunday preacher I am inwardly and painfully convinced that no persons more require the kind of monition which he [Mr. Thackeray the novelist] supplied than those whose regular business obliges them to tell other men of their wrong doings and temptations. Their function cannot therefore, I apprehend, supersede that of the Casuist. Clergymen may learn from him when they are preparing for their after work some of the perils to which it will expose them. . . .

[Casuistry] warns us against the quackery of these prescriptions; it shews us why we cannot obtain any diagnosis of other men's symptoms, except by acquaintance with our own. But it is not therefore profitless to those who encounter many troublesome diseases, and are beset with demands for prompt methods of curing them. That habit of looking for other men's faults to which I have alluded is often signally punished. A man who has yielded to it may begin to accuse himself as vehemently as he has ever accused any of his fellows. He may become the most laborious analyst of his own motives; he may turn his thoughts outwards, and may pronounce them all selfish and base. That kind of self-criticism will lead to no result or to very unwholesome results. It will be pursued for a while, and then the self-tormentor will beg for some anodyne or for some counter-irritant from an external penance; in time he will probably be weary of all such experiments, or will practise them only as formalities, and will determine that it is best to drift along wherever the currents of fashion and opinion may carry him. . . . [T]he Casuist would lead this curious enquirer into the different forces which are driving him to the right or to the left. . . . [H]e must be reminded that the Conscience in him is the man in him; he cannot divide himself from it; he cannot measure or weigh the fetters which bind it, but must above all things seek to be delivered from the fetters.

And the Casuist may help him in some degree towards this emancipation by one suggestion. He is not dealing honestly with himself when he says that there is nothing in him but what is mean and selfish. He may think that he is exhibiting a praiseworthy humility in saying so. It is not humility at all, nor is it the least praiseworthy. On the contrary, he is often secretly crediting himself with being better than he gives himself out to be, often thinking that he may make a little capital out of his self-depreciation. He will not be humble till he owns that there is a good always present with him, a good which he inwardly desires, a good which he ought to pursue. Then he will begin in very deed to feel the evil which is adverse to the good; he will understand that it ought in some way or other to be cast off. There is no work of the Casuist more important than this, or more needful in our days. Numbers presume that wrong is the law of their being, that right is only the exception to wrong. So far as they hold that opinion they never think that anything which they do is really wrong, however they may pretend to think so; they have no standard with which to compare it. Wrong for them is right. The Conscience protests continually against this horrible inversion. The conscience of a right which I cannot let go holds me up when I am most wrong. And the same Conscience says that the wrong into which I have fallen never can be anything but wrong; anything but a contradiction of the law under which I exist.

II. These are practical topics concerning every man, the most ignorant as well as the wisest. It is with such that the Casuist is occupied. He is to be testifying in season and out of season, that the subject which he speaks of is a subject for books only because it is a subject for men and women, and that it would remain the same if all the books that ever have been written were burnt to ashes. But for this very reason he must mingle in the battle of the books; he cannot overlook the systems which philosophers are constructing, and sending forth into the world. That is the second topic of which I meant to speak. We have heard in these Lectures that there are Systems, very popular in our day, which present men as the slaves of certain motives, which use the analyses of these motives to determine what men will be, must be, and therefore ought to be. We have heard again that as the necessary corollary from these maxims, they do not allow Right and Wrong to be ultimate distinctions. Such teachers may have done good in telling us what motives are likely to influence us in different circumstances; they may have done great good by correcting certain false impressions about these motives which have been made the basis of legislation or of individual actions. Of all this good the Casuist may gladly avail himself. But he is bound to struggle to the death against their primary assumption; that simply destroys what he maintains to be the root of a man's existence. If the System which starts from this denial were only a System, only for philosophical men, he might leave it to itself. But it embodies and justifies all those tendencies which I have just spoken of; those which take a religious form in some, a form of worldly Cynicism in others. They conspire with the popular taste for detecting and exposing other men's motives, with the more dangerous habit of detecting and exposing our own. Though they seem to treat all motives as inevitable and therefore as harmless, they do not involve the least tolerance or tenderness to those who commit what are to be called not sins or evils but only "acts inconsistent with the interests of the Community." A man against whom, under that title, Mr. Bentham hurls his anathemas, might, except for the honour of the thing, as soon be called a bad man according to the manner of the ancients. The Conscience of the philosopher slips in the obsolete phrases which he ridicules with the indignation which appertains to them. The Casuist who maintains the language of the Conscience to be the true language relieves the Benthamic curses of many troublesome circumlocutions; he may lead the curser to hesitate a little before he deals them out.

Similar remarks apply to that philosophy which would make our acts depend in a great measure upon our emotions and upon certain conditions of our physical organization. Whatever any *psychologist* may tell us about these emotions,—

even if he succeeds in analyzing the feeling of a mother to her child mainly into certain feelings connected with the roundness and smoothness of its cheeks—let us receive thankfully, in the last instance with the wonder which some of old deemed the first step to knowledge. Whatever wisdom the teacher has obtained at second hand from great *physiologists* about the brain and the nervous system, let us accept, so far as we can enter into it, with even more fervent gratitude. But the Casuist having done all homage to these lessons, will torment his instructor with these rude and troublesome notes and queries—"Yes! that is very remarkable indeed. And do these emotions then and this nervous system make me? Did not you say I had them? You might not perhaps think it worth while to give me the additional information who *I* am?" No! that is not in the bond. And therefore there is a function for the Casuist, who asserts that it is not only in his bond to consider that question, but that it is precisely the one which he has to consider. In this case also it is not the System which he is at all anxious to confute. But if there is a disposition in our days to make our emotions, our nervous system, or anything else, an excuse for not doing what we ought to do, or being what we are created to be—if that disposition as well as the faculty which I have claimed for our age are both flattered by the assurance that the highest philosophy is occupied in the analysis of these emotions, tracing the processes by which the nervous system becomes our supreme ruler; he must repel the negations of the system that he may maintain his own position.

So it is also with that doctrine about Society of which we have heard so much in these Lectures. Society has been used as a bugbear to frighten us; the Conscience must do what it bids or cease to be. If that is Society there are no terms to be kept with it. The Casuist's business is in the name of the Conscience to mock it and defy it. He must be more fierce in his mockery and defiance than he might have thought it necessary to be in any former age. For this theory is put forth as the last result of modern wisdom. It must spread wherever luxury abounds; wherever the passion for liberty is changed for any easy profession of liberality; wherever Opinion under one pretext or other is confounded with Truth. The worshippers of Society may soon tear each other in pieces when they have to settle how its votes shall be taken, who is to be the returning officer. But all lazy people will agree that somehow the strongest or the most numerous ought to decide what they shall do or leave undone. If the Casuist merged his work in that of the Moral Philosopher he could scarcely, I conceive, hold his ground in this conflict. He would then be always harassed with the doubt, "Am I to find the individual man somewhere outside of Society? Or am I to trace his doings in Society?" The satisfaction of that doubt seems to me this. You cannot contemplate the individual man out of Society: you will scarcely find him among savages if you look diligently for him. But you must vindicate his position in order that you may shew what Society is; of what it consists. If it does not consist of I's, of Persons, the Moralist has no concern with it. If it does consist of I's, of Persons, begin with asserting that character for it, then go on to investigate the relations in which the members of it stand to each other. That means, as I conceive, when translated into the book speech, "Begin with Casuistry; go on to Moral Philosophy. First make it clear what you mean by a Person; that you will do when you make it clear what you mean by a Conscience; then treat these Persons as if they did form real bodies, and tell us out of history, not out of your own fancy, what these bodies are." . . .

CHAPTER 4

Social Morality:
Twenty-One Lectures

SOCIAL MORALITY: WHAT IT IS AND
HOW IT SHOULD BE TREATED*

I have proposed to deliver a course of lectures on Social Morality. You may ask me what I understand by that phrase. If my sense of it differed from the ordinary sense I would begin by telling you what the difference is. But so far as I know, my sense is the ordinary sense. What that is I think we may ascertain if we question different writers on Society and the manners of Society about their object. If we can discover something which has been common to them all amidst the greatest disagreements of opinion, taste, and character, we may conclude that to be the aim of the Social Moralist as such. It might seem most natural to take the earliest of them first. My inclination would be in favour of that method. But the old writers are often said to be obsolete or to deal in book-wisdom, not in practical wisdom. I will begin with one who is open to no such suspicion.

In the last century a series of Letters appeared of which you have all heard, which some of you may possibly have read. They were addressed by Lord Chesterfield to his son. They were intended to form the manners of a young man, to cultivate in him the ease and grace which he may have inherited from at least one of his parents. If I said that Lord Chesterfield composed a Code of Manners for his son's use I should mislead you. He would have objected to the word "Code," as savouring of legal pedantry. Formal rules would not have produced the effect he desired. He would rather set before his pupil examples which were to be imitated or shunned. He had studied these examples in France as well as England; he possessed clear and keen habits of observation; he was himself the observed of all observers. For the kind of task which he imposed upon himself

---

*From *Social Morality: Twenty-One Lectures Delivered in the University of Cambridge* (1869; London: Macmillan and Co., 1886), Lecture 1, 1–20.

no one could be better fitted. The limits of that task were strictly defined. He did not care what it might behove men to do or to be who lay beyond the flaming battlements of "the world"; he only troubled himself about that class which, according to his charts, was comprehended within "the world." In them he sought not merely certain outward acts, but an internal habit, a something which would give to all their doings, words, gestures, evenness and order. He demanded of them for this end abstinence from many ways and practices into which if they did not count themselves members of a special circle they might fall. He assumed the existence of a standard to which they ought to be assimilated. Here is Social Morality as illustrated by one of its professors.

If we pass from these letters of Chesterfield to some of the very able and elaborate novels which were produced in the same century, we are presented with other and much more varied pictures of Social Morality. Fielding had probably no access to the sacred inclosure within which Chesterfield dwelt. He was a metropolitan Justice of the Peace; he had known personally something of those who came before him in that capacity, much also of the life of ordinary citizens and country squires, of schoolmasters and clergymen. In them, as well as in the servants who waited upon them, and in the highwaymen who were their terror, he discovered different exhibitions of character, different standards of behaviour, different apprehensions of justice and injustice, of right and of wrong. In every class there was evidently *some* standard; in every one some apprehension of justice and injustice, of right and wrong. If these had been absent, the members of such classes could not have been represented in any story; they would not have been subjects for a work of Art. The novelist does not pretend to try them by any canons of his; but he makes us feel that they had their canons, and denounced acts which appeared to them a departure from their canons. You see that unlike as Fielding was to Chesterfield, their aim was in this sense similar. It is with a certain disposition or habit or character that both are conversant. You may call it in either if you please an *artificial* disposition or habit or character. But it is by some means or other wrought into the man or woman. It becomes his or hers.

But observations upon one or another portion of English society could not satisfy an age which, however inferior to ours in facilities for locomotion, was yet becoming acquainted with a number of lands; an age which was hearing of the customs, inventions, hereditary wisdom of China, to which the falling Mogul Empire was disclosing the faiths and languages that had been buried within it. To compare the modes of thinking and belief, fluctuating or permanent, which prevailed in these lands with those of the West, became a favourite occupation of men of letters. They liked to imagine how a cultivated Chinese or Hindu or Turk or Persian would regard the manners and notions which he met with in England or France. Oliver Goldsmith, in his *Citizen of the World,* pursued this line of fancy, noting, in his quiet way, the effect which the follies of his countrymen might produce on a stranger. He was following in the wake of a man more thoroughly cultivated, if not more shrewd, than himself. About a hundred years before Mr. Morier published his clever *Hajji Baba in England*, the citizens of Paris were excited and charmed by a set of letters said to be addressed by a native of Ispahan to his friends, which criticised rather freely not only their external acts, but the conviction or want of conviction, the beliefs or unbeliefs, out of which the acts arose. The author of the letters, at first anonymous, proved to be a man of ancient family, the President of a Parliament in the South of France, a learned lawyer as well as an accomplished and vivacious writer. In a later time, after he had visited England, the President Montesquieu exhibited the genius which had produced the Persian letters in a work scarcely less lively, but more akin to the habits of his profession. His *Esprit des Lois* is, or was till lately, on the list of subjects for our Moral Science Tripos. It is, in fact, a Treatise on Social Morality. There was something Montesquieu perceived in every country besides the laws, written on tables or parchments; something besides its different institutions, Monarchical, Aristocratical, Republican. There was a mind which corresponded to these; it was fostered by them; in turn it sustained them; if it was lost they must perish. Whence it came, what accounted for the shapes which it assumed in diverse regions, what influence external circumstances such as climate might have upon it;—these were important questions about which conjectures might be hazarded. But at all events the fact of such differences could not be dissembled; it must be worthy of any attention that could be bestowed upon it. Montesquieu was hasty in his generalisations; he often trusted to records which could not endure severe criticism. But the value of his hints to historical inquirers, if they dissent ever so much from his conclusions, cannot be gainsaid. And immensely different as the wide observations of Montesquieu are from those of his friend Chesterfield, there is this likeness between them: they are both occupied with characteristics which are found in men; let them desire ever so much to note the appearances on the surface of society, those appearances point to volcanoes which lie beneath it.

Of such volcanoes some countrymen and contemporaries of Montesquieu were beginning to be conscious. The brilliant Parisian circle in which Chesterfield had moved was adorned by wits who declared that the traditions and maxims of the past were perishing; priests hovered about it who were deemed the conservators of those maxims and traditions, and were yet in many ways deepening the impression of their weakness which prevailed in it and had descended to other portions of society. There appeared a man, who stood about equally aloof from the wits and the priests, and who denounced in no measured terms those circles that paid alternate homage to either. He was the son of a watchmaker in Geneva. Though he had led a strange life and done acts which any school or man would have pronounced base—which he felt to be so while he confessed them—yet the old Protestant and Republican traditions of his birthplace had taken a mighty hold upon him. Even while he yielded to the impressions of his senses, he felt an intense and growing horror for what he regarded as the social corruptions of his day. Even while he described scenes which fostered the voluptuousness of cities,

he had a passion for the free air of the mountains. Geneva should not, he was resolved, derive its tone from the French capital; it should be a witness against the
tastes, manners, the whole social system of France. Rousseau began to be hailed
as the champion of natural and savage life against the civilisation of Europe. He
used language which justified this description. Yet he also used language which
might lead us to represent him as an imitator of those old Spartans who trampled upon nature, who sought to subdue it by a rigid education. This contradiction is especially apparent in his *Emile*, a book which has had a very powerful influence in every country of Europe. In it he denounced the schemes of nursery
discipline which he thought had destroyed all that was simple and natural in children. He declared that any reformation in society must proceed from a reformation of domestic life. His plans of reformation may often seem to us not less artificial than the practices against which he protests. We may think that a child
reared upon his system would have been extremely deficient in the simplicity
which he desired to secure for it. Nevertheless, whatever inconsistencies there
might be in his conception of the word Nature or in himself, he spoke to a conviction which was deep in the hearts of thoughtful men—nay, of the whole
French people. He shewed them that there was something in their Social Morality which needed to be reformed from its root.

Whether this reformation of Social Morality came or not, there did certainly
come a dissolution of French Society into its elements. How much Rousseau's
"Evangel," especially that contained in his *Contrat Social,* aided in producing this
result, Mr. Carlyle has told us. The French Revolution was a Social Revolution
in the fullest, deepest sense of the words. It was not a change of one kind of government for another; it was a decomposition of the whole body governing and
governed; a change of feeling respecting the relation of classes in the country to
each other; an attempt to overthrow classes altogether. Equality was affirmed to
be the basis of Society; of Society in France because of human Society; Frenchmen were equal because men were.

The Revolution therefore by its very terms rejected local divisions; it must embrace the world. All parts of Europe felt the shock of it; there was a vehement delight in the message which it brought; there was a vehement reaction against it.
Here in England the delight was felt in many youthful hearts; the reaction was
more conspicuous still. The distinction of classes was reverenced as a sacred
protest against the levelling doctrine; it was exalted above the distinction of Nations. When the universal Republic became a universal Empire the worth of *that*
distinction became evident to many who had sympathised in the first proclamation of Cosmopolitism; the other distinction became less offensive, when orders
in the state were contemplated not as an insult to the people but as a defence
against tyranny. Nevertheless the Revolution had left its stamp on these early
champions as well as on many who had always detested it. Not only such writers
as Wordsworth became poets of the poor; witnesses for the sanctity of common
life. The novels of Scott, lover of feudalism as he was, shewed a genuine unpa-

tronising sympathy with human nature in its humblest forms, of which it can scarcely be said that there were any clear traces in our literature since the time of Shakespeare. Evidently the doctrine of the illustrious plowman of his land, "a man's a man for a' that," had taken possession of his mind; courtly influences might weaken but could not expel it.—There were no doubt fashionable novelists who would gladly have restored the Chesterfield conception of life, and who had admiring readers in the middle class eager for what glimpses they could get about the doings of the highest. Such ambition there will always be in a country like ours, and writers willing, perhaps more or less able, to gratify it. But on the whole the tendency has been in the other direction. Those who have helped us to understand the forms of Society which are found under different conditions in all classes—of which we can in some measure judge for ourselves—have exercised the greatest influence over us. Even a writer like Lord Byron possessed by the feelings of his own order, not much honouring any other, was listened to not chiefly on that account, but because he shewed that beneath the artificial surface of his circumstances and of his character, there lay springs of terrible passion which belong to the kind, not the class.

In these instances, different as they are from those I spoke of before, the power of the writer, the interest of the reader, lies in the discovery of a certain character or *ēthos* first doubtless in some individual, but in him as connected with a Society smaller or larger, in him as showing what character makes the Society harmonious or discordant, stable or unstable. And when we examine how this *ēthos* becomes known to us, we see that there are certain permanent conditions of Society of which literature has taken account, and which, since the French Revolution more than in the centuries before it, have distinguished themselves from each other. I think you may perceive that Rousseau's hints (1) about domestic life, (2) about civilisation, (3) about a more general human Society than those names suggest, indicate three kinds of investigations in most respects unlike each other and yet all clearly falling within the sphere of Social Morality.

I. There has been a vast amount of writing during the last seventy years on the subject of Education, the ends at which it should aim, the persons whom it should benefit, the machinery which is available for it. But no part of these discussions has, on the whole, produced so much effect as that which has followed in Rousseau's line, pointing out the defects in domestic discipline and the way in which it may be reformed. Very able men have given us the fruits of their experience on this topic; it has especially called forth the quicker and more delicate observation of women, whether mothers themselves, or those who like Miss Edgeworth have performed the part of mothers to sisters, brothers, or strangers. However much the hints of such teachers have been directed to methods of intellectual culture, their object has been by one method or another to form a character; their chief skill has been shewn in tracing the influence of different members of a family on the characters of each other. The Family, small circle as it must be, has been found large enough for the discovery of innumerable varieties of feeling and disposition, every variety having some tendency to produce another by collision or sympathy. So those who have begun with the most practical purpose of improving household discipline, have also given us clear and vivid pictures of different households which they have seen or imagined. Historical novels have had a certain attraction for us. Brilliant pictures like those in *Ivanhoe* when painted by an antiquarian who is also a man of genius, must have an interest even when we suspect them as guides to the true knowledge of an age. But in general the portion of such books which is domestic produces by far the most powerful effect. The strictly domestic story has become characteristic of our times, not in this country only, but, as far as I can make out, in all countries of Europe. The morality may be of one kind or another. The Family may be merely a ground-plot for the display of sensational incidents. Still these incidents are found to be most startling, and therefore most agreeable to those who wish to be startled, when they are associated with outrages of one kind or another upon family order. Those who do not want such stimulants to their own feelings and fancies, and do not hold it an honest trade to mix them for others, have found in the quietest home-life materials for Art. All social harmonies and social contradictions, they see, may come forth in the relations of fathers and children, husbands and wives, brothers and sisters, masters and servants. There is a certain character, they are sure, which helps to make a family peaceful or miserable—a home out of which blessings or curses may diffuse themselves over the commonwealth. Even those who are impatient of national boundaries as too narrow, are yet occupying themselves with theories and controversies about the conditions of the family, some of them denouncing our ordinary conceptions of it as antiquated, some reviving *most* ancient theories respecting it, some maintaining that all the order of Christendom is due to the difference between its domestic forms and that of countries in which polygamy prevails, all its disease and disorders to the loss of the spirit which should quicken these forms. I am entitled therefore to claim the authority of the most thoughtful as well as the most popular writers, of all schools and of both sexes, for the opinion that Domestic Morality is not only an integral portion of Social Morality, but should be the starting point of any discussion respecting it. They are equally agreed that in treating of this topic our business is not chiefly with acts or modes of conduct, but with a character or state of mind from which the acts proceed, by which the conduct must be regulated.

II. The fierce onslaught of Rousseau upon the Civilisation which he found in France, and upon the very name of Civilisation—his preference for the life of woods—was endorsed in the declaration of Rights which inaugurated the Revolution. For in this declaration maxims determining what Society ought to be were deduced from a state prior to the existence of Society itself. The difficulties and contradictions of that assumption became every day more palpable; many who embraced Rousseau's doctrine concerning the sovereignty of the people were industrious in pointing them out. None again have been so much alive to the worth of Civilisation, and have been so eager to vindicate it from the charges of

Rousseau, as countrymen of his own who have shared in his dislike of the *Ancien Régime*. M. Guizot's work, which is so well known in England, and is so conspicuous for its learning and ability, represents the temper of the time in which it was composed. It is specially occupied in exhibiting Civilisation as the antagonist of Feudalism. Strictly, almost sternly, etymological, M. Guizot makes us feel that the word Civilisation points specially to that formation of towns, that development of cities, which counteracted the solitary influence of the territorial Proprietor in the midst of his land, the barbarism of those who were, in a great measure, *adscripti glebae*. With a critical knowledge of history to which Montesquieu could make no pretension, he distinguishes the different agencies, legal, personal, ecclesiastical—derived from the traditions of Rome, from Gothic kings, from the papal authority, from distinguished men, from the co-operation and clashing of these forces—which brought forth a civic life in modern Europe. He has made us perceive the meaning of this process which was working through so many ages. But he does not disguise from us or from himself that it was a mysterious process, which it requires an historical instinct to apprehend, which cannot be reduced under formulas now more than it could when the *Esprit des Lois* was composed. The lights of modern criticism have not tended, he shews us, to make Society, or the Manners of Society, more explicable by mere laws or systems of Government. On the contrary they have helped greatly to perplex the man who has thought that some one clue would guide him through the labyrinth—that he could determine, for instance, the condition of Europe, by attributing its blessings or its curses to the influence of the Clergy. They have brought with them blessings and curses which the faithful student of Civilisation, according to M. Guizot's notion of it, must equally recognise.

Mr. Buckle's work on Civilisation is in most respects very unlike Guizot's. At first sight it would seem not to concern my subject, since he was expressed in more than one or two very decisive sentences his opinion, that the further civilisation advances, the more will intellectual studies take precedence of moral. Such an opinion is in accordance with one part of the writer's scheme. He had an immense appreciation of statistics; a great confidence that by help of them we may be able to predict in what circumstances certain acts (e.g., homicide or suicide) will be frequent or rare. Now the intellect is no doubt chiefly conversant with such calculations as these; they are scarcely applicable to states of mind or feeling; it may be difficult to discover how these can be indicated by tables. But Mr. Buckle insists strongly on the difference between the nations of the East, which bow before the powers of Nature, and those of the West which defy them. That is a state of mind or feeling. Again, he deems it the grand test of a nation's civilisation that it loses the disposition to make war and to persecute for religious opinions. He does therefore in fact connect Civilisation with the formation of an *ēthos* or Social Morality, however he may trace that *ēthos* to certain external conditions or suppose it to be produced by certain exercises of intellect. The Morality which he scorned seems to consist of certain maxims. That he did not suppose these to be of much worth, may be accepted as a proof that he demanded a character which he found they could not of themselves produce. He is not therefore to be set down as an exception to our rule. As much as Montesquieu, or Guizot, he supposes Civilisation to consist in a certain social manner; one which cannot be expressed in formal edicts, which must be in the men who compose the society.

Here then we have another division of Social Morality. We might call it the Civil or the Political. But useful as both these words are, they are borrowed from countries in which the city had an absorbing importance that does not belong to it in later history. Such cities as Pisa, Milan, Florence, when they first attract attention in Mediaeval History, seem as if they might represent Italy, as Athens, Sparta, Thebes represent ancient Greece. But the Italian of this day will not tolerate that doctrine. He claims to be the member of a nation. London has never stood for England; the most popular writers among contemporary Frenchmen are careful to shew us that we must study the provinces and not merely Paris to know what France is. M. Guizot may be right in opposing Feudalism to Civilisation; but no German or Englishman or Spaniard could possibly refuse to regard feudal institutions as one element in the life of his people. All these considerations seem to shew that the epithet *National* will be more proper to denote the second branch of Morality, than either Civil or Political would be. If we adopt that we shall be in far less danger of missing the link between this portion of our subject and the first; in less danger of confounding it with the one of which I am about to speak.

III. The cosmopolitan aspect of the French Revolution has seemed to some its most characteristic aspect. The epithet has survived much of the disgrace which attached to it when it was supposed to indicate a contempt for national distinctions. The title human, or humane (as it used to be spelt), is open to no such objection. Humanity has been accepted as their favourite watchword by a set of philosophers who have devoted themselves most laboriously to the study of the principles of Society, who even boast that they have founded a new science worthy to be called "Sociology." I am not now considering the merits of this somewhat barbarous name. But I wish you to know that if there is any question as to Mr. Buckle's opinion about the dignity of Morality, there is none whatever as to M. Comte's. He does not for a moment postpone morality to the intellect; the great work of the positivist philosopher, he says, is to make moral considerations predominant over all other; the normal state of man according to him is that in which the intellect is subordinated to the heart. I may therefore claim him and his disciples as witnesses for that explanation of Social Morality which I have deduced from so many writers of other schools. I am delighted also to have their authority for recognising human morality as the centre in which both the other departments of Social Morality find their purpose and interpretation. Whether that agreement with them implies that Sociology is the highest of all sciences or the ground of all—whether the place I give to Humanity involves me in the

Comtist worship of it—we may inquire hereafter. Those questions have no place in a preliminary lecture; that ought only to fix the nature and object of the investigation on which we are entering.

But I cannot leave this distinguished school without saying that I desire on another ground to be a pupil in it. I wish to examine facts—*positive* facts if that adjective adds any dignity to the substantive—speculations only so far as they may have been offered for the elucidation of facts. If I speak of any theories about the superiority of one form of family life to another—and I shall quote some weighty remarks of M. Comte on that topic—it is only because I find the fact of our existence in families an indisputable one. If I am obliged to dwell on the difference of social forms in different Nations, it will be for the purpose of illustrating the fact that we are members of different Nations, and that one Nation cannot fix the form which is suitable for another. If I examine certain speculations of different philosophers respecting Human Morality, it is that I may shew how each one of these speculations is valuable as bringing into light Facts concerning our position as members of a Universal Human Society, constituted on a certain principle. In one respect, no doubt, I may seem to differ from M. Comte and his disciples. The Family is not lost in the Nation, nor the Nation in Human Society. They are coexistent; whereas M. Comte's first theological age gives place to a metaphysical age, and both are merged in the Positive. But I do not think that I am less adhering to facts, more plunging into speculations, because I am not able to adjust my thoughts to this great theory of succession, and only assume the common places which M. Comte as well as all other persons must recognise.

Here then I might stop; for I have sufficiently set forth the course which I propose to follow, and have justified it by a concurrence of modern authorities and examples. But though I have begun with these, I cannot forget that in this University we confess the dignity of older names and teach you to reverence them. Am I forsaking their guidance in submission to these newer lights? I think the books which we ask you to read may answer that question.

The purpose of Plato's *Republic* has been variously interpreted. Rousseau, with much plausibility, called it a Treatise on Education. No doubt it contains most interesting discussions respecting the methods by which the mind and character of the members of the Commonwealth are to be formed into harmony with the ends for which it exists. But that the education may be effectual, that we may understand the nature of it, we must learn what the principle of the Commonwealth is. That we may know this we must settle whether Justice is a reality or a fiction, whether it is only an individual principle or also a social principle, whether there can be a Society which does not confess it and is not held together by it. We are in fact engaged in the study of Social Morality. We are seeking to find what the *ēthos* of a Society—of Society itself—must be, and how that *ēthos* can be developed in the citizens of it. The controversies of modern times; the debate between Right and Might, which is carried on so fiercely in the schools and in the world; that most difficult of all problems, how the claims of the Individual and of the

Society can be reconciled; are all here. The manifold experiences of the Greek Republics, the subtlest wisdom of the greatest Greek thinker, are helping us to unravel threads which are spun about our own lives, which are embarrassing statesmen and common men of the 19th century.

If you pass to Plato's eminent pupil you encounter an intellect of a very different shape and texture from that with which you have just parted; in some of their leading methods of thought they are so unlike, that the saying has become current, "The Platonist and the Aristotelian can by no possibility understand each other." But in the point which I am considering now they are alike. One as much as the other would make Morality—Social Morality—consist in habits, in a character, not in outward acts, still less in formal maxims. The very word *ēthos* which I have used as the most convenient to explain this distinction is specially an Aristotelian word. Considering that Aristotle is reckoned so great a dogmatist—that he has composed such an Encyclopaedia of studies—it is marvellous how free he is from the temptations of the mere schoolman; how little he trusts in mere formulas; how every virtue of which he speaks is only a virtue as it becomes formed in a man. And if we join the Politics to the Ethics—as he tells us they must be joined—we discover that order of subjects which I am endeavoring to observe. In this respect the comparison of him with Plato, if it is greatly to his advantage, is for us most instructive. The *Republic* teaches us how the noblest student of Humanity in his eagerness to grasp the Universal is likely to lose sight of the Particular. In Plato's vast Communism the Family is lost. Aristotle acknowledges it as the very basis of political society; the relations of the household are the germs of the different forms of government.

Let no one persuade you then that these great teachers of former ages must be cast aside in order that you may profit by the wider experiences of your own day. Those who are not called to be students may turn their experiences to account; if members of a University despise the wisdom of the past, the present will not teach them; they will carry away a multitude of notions from a multitude of schools; each will trip up the other and make it useless. Plato and Aristotle if you use them rightly will shew you the worthlessness of mere notions, the impossibility of separating Morality from Life.

Mr. Buckle recalls to us the words "As you would that men should do to you do ye also to them likewise," asks triumphantly what they have effected for mankind? Speaking according to the lessons of the book in which they occur, I should answer, "Nothing whatever if they are regarded as mere words in a book; worse than nothing if they are taken as warrants for self-exaltation, as reasons for exalting ourselves as Christians above other men." The New Testament I need scarcely tell you is occupied from first to last—specially in the Sermon on the Mount—in shewing that acts are nothing except as they are fruits of a state, except as they indicate what the man is; that words are nothing except as they express a mind or purpose. Nor need I add that it is a Society—a Human Society— in which the preacher of that Sermon assumes that this *ēthos* is to be exhibited.

It might have sounded a commonplace of Divinity to tell you at the beginning of my Lecture that this is what I hold to be the meaning of Social Morality. We have now seen that no other is found to be satisfactory by any persons who have seriously meditated upon it. I might again seem to be merely following the order of the Scriptures in taking the Family, the Nation, a Society for all nations and kindreds, as the divisions of my subject. Since upon quite independent grounds that method has recommended itself to us, you will not deem it a less sound or desirable one because it has this sanction.

DOMESTIC MORALITY: PARENTS AND CHILDREN*

Many writers begin with considering mankind as a multitude of units. They ask, How did any number of these units form themselves into a Society? I cannot adopt that method. At my birth I am already in a Society. I am related, at all events, to a father and mother. This relation is the primary fact of my existence. I can contemplate no other facts apart from it.

Perhaps you will say, "For each of us separately that no doubt is true. But we want to consider the world at large." Well! and to what portion of the world at large is this truth not applicable? In what region do you find a man who is not born a son, who is not related to a father and mother? It is a fact for me surely, but it is a fact for you and for every man. And if you determine not to take notice of this fact, not to give it precedence of every other, the effect is, that instead of contemplating the world at large you will only contemplate yourself. *You* will be the unit about which all events and persons will revolve. Each man will regard himself as the centre of the universe. You will at last come to an understanding— a very imperfect understanding—that each must occupy this place in his own estimation; you will be forced to construct a Society on that hypothesis.

If, on the other hand, you start from the indisputable commonplace "We are sons," such a way of considering the Universe is from the first impossible. I cannot be the centre of the circle in which I find myself, be it as small as it may. I refer myself to another. There is a root below me. There is an Author of my existence.

If we adhere steadily to this which would strike any one as the true chronological order, some of the greatest difficulties will be taken out of our path; instead of being obliged to invent explanations of social existence, we shall find the explanations lying at our feet. We shall understand at the same time why men have been led to crave for such explanations, and to seek them afar off. The relation exists; there is a manner which answers to the relation, without which it becomes untenable, contradictory. But there is a tendency in each of us to break the relation, to lose the manner. We strive to be units, though by the order in

---

*From *Social Morality* (1869; London: Macmillan and Co., 1886), Lecture 2, part 1, 21–41.

which we are placed we cannot be. How this striving may ultimately become a blessing, how it may introduce us to other parts of our social order, we shall consider hereafter. At present I must insist that a son cannot be without a father, or a father without a son. To dissolve the relation into its elements is to remake the world.

As soon as I recognise an Author of my existence, I recognise an *Authority* over me. I do not mean of course that I know anything about the words Author or Authority; that I understand what binds them together. But I mean that in the very fact of Fatherhood Authority is involved, that I learn what it is through my filial relation. I will explain myself by comparing the word Authority with one which lies very near it, which is always in danger of being treated as synonymous with it.

I have *dominion,* say over a certain number of acres. There are on those acres dead stock and live stock: ploughs; cattle that are yoked to the ploughs; men that drive the cattle. All these are included in my dominion. Whilst I look upon them *only* as in my dominion I make no distinction between them. Dead stock, live stock, animals, men, they are all regarded as belonging to me, instruments for tilling my land. I begin to see a difference between them. I recognise a bond between me and the men who drive the animals. I do not cease to give them orders; but the orders are those of one who has authority, not only of one who has dominion. I may discover that the animals also submit to words rather than to force; that a certain authority can be exercised over them. I become *humane* to them. I cease to be a brute possessing brutes; I am a man directing them. I cannot refer either this sense of fellowship with men or this humane rule over animals to my separate Nature. Yielding to that, I shall merely try to assert dominion; whether I succeed or fail, it will be a battle of physical forces. But I am related to a Father, he is related to me. I cannot destroy that relation, though I try. It brings forth a manner in me. If the separate Nature prevails over this relation, there will in all cases be dominion, but no authority; subjection, no obedience; brutality, no manners.

In referring Society and the manners which make Society possible first to this relation, I am not, you see, resorting to any grand theory. I am merely asking you to take account of facts; of facts which must be wherever men have lived or do live; of facts which just as much belong to every English household of this year as to those of which you read in any records or legends of the earliest times. Authority and Obedience are as fundamental principles of Society now as they were in any Saturnian age; the demand for them is now as much as ever made first in the family; the seeds of them are there; the interpretation of them is there. If you try to explain them by the incidents of a later and more complicated state, you will be always at a loss. You will find something which you cannot account for by any arrangements or conventions: if you seek for it in laws, the laws will drive you back to some primeval order which is implied in them, which they did not create. Proof that this is so I hope to give you before I finish this lecture. First I would make one or two observations which connect what I have said with the lessons of other Moralists.

The more you study Aristotle's *Ethics,* the more you will be aware of a difficulty which he, with his customary honesty, takes no pains to hide. He speaks of certain habits which enable men to fulfil their work as men. Are not these habits part of our Nature? What else can they be if they are to be characteristic of our own selves? They cannot come to us from without. They must be internal. And yet they do not spring up in men without education. A most pregnant doubt, worth a hundred clever solutions. We are obliged to face it. Perhaps the Politics of Aristotle, which he never wished to be separate from his Ethics, may give us a hint about the way of facing it. There, as I told you in my last lecture, he refers us to the Family as the underground of all National Institutions. But if that be so, is not Education presumed in these Institutions, presumed in the life of each one of us? The father *must* educate his child; so far as he has any authority over him that must be an Education. For what end he educates is a question of immeasurable importance: that there should be some end is inevitable. He may train his son to mere exercises of brute strength; he may train him to revenge and malice. But, anyhow, we are saved from the necessity of considering the question what any child or man or boy would be if left to himself without education; because no one is. Each of us has had sufficient indications what he would have become if he had had his own way in any considerable degree; absolutely to have his own way is not given to child or boy or man.

Authority then under some conditions or other—authority, as distinct from dominion—is implied in the existence of fathers; its correlative, *Obedience,* as distinct from mere subjection, implied in the existence of sons. But I told those who listened to my lectures on the Conscience that Authority has been said to be another name for punishment; Obedience another name for the dread of punishment. I shall not repeat the objections which I made to that theory when I noticed it before. I wish you to reflect now that it is the best—the only— explanation which can be given of these two words and of all which they express, supposing the fact of the paternal and filial relation is overlooked, supposing it is not taken to lie at the root of human society. Then whatever difficulty there may be in settling who is to be the punisher; whatever difficulty in deciding the offences which he shall punish, or how his punishment shall produce any effect except that of shewing how strong he is, and how weak the subject of his punishment is; I yet frankly admit that the theory must be swallowed whole. The effort may be a difficult one, it may cause some disgust; but it must be made. On the other hand, if we assume the fatherly relation, the education which I have said is implied in it will include Punishment as one of its subordinate instruments. The punishment instead of being identical with authority will only have the slightest influence so far as the recognition of Authority precedes it. Obedience instead of being the dread of punishment may be destroyed by that dread; will only be promoted by punishment so far as disobedience is felt to be an irregular disorderly condition which inevitably draws punishment after it. How to temper punishment so that it may be a witness for authority, and may never express mere dominion—so that it may foster obedience and not stimulate disobedience—is one of the hardest problems of practical education upon which we cannot too earnestly seek for light.

If it is a maxim of advanced Philosophy that Authority is identical with Punishment, one cannot wonder that it should be proclaimed, as it so often is, to be the foe of Reason. Suppose parental authority to be, as I have maintained it is, the very ground of Education, we must believe that through it all the faculties and energies which belong to a child are developed, that without it they would lie dormant. The obedience of a son is shewn in receiving those influences and impressions from a father's authority which most tend to quicken his own activity. No true father wishes his son to present an image of his opinions. He knows that the copy will be probably a caricature; that an echo conveys the sound not the sense of the original voice. On the other hand, the son whose opinions are most unlike his father's has often learnt most from him; in his latest years he probably discovers how much the father's authority has helped to mould the very convictions which appear to separate them.

I have spoken specially of the father. In him most obviously dwells the authority which stamps itself on the life of a man. But the union of the mother's influence with the father's *helps* to distinguish authority from dominion; as well as to counteract any disposition which there might be in the male parent to demand of his son mere agreement with his conclusions. She never can regard a child as a possession; she never can appeal exclusively or mainly to his intellect. The authority is not weakened by her co-operation; it is divested of its inhumanity; it is made effectual for the whole of the child's existence, not for one section of it. I of course refer most to those cases in which there *is* co-operation— in which the two influences are not adverse. Even where they are so, we may clearly discern, by the disorder which the collision produces, what the true order of the household is.

I can never forget one sentence of Mr. Buckle, which I confess I prize above all his statistics and all his theories on civilisation. He said that no mere arguments for Immortality had ever had much weight with him, but that when he remembered his mother he could not disbelieve in it. Such a testimony from a man who so greatly exalted the Intellect, who in words at least treated Morality as poor in comparison with it, seems to me of unspeakable worth. It contains, as I think, a most pregnant hint concerning the parental relation generally, specially concerning the maternal side of it. I have said that the mother purifies and expands the principle of authority, therefore gives to the principle of obedience a simpler and higher character. Still more does she impart the true form to that feeling of *Succession* which this relation brings to light; the feeling which leads the father to rejoice in the prospect of a race. In later times—in developed societies— nay, to a very considerable extent in all societies—this anticipation becomes connected with thoughts of what the father shall leave behind him, of what the son shall inherit. The joy of the poor man who has nothing to leave, in the sight or hope of those who shall bear his name in after days, seems to a luxurious age incomprehensible; so much do questions of property in such an age blend themselves with the domestic felicity which they mar. But, as Mr. Buckle felt in his own case, there is something much more direct, more simply human in a mother's thought about the child that shall live after her; one wholly apart from any dream of possession, one that links itself directly with *personal* immortality. That thought communicates itself to the child; in the strictest sense he inherits it: not through a dogma which she has taught him but through his sense of a relation to her the thought becomes one of which he cannot divest himself.

But if this paternal relation, and this ēthos of Authority and Obedience which responds to it, are really what I have supposed, must there not be some signs of their effect upon the history of Mankind? Can it be only in particular families where the relation is exhibited amidst great varieties and contradictions that we are to realise the effect? You have a right to make this demand on me. If I cannot meet it satisfactorily, I shall admit that my method is a false one; that I am seeking to detect the rudiments of a Social Morality where they are not to be found.

Mr. Buckle draws a very striking distinction between the nations which have succumbed to the powers of Nature and those which have risen above them and defied them. He distinguishes also between those which have been the victims of superstitious fancies about the unseen world, and those which have been able to grapple with hard material facts. Suppose I found amongst the races whom he has disparaged on either of these grounds, instances of a Society which had been shaped and moulded by the authority of the father—whose history and legislation through a number of ages were stamped and penetrated with it—I might be answered "That is just what we should have expected. Such a race was likely enough to have an inordinate appreciation of domestic bonds, especially to regard with great awe the paternal relation." But suppose the people to whom I referred for my example was the one which had most courageously confronted the powers of Nature, and had overcome them, which had shewn the most capacity for dealing with material facts—with the prose of existence; suppose it deserved Mr. Carlyle's praise of being an eminently "thrifty people;" then it might perhaps afford a fair test of my doctrine. You will easily imagine that I am thinking of the Roman State, and of the influence which the *Patria Potestas* exercised over its institutions.

Certainly if we trusted to our schoolboy impressions that would seem a strong case in point. But those impressions may deceive us. Virgil has built Rome upon legends which modern criticism has exposed. Why should we attach any worth to his notion that piety to a father had more to do with the foundation or preservation of the city than its fancied Trojan ancestry? Why should the name of fathers given to senators, or of father to the Lord of the Capitol, be more than fictions? Why should we endow these names with any significance?

I can answer these questions best by referring you to a book containing the ripest modern scholarship applied to the examination of Roman Institutions. Sir H. S. Maine has assuredly no prejudices in favour of the stories which were always suspected, and which our age generally discredits. He has not written on Social Morality, but expressly on Ancient Law. In his exceedingly able book he has discussed at considerable length the subject of the *Patria Potestas*. What he says about its influence on the latest Jurisprudence of Rome and of Modern Europe, is highly important. What he says about the grounds of it, and of the necessity of looking for it in a Society antecedent to all legal forms, concerns our present purpose still more.

One or two short passages will explain Mr. Maine's view of the bearing of the Patria Potestas *on* Roman Law: "It may be shewn I think that the Family as held together by the Patria Potestas is the *nidus* out of which the entire Law of *Persons* has germinated." (*Ancient Law*, p. 152.)

He expresses this opinion though he has taken pains to shew how much the power of the Father over the *person* of the Son, which existed at one period, was modified by later legislation or by the force of opinion. "But," he remarks (p. 141), though "the power over the person may have been latterly nominal, the whole tenor of the extant Roman Jurisprudence testifies that the father's rights over the son's *Property* were exercised to the full extent to which they were sanctioned by law." The law of *Persons*, the law of *Property*, then, were both in the most marvellous way affected by this institution, and the habits of the people as much as either. He goes on:—

"There is nothing to astonish us in the latitude of these rights when they first shew themselves. The ancient law of Rome forbade the Children under Power to hold property apart from their parent, or (we should rather say) never contemplated the possibility of their claiming a second ownership. The father was entitled to take the whole of the son's acquisitions, and to enjoy the benefit of his contracts without being entangled in any compensating liability. So much as this we should expect from the constitution of the earliest Roman society, for we can hardly form a notion of the primitive family group unless we suppose that its members brought their earnings of all kinds into the common stock, while they were unable to bind it by improvident individual engagements. The true enigma of the Patria Potestas does not reside here, but in the slowness with which these privileges of the parent were curtailed, and in the circumstance that, before they were seriously diminished, the whole civilised world was brought within their sphere." (Pp. 141, 142.)

To what does this Institution point, fixed as it was in the heart of the strongest of all commonwealths, the one which has done so much to mould the Society of modern Europe? A longer extract is necessary that you may understand what our author teaches us upon the subject.

"Archaic Law is full, in all its provinces, of clearest indications that society in primitive times was not what it is assumed to be at present, a collection of *individuals*. In fact, and in the view of the men who composed it, it was *an aggrega-*

tion of families. The contrast may be most forcibly expressed by saying that the *unit* of an ancient society was the Family, of a modern society the Individual. We must be prepared to find in ancient law all the consequences of this difference. It is so framed as to be adjusted to a system of small independent corporations. It is therefore scanty, because it is supplemented by the despotic commands of the heads of households. It is ceremonious, because the transactions to which it pays regard resemble international concerns much more than the quick play of inter-course between individuals. Above all it has a peculiarity of which the full im-portance cannot be shewn at present. It takes a view of *life* wholly unlike any which appears in developed jurisprudence. Corporations *never die*, and accord-ingly primitive law considers the entities with which it deals, i.e. patriarchal or family groups, as perpetual and inextinguishable. This view is closely allied to the peculiar aspect under which, in very ancient times, moral attributes present themselves. The moral elevation and moral debasement of the individual appear to be confounded with, or postponed to, the merits and offences of the group to which the individual belongs. If the community sins, its guilt is much more than the sum of the offences committed by its members; the crime is a corporate act, and extends in its consequences to many more persons than have shared in its ac-tual perpetration. If, on the other hand, the individual is conspicuously guilty, it is his children, his kinsfolk, his tribes-men, or his fellow-citizens who suffer with him, and sometimes for him. It thus happens that the ideas of moral responsi-bility and retribution often seem to be more clearly realized at very ancient than at more advanced periods, for, as the family group is immortal, and its liability to punishment indefinite, the primitive mind is not perplexed by the questions which become troublesome as soon as the individual is conceived as altogether separate from the group. One step in the transition from the ancient and simple view of the matter to the theological or metaphysical explanations of later days is marked by the early Greek notion of an inherited curse. The bequest received by his posterity from the original criminal was not a liability to punishment, but a liability to the commission of fresh offences which drew with them a condign ret-ribution; and thus the responsibility of the family was reconciled with the newer phase of thought which limited the consequences of crime to the person of the actual delinquent. . . . In most of the Greek states and in Rome there long re-mained the vestiges of an ascending series of groups out of which the State was at first constituted. The Family, House, and Tribe of the Romans may be taken as the type of them, and they are so described to us that we can scarcely help con-ceiving them as a system of concentric circles which have gradually expanded from the same point. The elementary group is the Family, connected by com-mon subjection to the highest male ascendant. The aggregation of the Families forms the Gens or House. The aggregation of Houses makes the Tribe. The ag-gregation of Tribes constitutes the Commonwealth. Are we at liberty to follow these indications, and to lay down that the commonwealth is a collection of per-sons united by common descent from the progenitor of an original family? Of this we may at least be certain, that all ancient societies regarded themselves as having proceeded from one original stock, and even laboured under an incapacity for comprehending any reason except this for their holding together in political union. The history of political ideas begins, in fact, with the assumption that kinship in blood is the sole possible ground of community in political functions; nor is there any of those subversions of feeling, which we term emphatically revolutions, so startling and so complete as the change which is accomplished when some other principle—such as that, for instance, of *local contiguity*—establishes itself for the first time as the basis of common political action. It may be affirmed then of early commonwealths that their citizens considered all the groups in which they claimed membership to be founded on common lineage. What was obviously true of the Family was believed to be true first of the House, next of the Tribe, lastly of the State." (Pp. 126–129.)

Sir Henry Maine goes on to explain, as Niebuhr had done, that the supposition of an ancestry was often a gratuitous one, "that men of alien descent were grated into the original brotherhood," that legal fictions were invented to connect the old feelings of kinsmanship with the later principle of *contiguity in place*. To these remarks I must recur in the second part of these lectures, when I arrive at that period of social development in which Sir H. Maine is most interested, the strictly legal period. I must however give you the words in which he sums up his observations on the Family.

"The Family then is the type of an archaic society in all the modifications which it was capable of assuming; but the family here spoken of is not exactly the family as understood by a modern. In order to reach the ancient conception we must give to our modern ideas an important extension and an important limitation. We must look on the family as constantly enlarged by the absorption of strangers within its circle, and we must try to regard the fiction of adoption as so closely simulating the reality of kinship that neither law nor opinion makes the slightest difference between a real and an adoptive connexion. On the other hand, the persons theoretically amalgamated into a family by their common descent are practically held together by common obedience to their highest living ascendant, the father, grandfather, great-grandfather. The patriarchal authority of a chieftain is as necessary an ingredient in the notion of the family group as the fact (or assumed fact) of its having sprung from his loins; and hence we must understand that if there be any persons who however truly included in the brotherhood by virtue of their blood-relationship, have nevertheless *de facto* withdrawn themselves from the empire of its ruler, they are always, in the beginnings of law, considered as lost to the family. It is this patriarchal aggregate—the modern family thus cut down on one side and extended on the other—which meets us on the threshold of primitive jurisprudence. Older probably than the State, the Tribe, and the House, it left traces of itself on private law long after the House and the Tribe had been forgotten, and long after consanguinity had ceased to be associated with the composition of States. It will be found to have stamped itself on all the great departments of jurisprudence, and may be detected, I think, as the true source of many of their most important and most durable characteristics. At the outset, the peculiarities of law in its most ancient state lead us irresistibly to the conclusion that it took precisely the same view of the family group which is taken of individual men by the systems of rights and duties now prevalent throughout Europe. There are societies open to our observation at this very moment whose laws and usages can scarcely be explained unless they are supposed never to have emerged from this primitive condition; but in communities more fortunately circumstanced the fabric of jurisprudence fell gradually to pieces, and if we carefully observe the disintegration we shall perceive that it took place principally in those portions of each system which were most deeply affected by the primitive conception of the family. In one all-important instance, that of the Roman law, the change was effected so slowly, that from epoch to epoch we can observe the line and direction which it followed, and can even give some idea of the ultimate result to which it was tending. And, in pursuing this last inquiry, we need not suffer ourselves to be stopped by the imaginary barrier which separates the modern from the ancient world. For one effect of that mixture of refined Roman law with primitive barbaric usage, which is known to us by the deceptive name of feudalism, was to revive many features of archaic jurisprudence which had died out of the Roman world, so that the decomposition which had seemed to be over commenced again, and to some extent is still proceeding." (Pp. 133–135.)

The more you reflect on these passages, the more you will perceive that what I have assumed for obvious reasons to be the right chronology of our own lives is also the right chronology of human society. Sir H. Maine's opinion upon this subject is very distinctly expressed in an earlier passage which I passed over that I might not distract your thoughts from the evidence concerning Roman history, and that I might not take advantage of any apparent confirmation of my statements in the sacred records.

"The effect of the evidence derived from comparative jurisprudence is to establish that view of the primeval condition of the human race which is known as the Patriarchal Theory. There is no doubt, of course, that this theory was originally based on the Scriptural history of the Hebrew patriarchs in Lower Asia; but, as has been explained already, its connexion with Scripture rather militated than otherwise against its reception as a complete theory, since the majority of the inquirers who till recently addressed themselves with most earnestness to the colligation of social phenomena, were either influenced by the strongest prejudice against Hebrew antiquities or by the strongest desire to construct their system without the assistance of religious records. Even now there is perhaps a disposition to undervalue these accounts, or rather to decline generalising from them, as forming part of the traditions of a Semitic people. It is to be noted, however, that the legal testimony comes nearly exclusively from the institutions of societies belonging to the Indo-European stock, the Romans, Hindus, and Sclavonians supplying the greater part of it; and indeed the difficulty, at the present stage of the inquiry, is to know where to stop, to say of what races of men it is *not* allowable to lay down that the society in which they are united was originally organised on the patriarchal model." (Pp. 122, 123.)

Of this (so-called) patriarchal theory I have said nothing, because I wished to rest my case on the evidence of facts with which we are all familiar. Those facts, as I may try to shew you hereafter, help to explain some of the legal fictions of which Sir H. Maine speaks, for they tell us why of necessity the relations of the family must interpenetrate the later order of the Nation, and impress their own character upon it.

Leaving these more general remarks, much as they concern our subject, and recurring to the particular Roman Institution about which we first consulted Sir H. Maine, I think he has made it clear that the conclusions suggested by our ordinary reading will endure strict investigation. Virgil was not mistaken in his belief that the ground of his nation's stability lay in the reverence for fathers; that the authority of the Consul rested ultimately on the father's authority; the obedience of the soldier on the obedience of the child. The power of the Roman over material things must be traced to the same source. It does not appear that any peculiarities in the atmosphere of Rome enabled those who dwelt in it to make roads and drain marshes. The habit of obedience, grounded upon a personal relation, made them victorious over things, victorious over the men who wanting that obedience stooped to things. It is delightful to find a court poet still retaining his interest in the growth of vines and the assemblies of bees: it is more delightful to find him still hoping for the restoration of manners in Romans through the revived recollection of the sacredness which they once attached to the paternal name.

Sir H. Maine laments his inability to trace as accurately as he would wish the alterations in the *Patria Potestas* in its different periods; how it was modified by laws or circumstances or opinions. Such a historical survey, were it possible, would I believe throw a clear light upon that distinction on which I have insisted between Authority and Dominion. To the paternal *authority* Rome owed its strength and freedom. The claim of paternal Dominion resulted in Imperial Tyranny. In the third part of these lectures I shall have much to say respecting the influence of the paternal relation, and the Authority which assumed it as its foundation, upon the manners of the modern world. Here I will only observe that though the institutions of Rome especially testify to the authority of the father or his dominion, the influence of the mother is never forgotten in its most characteristic legends, in its most trustworthy records. They shew how deeply the most masculine of all Societies was indebted to the female for the preservation, because for the softening and the humanising, of its strength; how much the degradation of the female was involved in its degradation.

While I speak of this combined influence on the most organic of all commonwealths I am reminded of a poem which turns on the density of the most inorganic of all tribes. You will guess that I allude to the *Spanish Gypsy* of George Eliot. That remarkable and beautiful drama has been represented by some of its critics as an extravagant testimony to the influence of Race in overcoming the effects of education, in breaking the chains of a passionate attachment. To me it

reads much more as a testimony to the might of paternal authority. With what
admirable truth the struggle of Fedalma against that might is told; how every
feeling that is deepest as well as tenderest rebels against the inexorable command
of the outcast and prisoner who claims her as his daughter; most of you well
know. But the victory was complete. The lover is given up for Zarca; the heart-
broken girl undertakes the task of which she despairs.

> Father, my soul is weak, the mist of tears
> Still rises to my eyes and hides the goal
> Which to your undimmed sight is clear and changeless.
> But if I cannot plant resolve on hope,
> I will stand firm on certainty of woe.
> I choose the ill that is most like to end
> With my poor being. Hopes have precarious life.
> They are oft blighted, withered, snapped sheer off
> In vigorous growth and turned to rottenness.
> But faithfulness can feed no suffering
> And knows no disappointment. Trust in me!
> If it were needed, this poor trembling hand
> Should grasp the torch—strive not to let it fall,
> Though it were burning down close to my flesh,
> No beacon lighted yet; through the damp dark
> I should still hear the cry of grasping swimmers.
> Father, I will be true!
>
> *Spanish Gypsy*, Book III, p. 253

That is certainly the sublime of obedience, scarcely conceivable in a Roman
son, possible perhaps for the daughter of a Gypsy. Beneath the profound melan-
choly of this passage and of the whole poem, I cannot but fancy I see a glim-
mering of promise. It may be that abject races, which cannot rise to a new life
through the influence of Joint Stock Companies and competitive Examinations,
may yet have seeds in them which a domestic culture might call forth. It may be
that races perishing in a worn-out civilisation may awake at the stern summons
of a father's voice coming to them softened and deepened through notes of feminine devotion and self-sacrifice.

NATIONAL MORALITY: LAW*

I spoke in the last Lecture of the School as the passage out of domestic life into
the life of neighbourhood, which is also the individual or personal life. A line
from George Herbert, which I quoted in a former course, defines this transition,
"Then Schoolmasters deliver us to *Laws*." The school is the preparation for

---

*From *Social Morality* (1869; London: Macmillan and Co., 1886), Lecture 8, part 2, 119–32.

National Life. When we contemplate men in a Nation, we contemplate them as under a Law. The expressions are interchangeable.

Under a Law, you observe; that is the marvel we have to consider. There may be a great many theories about the making or unmaking or remaking of laws; who are to be the agents in making or unmaking or remaking; what principals employ the agents. But apart from all these disputes, there is for each of you and for me this fact. We find a Law; it claims us as its subjects; we learn by degrees that we *are* subject to it. That is a very great discovery. We are slow in arriving at it; very slow in confessing the full force of it. Just so far as it is brought home to me I know that I am a distinct person; that I must answer for myself; that you cannot answer for me. I perceive also that each of you is a distinct person; that each of you must answer for himself.

That is the effect of Law; that effect warrants me in connecting it with Social Morality. If you recollect the principles which I laid down in my first Lecture, and which appeared to be recognised by writers of the most opposite opinions, you may suppose that I have nothing to do with Law; that Law and Morality stand wholly apart from each other. For I said that the Moralist is primarily occupied with a certain State or Character; only with acts as they exhibit a character. And I think, as most people think, that Law is chiefly concerned with Acts, that it cannot undertake the task of forming the character from which acts proceed. It forbids murder and robbery; if it tries to produce good temper or charity it will try in vain. I will go a step further. If it tries to make us just it will try in vain. Justice, as we shall find, is nearer of kin to Law than Charity is. But Justice, like Charity, is a Disposition or Habit; and of Dispositions and Habits the Law cannot take cognisance. The Lawgiver may find good habits to be very necessary. He may inquire earnestly how they can be formed. He will certainly be compelled to own that he cannot form them.

I find myself under a Law. A Law, what is that? I have been used to hear commands from a Parent. I have learnt to recognise his authority over me, to distinguish it from force. When he tried to compel me by force I could resist. His authority was a subtler thing. I did not know exactly with what weapon to strive against that. But here is no parent. It is a command which has issued from I know not where. He who repeats it to me, he who enforces it upon me, does not pretend that he has invented it. He assures me that he has not; that he is as much bound by it as I am. He has the same facilities—probably much greater facilities for breaking it than I have. He says he *must* not break it. What is this *must* not?

When Bellario, the jurist of Padua, sent the most charming of messengers to represent him at Venice in the great cause of Shylock against Antonio, she said, having heard of the bond,

Then must the Jew be merciful.

A harsh voice answered,

On what compulsion *must* I? tell me that.

And Portia, after making her splendid speech on the quality of mercy, admitted in her legal character that Antonio must pay the penalty, that the State of Venice would not be safe if Covenants were not observed to the letter. Here is the true faith of a legal, commercial Community, such as Venice was. There is an Obligation upon each individual of the State; there is an Obligation upon the State itself. Nothing can break or set aside either. Against the most popular and beloved citizen it must be maintained, in favour of the most detested. The position is all the stronger, because it comes forth in a poetical legend, not in a legal treatise. Shakespeare adopted it; for it was the only maxim upon which English Society, in the days of Elizabeth, could stand.

Very mysterious assuredly this sense of Law is. It breaks through such prejudices as those which surrounded the person of the Jew in the middle ages. It sets at naught the dignity of birth, the advantages of position. It mocks even the ecclesiastical indulgences which appealed to a power above Law. I cannot explain it away by any philosophical phrases. I can merely bid you take notice of the facts. They are, you see, vulgar facts. I have purposely dwelt upon the commercial character of Venice, that you may connect this authority of Law with the incidents of property. It springs out of no dreams of sentiment; rather, it scatters all such dreams. A bond! a contract! what a commonplace thing that is. Very commonplace, referring, in this case, to a loan by one merchant to another; enforced by the penalty of a pound of flesh. But the loan did not create the reverence for the Law which protects it; the penalty did not create it. The loan could not have been, the penalty would have been nothing, but for the sense in the mind of Christian and Jew that there was a Law, that it was mightier than both.

Now no sort of moral sympathy was produced either in Christian or Jew by this Law. The Christian did not spit on the Jew less for it, did not call him less foul names for it. The Jew did not hate the Christian less for it, did not the less desire to ruin either his faith or him. Nevertheless the Law spoke to both; threatened both; protected both. Each had an interest in twisting it; the Christians being in the ascendant had the power to twist it. Still they bowed to it. The Jew feeling himself a proscribed man could yet evoke the Law of the very people which proscribed him. They might interpret it falsely, they might exalt force against it; but if they did they were overthrowing their State; that State stood by Law, meant the triumph of Law over force.

Therefore though this mighty and mysterious Law is incapable of moulding the mind or character of any individual, it has *this* faculty. It makes him feel that he is tied and bound, that, whether he likes it or not, there is a yoke over him to which his neck must adjust itself. There is an *obligation* upon him; no other word but that expresses his position; he can substitute no other for it. "Why am I obliged? Why may I not have my own way? Who obliges me?" All these questions I may ask. And I may find answers to them, such as these: "It is the will of a Majority of these among whom I am dwelling." Yes! and supposing the Majority should agree to dispense with all Law; should say, "We will have nothing to do with it," what then? There would be an Anarchy. Just so. And if in the midst of that Anarchy some two or three should proclaim the dignity of Law, and should say, "We at least will obey it," those one or two would constitute a State, and till the Majority joined with them, the Majority would be no State at all. You may say again, "The penalty of violating the Law leads me to observe it." Possibly; but who attached the penalty to the Law? who keeps it attached? If the majority do not choose to enforce the penalty, as in the case I have supposed, what will the penalty avail for any individual? We may go round and round in this circle; we shall find that at last we take for granted the Law, and an obligation in us to keep the law; that neither the Will of the Majority nor any terrors for transgression mean anything unless I assume something which governs the Will of the Majority, something which it as well as every individual can transgress.

Looking at Law simply as Law its action upon the members of a nation is this. It makes each of them aware of an obligation; it makes each of them aware that there is a line which he has an inclination to pass over, and which he is not to pass over; it awakens in him the feeling of a wrong which he may do to another, of a wrong which another may do to him. Taken by itself Law awakens me to these convictions; that is its office. But Law cannot be taken by itself. It finds me one of a family. It is unable to dissolve any of the relations in which I exist before I became aware of its claims. All of us to whom the Law speaks are sons. It does not add anything to the affection of the son for the father, or the father for the son. It cannot call forth an affection which does not exist. But it stamps an obligation upon the Relation. There is something which every son owes to his father and mother because they are his father and mother. So again, it stamps an obligation on marriage. It does not form the union; it cannot beget any trust in those who are united. But it guards every marriage-bed. It denounces adultery. The movement onwards into the age of Law—revolution as it is—yet gives all that preceded it a sanction. The Law takes under its care not only me and my neighbour, but all the conditions under which it finds me and my neighbour.

The change even in this respect is very great, the progress very remarkable, though it seems to be only the ratification of that which was already established. It is one thing for a man to feel a tie to his parent or his wife; it is quite another to contemplate that tie as one for his neighbour. The relation is not only for his household; it is for a multitude of households. And yet how clearly the individuality of Law makes itself manifest. Each man is taken apart from every other. Each one is met with a "Thou." The Law is over families, but it is addressed to every one who hears it separately, without reference to his ancestors or his descendants. The corporate feeling descends upon the Law, as Sir H. Maine has shown so admirably, from the House; the Law accepts the legacy with some awkwardness; but its own formula excludes all participation in responsibilities, recognises each one as the doer of his own acts and the sufferer from them.

Does the Law then only confirm that which was already to some extent characteristic of the Family?

1. With respect to human life it introduces what must be called an altogether new conception, though one which does not really clash with older conceptions, but unfolds and deepens them. The life of the child, of the sister, of the wife, is bound up with the life of the father, of the brother, of the husband; the kinsman has a difficulty in contemplating it except as the life of a kinsman. The life of his ox, or his sheep, is also precious in his eyes; he may claim the power of taking it away for the food of his own household; but it is surely more precious than that of an invader from any other household. He has not yet learnt to distinguish the life of a man as such from the life of another animal. Both are contemplated domestically, if I may so speak. It is difficult to express oneself with perfect accuracy; as it is difficult to distinguish the streaks of dawn from the light of the risen sun. But there is a clear difference between the sense of the sacredness of a man's life, in a legal and in a merely patriarchal community. The difference arises from the growth of a consciousness that a man is not accidentally but essentially different from a beast; that men form a Society of which beasts are not a part. There may on this account be often less of humanity to animals in the more developed than in the more primitive Society; the Arab's care for his horse may be an example to those who have a sense of legal bonds to which he is a stranger. Apparent—nay real—retrogressions may accompany a veritable progress; they should not hinder us from recognising the distinction of the human life from the animal life as one of the greatest of all the blessings which Law confers on us.

2. As each man is brought forth into distinct prominence by the Law it becomes evident that he needs protection for something besides his bodily life. He has a reputation which may be injured; words can inflict a wound upon him as well as swords. That is a subject which we shall have to consider more particularly in the next lecture. I advert to it here because it denotes very remarkably what kind of advancement it is which I am describing. Each man acquires an importance in himself. Each man is obliged to recognise the importance of his neighbour to himself. An injury to character falls into the circle of positive acts of which the Law takes cognisance. Its function is not the least to mould a man's character but it can decree that his neighbour shall not interfere with this more than with his visible possessions.

3. The last sentence reminds me that I have not yet spoken of that which is in some respects the most important topic connected with the legal or national state as distinguished from the domestic. How can I dare to speak of *Property* in these terms when I have already treated of *Life*—emphatically of human life? I use this language precisely because I wish you to be aware of the transcendent superiority of Life to Property, and because there is the greatest fear that you may lose this feeling altogether if I am not careful in pointing to you how Law and Property are related to each other and what position Property assumes in the crisis of Society which I am now examining.

Two observations have presented themselves to us in the lectures on Domestic

Morality: one is that Property in its strict sense does not exist in the Family, that there is a common stock, which is vested in the father and is only dispersed among the children when the family is broken up; the other is that a craving for separate possession may be always traced among the members of a family and is the chief interruption of their fellowship. Now the Law by its primary condition of treating each man as separately responsible, though it cannot destroy the family relations, though it cannot more than to a certain point disturb the custom of succession or inheritance which it finds, yet does unquestionably give an altogether new weight to Property, does ratify the disposition of each man to say "This is mine." A Law attempting to create a Communism or assuming Communism as its basis is a contradiction in terms. It must recognise separate ownership; it must forbid each man to interfere with that which his neighbour owns.

This truth has impressed itself deeply upon the citizens of nations and the rulers of nations. With it has been combined the observation—brought home to them by accumulated evidence—that questions of property are those which disturb, more than most others, the peace and order of a community, tend specially to provoke assaults upon the life or reputation of its members. The inference seemed natural, "The main function of Law must be to grapple with these questions; to devise means for preventing the holders of property and the seekers of property from coming into collision with each other; to settle their disputes when they arise." And when legislators have found themselves defeated in their experiments for these purposes, even in those which seemed best contrived—suggested by the experience of practical men as well as the wisdom of philosophers—they have begun to think, "Law after all wants some support besides its own authority; whence must the support come?" The most popular answer has been, "It must come from a sense in the holders of property and the seekers of property, of that which is for their own interest. If they perceive *that* they will devise reasonable laws; they will know where it is best to dispense with Law." All this sounds very plausible. I do not say that it is only plausible. But you observe that it changes our position altogether. We thought Law was to guard property; to protect men from invading each other's property. Now it appears that property is to guard Law. The feelings, or if you will the intellectual perceptions, of men about what it is good for them to have and good for their neighbours to have are to prescribe what the Law shall be. I venture to think that those very facts which would be appealed to in favour of this doctrine directly confute it. The latest experience that I know of is that of the gold-diggers in California. The story is told at considerable length on the authority of an eye-witness in a chapter of Sir C. Dilke's *Greater Britain*. I wish you would read that chapter and consider it carefully. It shews unquestionably that a set of reckless vagabonds who had come from every country to seek for property, and who committed the most ferocious acts against each other in order to obtain it, were at first restrained by an extemporised Lynch Law, and at last became an orderly Society. Can we infer from these facts that the lust of gold suggests the policy of confining the lust within certain bounds? or may we rather conclude with Sir C. Dilke that a few people having the sense of Law derived from the traditions of a "law-governed" community were able at last to awe a multitude of ruffians much stronger than themselves—were able to call forth in the very people who were to be restrained—and whom mere force could not overcome,—the sense of an order which they must not transgress? Looked at in the last aspect I know of no recent record which is so cheering, none which throws a more brilliant light upon the testimonies and the beliefs of other days.

Turn back, for instance, from these recent facts to that splendid fiction of which I spoke before, a fiction embodying the principle that is hidden in a great many facts. The faith of Shylock in law—even a law which was to be administered by the Courts of Venice—strikes me as magnificent; it proves him to be the member of a race which, more than any other, has borne witness of Law, has diffused the reverence for Law through the nations of the West. He is sure that Law must somehow prevail; he recognises in a Christian who expounds it honestly "a Daniel come to judgment." If that had been all, his character would be not ignominious but sublime. What makes it ignominious? He regards Law only as an instrument for securing his property. He is not without family affection, but he cannot separate his ducats from his daughter. There is the reverse of the medal; there is the mean Mammom worshipper. The two tempers may dwell in the same man; because there is a deadly war within him; because hostile principles are struggling for the mastery of him. But the craving for Property will never beget reverence for Law. And the Law, instead of fostering his covetousness, will make the man conscious of it, will make him know how much it interferes with his submission to that which in his heart he honours most.

4. That is another of those great functions which Law performs for morality— functions all the more valuable because they prove how utterly unable it is to make us moral. The Law, taking each of us apart, treating each man as an individual, brings him to perceive what there is in that very individuality which leads him to struggle with Law, to be at war with Society. He wants something for himself; he wants something which is his neighbour's. The Law which forbids him to meddle with another's property shews him that he has a *wish* to meddle with it, leads him to doubt if that wish can be separated from himself. That makes Law so terrible—not its punishment for any specific transgression, which he need not incur, which he could easily endure; but the detection in him of that which appears to be hopelessly at variance with the condition under which he does exist and must exist. The sense of obligation to his neighbour ends in the discovery of an intense dislike to the obligation, of a passionate longing to be free from it; while at the same time he eagerly insists that his neighbour is obliged to him; he must have the forfeit of *his* bond.

Were this the only effect of Law, or were there nothing to qualify it, we might shrink from the national state as from one that only lays upon us a heavy burden of which in the earlier stages of life we had no experience. No doubt each step as we advance does make us more aware of that which we have to lift; *this* stage teaches us that the heaviest weight which a man has to bear is himself. That is surely a hard lesson if there comes with it no promise of a way in which he may throw off himself. He has had hints upon that subject in his previous experience. Each family relation has said to him something about the possibility of losing himself in another; has taught him that he only realises a blessing when he confers it. This remembrance is not enough for his present growth; his personal distinctness has been discovered to him; he cannot merely fall back upon domestic sympathies. But they may remain to illuminate the new road which he has entered; there may still be a way, by which he can lose himself and so find himself.

In the mean time the Law does not only bring to him the conviction that there is something wrong in him; something very close to him, a part of himself, if not his very self, from which he needs to be emancipated. There can be no Wrong if there is not a Right; he cannot be unjust to his neighbour or his neighbour to him, if there is not some justice which is over them both. The sense of being under a Law forces that belief upon us. We may explain it away afterwards. Philosophers may shew us that we have been misled in the use of the word "justice," or that it can be resolved into elements altogether unlike those of which we have supposed it to consist. For this we must be prepared. But though the explanation may remove the impression which Law has made upon us, that is the impression. That is what it has made upon all nations. When they have been submissive to this Law it has been because they took it to be what they called just, when they have protested against it they have named it unjust. Wise men may expose the folly of this vulgar speech; but that it is this kind wherever nations exist, there is no question. That fact is all I am concerned with at present. I am considering the operation of Law upon us; if its operation is to deceive us, still I am bound to notice the deception. Many acts may be deemed wrong in one place which are not deemed wrong in another; many acts may be praised here which are blamed there. But the epithets are given, the praise and blame are bestowed. "Ah, but perhaps wrongly." Perhaps so; but you are resorting to the very word which you wish to banish from our discourse.

Justice has unquestionably a relation to law which mercy or charity has not. But as I said at the beginning of this Lecture, that Law could as little produce habits of Justice as habits of Mercy, so I say at the end of it that there is a sense in which the formula of Law may be applied to Mercy. "Then *must* the Jew be merciful" was Portia's language. She spoke as a woman, doubtless, but the phraseology of her adopted character suited well with her own. She felt that there is an obligation to shew mercy. I do not imagine we shall ever shew much if we think otherwise. Sentiment is but a weak support for one part of morality or another. It must rest at last on a Command. Whence that Command issues, why it must enjoin Mercy, is a question for a future Lecture.

UNIVERSAL MORALITY:
THE MODERN CONCEPTION OF HUMANITY*

Many writers on the French Revolution have maintained that the two cries for Liberty and Equality interfered with each other, that the destruction of Orders was the preparation for the Empire, and therefore for the loss of Freedom. It may be a question whether the Orders had not destroyed themselves before the voice of any popular assembly declared them to be no more; otherwise I can have no objection to a remark which is so much in accordance with those which I made respecting the dissolution of the Roman Republic. But for my present purpose it is of more importance to inquire how the third cry for Fraternity affected both the others. So far as Fraternity meant the union of all nations, the first Napoleon might boast that he had accomplished what the Assemblies had only decreed. French, Spaniards, Austrians, Prussians, Swiss, all were comprehended in his embrace; if Russia and England refused it, that was the fault of their exclusiveness; he would have cordially hugged them both. But Fraternity did not mean only or chiefly the removal of the barriers which language or customs or laws had raised between the different portions of mankind. It meant first of all a union for Frenchmen. Other nations might become brothers. France should set them the example, should shew them under what conditions Brotherhood was possible. These conditions it was evident were not exhibited by the Empire. If that had not quite satisfied the demand for Equality by putting down old distinctions to raise up others in their place, if it had met the appetite for liberty by establishing a marvellous and mysterious Police, it had certainly done nothing to make citizens feel themselves members of a Family. Was the conscription the sign of their adoption into it?

But the craving which this word expressed was too deep a one to be extinguished because rulers, the most popular and triumphant, failed to provide any food for it. Philosophers, theoretical and practical, girded themselves to the task. It might have been foreseen that they would be most numerous and most comprehensive in the country which had been giving birth to the Revolution. All those of whom I spoke in the last Lecture were brought up in a Protestant atmosphere, under the influence of its individualising tendencies. Some, perhaps all of them, might be provoked to a reaction against these tendencies, might strive to throw them off. Hobbes and Hume both lived much in France, and for different reasons corresponding to the difference of their characters preferred French to English Society. Yet every one, from the philosopher of Malmesbury to the philosopher of Königsberg, shewed that he could not begin from Society, that whether he talked of Motives or of Ideals or of Consequences or of pure Duty or even of Sympathy, he was still, consciously or unconsciously, contemplating each man in himself before he contemplated a body of men. The air

---

*From *Social Morality* (1869; London: Macmillan and Co., 1886), Lecture 19, part 7, 352–70.

which Frenchmen breathed was of a most different quality. They were social by
instinct, social by tradition, social by the faith in which they had been educated,
social by the influences of the Revolution which had cast off that faith. There had
been a Calvinism in France which had added, I conceive, much to its health and
vigour. The desertion of it by Henri IV, the persecution of it by Louis XIV,
helped to destroy the moral fibre of the land. But it was an alien plant in the soil.
The efforts of kings to uproot it would have availed little if the heart of the people had cherished it. But unbelief and belief, the contempt of the *esprits forts,* the
passionate zeal for Reform in the body of the Nation, seemed equally to stand
apart from what we might suppose would have supplied some justification to the
one, and have helped forward the other. The French love of organisation was impatient of any practice or any theory which did not promise first and above all
things combination and fellowship.

Such a disposition offered a great encouragement to the champions of Catholicism who had seen it trampled down in the revolutionary fury. When that fury
had spent itself there was sure to be a cry for some constructive power, some fus-
ing principle, which might bind the fragments of Society together again. The
more worldly Churchmen might accept the doubtful compliment of Napoleon,
that the Papacy was an institution which it would be worth while to create if it
did not exist; the religious would expect it to prove its unfailing vitality, to shew
that no human hands could have created it. Jesuitism,—as a protest against all
tendencies to separation, in behalf of a mysterious unity,—could not despair of
being welcomed back from the banishment to which the past age had consigned
it. The name of Brotherhood was itself mediaeval. The Church had called religious Brotherhoods into existence, which had ministered in many ways to order
and civilisation. Trade Brotherhoods had been produced by the same impulse,
had borne the same stamp. Might not the watchword of the Revolution be re-
claimed by ecclesiastical wisdom, be consecrated to an ecclesiastical use?

Though such thoughts might hover about a number of minds, might penetrate into some hearts, the Papacy was evidently too much terrified by the destructive symbol—too much inclined to suspect mischief in all who gave it even
a half spiritual sense—to seek help from popular sympathy, when the old Governments were restored. Its simple policy was to ally itself with them; to discourage all associations which savoured of freemasonry; to treat the protection
and preservation of property as the supreme interest of the Church no less than
of particular States. If the States felt that it was performing this function for them,
they might be willing to keep down heretics within their borders; to enforce, as
far as they could, reverence for the Priesthood.

But a higher interest than this it was felt must be vindicated by some Society,
whether it was called the Church or by any other name. The idea of a Brotherhood for men as men which had taken hold of France if not Europe at the Revolution, could not be realized by institutions which merely contemplated possessors, and sought to secure them in their possessions. Wherever there had been

the conception of a Universal Society by the most exalted philosophers, by the simplest peasants, a certain Communism had mingled with it. States might regard the word and that which it represented with dread; might resolve to keep it at a distance. But were they not narrow in their objects; tied by traditions and genealogies and class distinctions? Were they for ever to divide the world?

If I tried to notice in this Lecture even a few of the schemes to which this prolific thought has given rise I should do both them and you injustice. I might lead you to think of them as merely visionary when they were the result of much practical observation and experience. I might exhibit some of their weak points when it would do us much more good to perceive where they were strong. I might connect them with titles which have become opprobrious when the objects of their propounders were benevolent, when they desired to promote order not confusion. I would only make these two remarks, which you may find useful. The first is that for the reasons I have given already the most carefully elaborated of these schemes will be found to have French authors, though no doubt opportunities have been afforded by the freer life of Great Britain for practical experiments limited in extent, but of great interest and value—e.g. that of Mr. Owen at Lanark. The second is that beneath all the schemes, great or small, however diverse in character and design, lies the conviction that somehow or other there must be, or there must be formed, a Human Family. If only a few compose it, still it must in virtue of its principles be capable of embracing all men.

I am thus drawn on to consider what I have called in the title of this Lecture the modern conception of *Humanity*. Inattention to the nomenclature of different periods or, what means the same, to the nomenclature of the most eminent thinkers in different periods, often leads us into fatal misapprehensions respecting their distinctive qualities. We may easily confound the *Human Nature* which was the favourite and common subject of study in the last age with the *Humanity* which has begun to be so much spoken of in ours. If we do, I suspect we shall not appreciate the step which we have taken in advance of our immediate predecessors; we shall understand even less where we stand in relation to those who were before them. We shall be embarrassed with schools, each of great historical and even present importance, but partial and contradictory; when we might ascend through them to a living and practical moral ground.

The disciples of M. Comte maintain that it is he who has brought us to this higher ground, that he has interpreted the earlier experiments of this century, and has embodied them in a comprehensive system. I am not at all anxious to dispute these claims, or to set up any rival who can challenge a share of them for himself. I assume that his philosophy does represent the modern conception of Humanity. Probably it is nowhere so completely expressed as in his writings. He has explained to our generation the desire of former teachers to build up a Universal Society, and a Morality which should be adapted to it; their eagerness to associate this Human Society and Human Morality with physical studies; their impatience of theology and its traditions and associations; their resolution that whether or not it was necessary in other days it should be banished from the new age. It seems to me that he has brought these questions to a more distinct and intelligible issue than any previous thinker. As a clergyman and a Professor of Moral Theology, I feel myself under unspeakable obligations to him. For he has cleared the ground of much rubbish which hindered us from knowing where we were standing; he has compelled us to abandon all apologies for our faith, and simply to ask ourselves what we mean by it, and what we suppose it can do for mankind. If it can do nothing, if what we have called the Kingdom of Heaven is not concerned about the reformation or regeneration of the earth, we must confess that we have been walking in a dream, or have been deliberately imposing a lie upon our fellow creatures.

1. M. Comte has dwelt much upon the fact that since the time of Bacon,* Moral Philosophy has been more and more inclined to assume a physical, and to discard a theological foundation. The truth and importance of this remark I fully recognised in my last Lecture. I did not merely accept it as a general proposition; I endeavoured to illustrate it in a number of particular cases taken from the representatives of schools utterly opposed to each other. The period between our Civil Wars and the French Revolution presented a series of experiments all conducted upon the maxim which M. Comte supposes to have established itself for ever as the only reasonable or possible one. I recognised a great value in each of these experiments; an undoubted result from each. But upon that maxim which these students assumed, they could not be reconciled, they must be at war for ever. Introduce the maxim which they agreed to cast out and which yet continued to subsist as the acknowledged basis of the people's faith in all countries of Europe, and we could do justice to all these results; it was impossible to part with any one of them.

2. The agreement of such remarkable men—so different as those I have enumerated—that theology had been used up at least for moral and political purposes, that a physical age had set in, offers surely a great excuse for M. Comte's grand generalisation, which Mr. Mill reckons his most characteristical one. The study of physical facts, he says, must be taken as the sign of the world's maturity; the study of theology of its infancy; a middle period of metaphysical speculation being the transition from one to the other. No man who has heard such a proposition enunciated can forget it, or can fail to find instances in history which seem to establish it. What will have really far greater weight with most men than these instances, what will give *them* weight, will be their own personal experiences. "Were not we," they ask, "theologians in our nurseries? Did we not stumble about in strange metaphysical puzzles of which we could find no solution, when

---

*M. Comte joins the name of Descartes to that of Bacon. I am not competent to estimate the kind of impression which that illustrious thinker has made on his own countrymen. If I am not mistaken, his influence on England, where his physical speculations are little prized and where his search for a ground of his own thoughts has affected the most earnest students at some stage of their lives, has been rather to counteract than to promote the tendency which I spoke of in my last Lecture.

we first became capable of exercising our thoughts? Do we not discover as we become men that our business is with 'positive' things; with the outward world, of which in the earlier periods we knew nothing?" There is a force in reflections of this kind which those who submit to it are not aware of. And it is a force which affects ordinary men of the world even more than students. For the name "positive" covers much ground. It may be taken loosely to express the processes or the results of scientific inquiries. But that is not its obvious or natural signification. It denotes rather the material on which these processes are exercised, that with which men are concerned who buy and sell if they never trouble themselves about science. In this sense practical men may exclaim that they have been talking Comtism all their lives without knowing it, because they have said to each other: "It is very good for children to say prayers with their mammas in the nurseries. It does not much signify what nonsense they talk about their minds and souls at College. When they become lawyers or merchants or Members of Parliament, they soon tame down into common sense. Then what they care about is the prices which things or men will fetch in the market." Discourse no doubt denoting a high civilisation, but one which cannot be appropriated to the 19th century. Opinions similar to it in all essentials are attributed to citizens of London in Ben Jonson's Comedies, to citizens of Rome in the Epistles of Horace.

But this assuredly is not orthodox Positivism, not what M. Comte meant by the third or mature stage of human existence. That Experimental Philosophy, in Bacon's sense of that word, has been reserved for this last stage and has been one of the greatest gifts to mankind, I take to be his doctrine; surely a very sound one. I do not feel less gratitude to him for this announcement, that he has expressed it in terms which are open to the other construction. The ambiguity will be useful to us if it teaches us that there are two possibilities; one of ascent from our infantine wisdom, one of descent. We may rise to a scientific apprehension of the meaning of facts, we may sink into the habit of considering them only as they affect our private interests. We may become human, we may drop into a positive money-worship which is merely brutal. That we should avoid the degradation and attain the elevation would have been surely M. Comte's desire.

What I maintain is that the hindrances to experimental philosophy were also the great hindrances to theological belief. As long as men are counted infallible the investigation into the meaning of facts will be checked, precisely because the belief in a God of truth, in a God who stirs men to pursue truth and leads them on in the pursuit of it, is checked. The practical denial of God, not faith in Him, makes us afraid that if we seek we shall not find, if we knock it will not be opened to us. Those nursery prayers which the Club sage thinks were so good for the child, so inappropriate to the man, ought to be so regarded if the man's ultimate vocation is to get all he can for himself. But in that ripest period he will look back upon his childhood, and fancy it must have been the sunniest and most blessed moment of his existence because he cherished delusions which have passed for ever away. Whereas, if his vocation is to know truth and to be true, he may have then had his first glimpse of the vista which through ages upon ages he is to explore. He may have been shewn who would be his guide through the bewildering, but most needful and precious questionings, respecting himself and his fellows into which he enters as he grows older; he may feel that he first knows the full need of his mother's lessons when he grapples with the mysteries either of the outward Universe or of Human Society.

3. So I come to that great development of the doctrine, that Physical or Positive studies should be the induction to Human studies, in which M. Comte supposed the glory of his system to consist. Here I feel myself in a difficulty which I must state frankly, and about which I greatly desire light from those who can give it. M. Comte supposes that there is an order or hierarchy of studies, that Humanity is at the summit, but that Mathematics, Chemistry, Biology and others lead up to it. Now I am utterly unable to ascend this scale. I do not affect to be a Mathematician, a Chemist, or a Biologist. It would be the greatest quackery to pretend that I can judge whether M. Comte's arrangement of these subjects is right, or how well or ill he has treated any one of them. Am I therefore unfit to understand his doctrines so far as it bears on Humanity? Is it impossible for me without this qualification to become a Comtist? Or can I only acquire that qualification by taking for granted all that is said in M. Comte's course on topics about which I am ignorant? In the first case it strikes me that the limits of the school must be drawn very closely; that the conditions under which it is entered are severer than those which any sect in the world has laid down. But I open a book written in a popular style and addressed to all Europeans and Americans; there I find people of every class and tongue urged at once to become proselytes of the new faith. That book sometimes leaves a painful impression upon the mind that the second alternative—that of implicit faith—is demanded of us. Much is said to have been done by "Positivism" behind the scenes; we seem sometimes to be told that we *must* receive its lessons on Humanity, they being inevitable deductions from doctrines previously established respecting Mathematics, Chemistry, Biology. When, however, I meet with Comtists, men of the highest worth and honesty, who do not profess any deep acquaintance with these subjects—who, at the same time, would never submit to the infallibility in a philosopher which they deny to a Pope—I feel that I must have misunderstood them on these points; that they do not mean to exclude us from the benefit of their lessons upon what they deem the highest of all topics, because we are not competent to pass an examination in the lower. Although therefore I should like some more confident assurance that I am not venturing on sacred ground without the proper initiation, I shall assume that it is lawful to claim my portion, ignorant as I am, in the Humanity of which the Comtists speak. I think they will find hereafter that men will not care as they ought to care for Mathematics or Chemistry or Biology, if they are not first induced to assert their rights as men. I may fully accept M. Comte's doctrine that Humanity is the climax of these studies. I must also believe that it lies beneath them, and must in some way be the preparation for them.

4. If this point is settled we can do much greater justice to the comprehensive Humanity of this teacher. That he refuses to confine it by any sectarian limits, that he would recognise men of all kindreds and nations as sharers in it, is a valuable and necessary protest, it seems to me, against opinions which have prevailed in all parts of Christendom. What the humanity of the Eastern Empire was I have tried to shew you. How the West became more and more Latin in all its thoughts and conceptions; how Protestants rebelling against this limitation introduced others still narrower, so that the rejection of what is common to man seemed to be the badge of their circles, I have also been compelled to explain. We may not have learnt these facts from the Comtists' preaching; yet we may be heartily thankful to it for not allowing us to forget them or explain them away. As little can we deny the service it has done us by declaring that the mere Roman Virility must not be confounded with Humanity; that we cannot feel the length and breadth of that word till we acknowledge the grandeur of the woman's position. Once more we must rejoice that they have not permitted these to be barren maxims, that they have insisted upon them as truths which must affect the politics of the world; which must be tested by the circumstances, not of other times, but of our own. Such hints are most salutary and bracing; they speak not of compromises but of battle; if we are to be swept away in the battle, as they threaten that we shall be, we must nevertheless prepare ourselves for it.

5. If I recognise the worth of this conception because it protests against the attempt to exclude any portion of the race from the circle of Humanity, I honour it quite as much because it treats Humanity not as degraded but as glorious. On this point also I have been forced to own that it is at war with the lessons which different portions of Christendom have derived from their teachers, with those which prevail in Protestant sects as well as among Romish Orders. It is at variance also with the doctrines of philosophers so little in sympathy with either as Thomas Hobbes. The difficulty indeed of combining a view of Humanity which is inclusive with one which is elevating has been felt in all ages and by all thinkers to be enormous. Is it not a truth that a majority—a vast majority—of our species are gross and animal; nearer—to use a phrase which an illustrious statesman has made classical—the ape than the angel? Does not every new investigation bring this truth more home to us? Is not Science endorsing it? The consequence is that from whatever point theorists start, they commonly end with adopting under some form or other, the doctrine which they complain of when it assumes its Calvinistic form. They hold whatever is good among men to be exceptional. The Comtists bravely resist this conclusion. They will pay the highest honour to Humanity as such. If they contemplate it in particular specimens, that is, if I do not mistake, because they suppose the characteristics of it to be most fully exhibited in those specimens.

6. And they suppose the human characteristic, that which all are to strive for because it is human, to be not selfishness but love; only when each man seeks not his own interest, but the interest of the whole society, is he truly human. That is

the goal which we are to keep in sight; not the obtaining of rewards, not the escape from punishment, but this sublime and perfect charity. Great as the intellect is, it must bow to the heart; all efforts after knowledge, even if pursued according to that wonderful system which M. Comte elaborated, are still conducting to this higher end; only when that is attained has Positivism fulfilled its mission.

Portions of this language may sound not altogether new to us. Do you think we can safely dismiss them on that plea? Have we understood them so well—have they penetrated so far into our practice—that we can afford to part with any one who sings them afresh to us, mingled possibly with some sharp notes of denunciation and contempt? If Comtists know the secret of combining reverence for all mankind with resistance to the selfishness to which we feel that each of us has continually yielded, surely we should listen earnestly while they impart it. If they do nothing but cause us some shame, that may be the very good we want; those who stir us to that may be our highest benefactors.

What is the secret then? It is this: "Part with your theology. Exalt Humanity into the place which it has occupied." The words have a most tempting sound. There are numbers who are eager to accept them. I think I have partly shewn you why. If I gave you different passages from M. Comte's books which shew what he supposed theology to be, you would be still better acquainted with his reasons. He often compliments the theology of the Catholic Church for vindicating the feelings against the mere glorification of the intellect by philosophers. But Positivism, he says, does that more perfectly; it exalts the heart to its right place, to its highest honour. Theology has worshipped a woman in the person of the Virgin. How much better does Comtism fulfil the same object! Theology has kept up a certain notion of a Society not confined to one nation with a Supreme Dogmatist over it. That was very well for the Middle Ages; it was better than the anarchy which the brutal conflicts of the different States might have produced. It suggested the thought that there is an educational power as well as a merely governing one. But Positivism has adopted all that is good in this doctrine into itself. A supreme Dogmatist must give place to a perfect System; a wider Humanity must displace what was merely the preservation and development of certain maxims originating with a set of Hebrew teachers. Then theology has its direct mischiefs. It encourages selfishness. It leads men to abandon the interests of the earth and mankind for the sake of rewards which are to be obtained in some future world. It is also adverse to fixed principles such as Science craves for. It introduces uncertainty and fluctuation by promising continual interferences on behalf of particular favourites.

Now you will perceive how much excuse there is for these charges; how little right any one of us may have to say, "They do not apply to me." But did it not occur to M. Comte that there was another way of judging what the theology of Christendom is besides an examination, which must be somewhat loose and hasty, of the tenets and practices of its particular teachers? Might he not, just for a moment, have looked at those very short documents to which I have referred so often, seeing that they are recognised by all the teachers, and also are the language of the people? If he had done so he would have discovered exactly what is the difference between his conception of Humanity and the theological one; he would *not* have discovered any one of those characteristics which, either for praise or blame, he has imputed to theology.

He would not have found that the Creed of the West speaks either of the feelings or the intellect. He would have read in it of God a Father who is the Creator of Heaven and Earth, that He is emphatically *not* a capricious Being who interferes on behalf of a few favourites, but one who had made himself known to men through a Son—that Son entering into the nature of men, dying the death of men, rising for men, exalting His manhood at the right hand of God, being the Head and Judge of men. Here is the common Humanity of men; here is that Humanity exhibited not in some partial examples, but in a Central Object to whom all may turn, in whom all may see their own perfection. And that perfection is emphatically the perfection of unselfishness, of one who sacrifices Himself for the good of the kind, for the pure love which M. Comte deems the supreme good of man. M. Comte, if he had continued the perusal of this simple manual of theology, would have heard of a Uniting Spirit who builds up a Society of men, who sets them free from sins, who promises to raise up their bodies out of death, who gives them the Life of the Eternal God which has been shewn to be the Life of the Eternal Charity. Certainly not a limited Latin or Greek Society, not one held in subjection to any Supreme Dogmatist or to the rules of any sect.

What is it that M. Comte calls upon us to exchange for this obsolete infantine Theology? We are still to believe in Humanity, only in a headless Humanity. It is a Humanity which has no deeper root than our own nature, which can only be understood and adored in ourselves and in our fellow-creatures. It is no metaphysical abstraction. Positivism abhors metaphysics. It must therefore take concrete forms; it must be reverenced and adored in those. Every one who reads history, who knows anything of himself, must perceive how plausible such a doctrine is, how highly probable it is that it should bring forth practical fruits. M. Comte has produced the most clear and complete Philosophy of Idolatry that exists in the world; the fullest justification and apology for all the worships that have divided Humanity. The only question is whether such a Philosophy is the way to a United and Universal Humanity.

I think it may be, if it has the effect which it ought to have, of leading us to see how much we have, one and all, been acting on the maxims of this philosophy, how much we have been deifying our own partial tastes and conceptions, how little we have been confessing a Centre from which the life of all human creatures is derived, in which they may find a fellowship amidst all their diversities. What honour do not Comtists deserve of us—what columns and statues can be too magnificent for their high priest—if they bring us back to the belief that the Love which they say is the sublimest quality of men is indeed, as St. John said, the very being of God; that which was manifested to men in His Son; if in the bitter despair of becoming by any effort of ours what they tell us that we ought to be, in the full consciousness of all the selfishness which Hobbes imputes to our nature, we are led to confess a Spirit who can raise us to a participation of the divine Nature? For my own part I do not profess the least skill in confuting Comtists. I am glad to be confuted by them, since their exposure of my theology compels me to understand how little I have appreciated it, and what the worth of it is.

I am anxious to distinguish between any Social arrangements which Comtists may recommend and their fundamental principles. Their dogmas about the relations of Labourers to Capitalists are entitled to the same respectful consideration as all others that have been propounded by Frenchmen or Englishmen who have devoted thought to that subject. If they seem to contradict others which have commended themselves to our judgments, we need not be in a hurry to reject either. Still less ought we to despair of a solution of the most difficult problems, because our assent is demanded to so many different solutions; every student, every practical man may contribute some hint which we cannot afford to lose; in action we may discover the use of one and another that we have slighted. If Comtists sometimes appear as decisive in their conclusions upon those points which must be open to the influence of varying circumstances as upon the most universal principles, that is the ordinary infirmity of young and vigorous schools bent upon showing that they are not content with figures in ivory or pasteboard, but must have actual pawns and bishops and kings to play with. And surely it is well for us to be reminded that all our principles must be tested at last by what they can do for our own characters and for mankind.

From those applications of this system which concern the intercourse of nations with each other, we may all I think derive much instruction; many grave warnings as to immoral notions and habits which we have tolerated in public men, and have perhaps cherished in ourselves. As long as they adhere to the word "international," I can listen to them gratefully; for that word recognises the distinctness of the bodies which hold fellowship with each other; it excludes the imperialism in which nations are lost. But there is in this system such a dread of the individuality which I believe is involved in the existence of nations; such an evident hankering after the "death" of Jesuitism if it could be secured without the name which Loyola adopted, and (as I hold) dishonoured; the founder and disciples of this school have such an admiration for Charlemagne's doings in the West, such a liking for the civilisation of China, even though the "Progress" which they admire is not quite compatible with its "Order"; that one cannot but perceive an Empire looming through all their speculations, however much it may at present be kept out of their own sight as well as ours.

If that vision did come in its fulness upon some of the disciples of this school, if they saw that they must in deed as well as in name renounce the liberty which was once dear to them, I suspect they would begin to reconsider with great seriousness the steps by which they had arrived at such a result. I should be very sorry if their reflections led them into an angry reaction against their teacher or his lessons. Those who have known most of these reactions in themselves or seen them in others would be guilty of a crime if they tried to produce them in any one. I hope that instead of revolting against M. Comte, his disciples may always remember him as the discoverer to them of the great truth that there must be some Universal Society for men. That society, as I have tried to shew you, may take the form of an Empire; then it will be but a repetition of the experiments against which the cry in men for a Brotherhood has ascended to heaven. It may take the form of a Family; then it may satisfy that cry, if indeed there is a Father in Heaven who adopts men of all nations and kindreds into His Family, and teaches them what are their places in it.

UNIVERSAL MORALITY:
DEMAND IN THE NEWEST CIRCUMSTANCES
FOR A DIVINE GROUND OF HUMAN LIFE
AND HUMAN MORALITY*

When I spoke to you in the last Lecture of that which I called the Modern Conception of Humanity, I did not intimate any purpose of adding to this conception some theological tenets modern or ancient. If I undertook such a task, I should not only be forsaking my proper province as a Moralist, I should be making all that I have said to you about morality unintelligible. I have not tried to shew you that something is desirable besides the Universal or Human Morality which has been the subject of this course; I have wished to ascertain what is the foundation of that Morality; how it can be in very deed a Morality for men as men, a Morality for you and me. I believe, as I have said, that all the partial conceptions of Humanity and of Human Morality which the inquirers of the 18th century bequeathed to us, as well as that more comprehensive one which has been elaborated in our own day, afford us the greatest help in understanding the lessons of those periods which we had examined previously. But I fully admit that the test of all principles affecting to be moral and human must be their application to the circumstances in which we are placed. What signifies it to us if they were adapted to Palestine in the 1st century, or to Constantinople or Rome in the middle ages, or to the Teutonic nations at the Reformation, if they do not explain our lives, if they cannot direct our practice in this year 1869? We may respect them as fragments of antiquity, we may deposit them in museums, but we must have something else for our common daily business. Because I can find no other which is adequate to our emergencies, I go back to the principle of a Universal Family which was announced eighteen centuries ago, and which has been subject to so many contractions and mutilations in subsequent periods. I accept the principle in that primitive form which has been preserved among the people of Christendom, whatever may have been the opinions of its different doctors.

---

*From *Social Morality* (1869; London: Macmillan and Co., 1886), Lecture 20, part 8, 371–96.

I. That a Fatherly Will is at the root of Humanity and upholds the Universe was the announcement which shook the dominion of capricious daemons and the throne of an inexorable fate in the Roman Empire. The circumstances in which it was first proclaimed shew how much the Universality of the announcement was involved in its essence. The resistance to it came from the Jews, because they said they were the chosen people of God, the only favourites of Heaven. The Apostle of the Gentiles, whom it is the most modern fashion to credit with the characteristic peculiarities of Christian Theology, affirmed his privilege as a Jew only to be this, that he might proclaim his Gospel concerning God to all nations. His cause would have been lost, every argument which he used would have been stultified, his sufferings would have been wasted, his influence on mankind would have been nothing, if he had not delivered this as a message to men just as he found them, not after they had entered the Church, but as the reason why they should enter it. Every attempt that was made afterwards by any church or any school to make the truth of the announcement dependent on the acceptance of it by one set of men or another was a defiance of his express words; must deprive the morality which he deduced from it of all reality for them or for their race.

Now the circumstances which are at this time creating the greatest suspicion of Christian Morality are these. We know that an immense world has been discovered of which the Palestine fishermen and the tentmaker of Tarsus knew nothing. "While it was possible to contemplate Christendom as constituting the world, or at least all that is sacred in it, the morality of these teachers, it is said, might be accepted as sufficient. It led to great crimes and brutalities when new regions of men were revealed to the sailors of Spain or Holland or England. Those who lay outside the fold might be treated with unbridled ferocity, or be compelled by such ferocity to come within it. Afterwards when along with commercial intercourse and civilisation some notion of a common Humanity began to prevail, the Churches caught a little of it, talked with pity of the poor exiles from God's mercy, and when no longer able to persecute them, made considerable efforts to persuade them that the European faith in some one of its forms was better than their own. But though in these efforts some gentleness towards people of other religions may have been called forth—though that may have been found on the whole the most useful policy of the proselytisers—what fellowship can they have felt with those whom they warned under the most terrible penalties to become like them; how can they have confessed that there was any common moral standard to which they might appeal?"

I am not careful to consider the numerous exceptions to this charge which the records of every sect and nation might offer, because I wish you to observe, that if it was true absolutely and without any exception against all Christians, it would only shew what had been the effect of neglecting the maxim from which they started. It is equally true that every instance of the behavior towards men of other races and faiths which is the opposite to this has been an adherence, whether intentionally or not, to that maxim. Suppose a man to hold it fast, he must trace all sense of justice, veracity, equity, kindliness in himself to that which he affirms to be the perfectly good Will; he must acknowledge every unjust, untruthful, unfair, unkind act of his as a rebellion against it. He must attribute all the imperfection of his acts either to a confused apprehension of this Will, or to some perverse influence which hinders him from giving effect to his apprehension of it. And this judgment of himself must be also the one which he forms of all with whom he is brought into contact. Whatever sense of justice, veracity, equity, kindliness is found in them must have its source in that same Will, cannot have any other source. Whatsoever in them is unjust, untrue, unfair, unkind, must come from a confused apprehension of this Will, or from some false influence which prevents them from giving effect to their apprehension of it. The principle in both cases is precisely the same. And the treatment of the cases must be in all essentials the same. To set up a Western standard of morals against an Eastern is to deny our principle; to exalt ourselves in any degree, either on the plea that our civilisation is better, or that our religion is better, is to confute the claims of each. The man who boasts of *his* peculiar civilisation boasts of his narrowness, of his incapacity to recognise the distinctions and varieties which are found in the society of men as in the natural Cosmos. The man who boasts of his religion, boasts that he has some special God who is not the Father of all the Families of the Earth, who is not the root of all that is right and true in himself and all men, who does not abhor what is wrong or false in him as much as in all other men.

There can be no doubt that any one who is uniformly just, fair, kindly in his dealings with those of another faith, still more that any one who deliberately exerts himself to improve their condition, to elevate their thoughts, to make them partakers of all that he finds most precious to himself whatever it be, does undermine the worship of separate local gods, still more the worship of unjust and cruel gods, even though he never speaks a word against them, though he enters into no argument to withdraw any one from them. On the other hand, if, under any pretext, we assume right to insult or bully or corrupt or cheat any man in any country whom the chances of dominion or diplomacy or trade throw in our way, we do what in us lies to confirm that man in the belief of insulting, bullying, corrupting, cheating gods; we lead him to pay them homage as the best means of securing their connivance or support, and of counteracting our violence or our tricks. This effect we shall produce, because we are, in our inmost hearts, doing homage to these gods ourselves, because we are invoking them, if not at public altars and temples, yet in our daily transactions, in our secret thoughts. It is well that we should thoroughly understand this. Comtists or others may talk to us about getting rid of theology. We can very easily get rid of that theology of which I have spoken to you in these Lectures—of that theology which recognises a Righteous Will, a Fatherly Will, as the ground of us and of the Universe. We do get rid of that continually; we shake it off as a most inconvenient burthen. But we cannot get rid of *some* theology. When we have rejected the name or names that men have worshipped, the substance, the character which the names represent, cleave to us as closely as ever. The more we feel that there is no object above our nature—no ground beneath our nature—the more will those tendencies, appetites, antipathies, which we find *in* our nature, present themselves to us as irresistible powers which we must obey. They will associate themselves, as they have done in all mythology, with the powers of the outward world; then in spite of all our knowledge of that world, these powers will combine with those which we feel characteristic of ourselves to terrify and enslave us.

I believe the circumstances of our time are compelling us to take notice of these facts, that men in all directions are taking notice of them. Those who speak most of the moral corruptions which are to be discovered in Hindustan, Japan, in any Eastern land; those who complain that we will not recognise the nobler qualities which are to be found in the natives of all these countries; those who ask whether the same evils which Christians have denounced as the results of heathen worship are not to be seen in their own actions—all alike, however they may wish to fix our attention upon one set of facts, and to make us incredulous of others which rest upon evidence as strong and decisive, are leading us to the same result. They all point to a standard of which they are conscious, of which they discover a consciousness not only in particular men, but in whole societies of men; they recognise in each particular man, in every society of men, a departure more or less violent from that standard. The question how if that is so we are to account for the dissimilar maxims which men have proposed to themselves, and by which they have tried to regulate their conduct, may seem to become more difficult as our experiences become more manifold. In fact those manifold experiences are driving us to a practical solution of the difficulty, are interpreting the old solution of it. Not that which is peculiar, not that which is exceptional, is most elevated; but that which has the largest, most comprehensive sympathy, which can most enter into the conditions of those who are lowest and most degraded. Whence can such a sympathy have issued, whence can the desire of it have issued? If its source is in our circumstances it must soon be exhausted; those circumstances, by their varieties and contradictions, are exhausting it. If the source is in ourselves, the self of each man must extinguish it. The circumstances have given rise to those partial conceptions of worth which men in different regions have formed, which they have exalted into gods. The selfish instincts have made these conceptions incapable of reconciliation. Suppose the sympathy to have sprung from a Will which has called Man into being, which is the origin of Life and Order to the Universe, there is at least the dawn of light upon this great paradox, the promise that all our acts, thoughts, and habits may not for ever be entangled in the meshes of it.

II. But a Fatherly Will must always seem a monstrous and incredible dream to human beings living in a world such as we live in, if they have been left to destroy themselves and each other according to their whims and fancies. If that is the Will or the Fate which governs the Universe, there must be some Deliverer from that Will or Fate; some Prometheus who shall steal the fire that is to hinder human creatures from being utterly wretched, utterly at the mercy of the Tyrant. Such redemptions every mythology is full of—full in proportion to the experiences which there were of human misery in the land that produced it. There must be some friendly daemon, some co-operator with the poor victims of mortal oppression or of Death the common oppressor, one who shall at least alleviate the wretchedness of some district or family or time if he cannot remove it. To secure such aid and co-operation what prayers must not be poured forth, what sacrifices offered! If a child will secure the help of the intercessor, if it will buy off the wrath of the enemy, can that be grudged? More and more the enemy is contemplated as absolute and supreme; the helpers as temporary and accidental. And supposing they are habitually well disposed—supposing they have not been alienated by any offences of their votaries, what do they know about the wants of their votaries? There may be pity; what participation in woe can there be? A modern poet has given admirable expression to the sense of hopeless separation between the inhabitants of the earth and its supposed rulers and to the cry which it suggests. He may or may not be right artistically in attributing such sentiments to a Greek Chorus, but they are in themselves most striking and true.

> But up in heaven the high gods one by one
>   Lay hands upon the draught that quickeneth,
> Fulfilled with all tears shed and all things done,
>   And stir with soft imperishable breath
>   The bubbling bitterness of life and death,
> And hold it to our lips and laugh; but they
> Preserve their lips from tasting night or day,
>   Lest they too change and sleep, the fates that spun,
> The lips that made us and the hands that slay;
>   Lest all these change, and heaven bow down to none,
> Change and be subject to the secular sway
>   And terrene revolution of the sun.
> Therefore they thrust it from them, putting time away.
>
> I would the wine of time, made sharp and sweet
>   With multitudinous days and nights and tears
>   And many mixing savours of strange years,
> Were no more trodden of them under feet,
>   Cast out and spilt about their holy places:
> That life were given them as a fruit to eat
>   And death to drink as water; that the light
>   Might ebb, drawn backward from their eyes, and night
>   Hide for one hour the imperishable faces.
> That they might rise up sad in heaven, and know
> Sorrow and sleep, one paler than young snow,
>   One cold as blight of dew and ruinous rain;
> Rise up and rest and suffer a little, and be
> Awhile as all things born with us and we,
>   And grieve as men, and like slain men be slain.
>   —From Swinburne's "Atalanta"

The answer to this passionate demand according to the Christian theology has been given once and completely. He whom it recognises as the Creator and Life-giver of the Universe "has grieved as men, and like slain men been slain." He endures the tyranny which is triumphant over man's nature that He may redeem the wills of men from subjection to their nature and to all the accidents which befall their nature; that He may ultimately raise their bodies as well as their wills out of the death to which He submits.

If you fancy that you can trace in modern Europe—in any of those who have accepted the Christian Revelation—that very confusion which has mingled with the mythologies of the old world, and with those which Oriental scholars bring under our notice; if you see among the people of Christendom and even among their teachers a disposition to think of a Redemption from the Creator instead of by Him, of a Sacrifice to change His Will rather than to accomplish it: that is only a proof how little we can trust the opinions or notions of men in one region or another; how common a gravitation there is in all these notions and opinions towards narrowness and self-seeking: how habitually, if we would think as the Apostles thought and speak as they spoke, we must look not to men but to Him of whose Will they testified, whose redemption they proclaimed, to sustain our confidence in either. And all modern circumstances, it seems to me, by bringing into clearer light the feebleness and insecurity of our judgments and, at the same time, the needs of Humanity in every region of the earth, are urging us to adopt the original language, undiluted by the least sectarian mixture, which declared that a Redemption had been accomplished for mankind by the obedience of the Son of God, by the sacrifice of the Son of man.

III. The announcement of a Fatherly Will as redeeming human creatures from their bondage to evil and death by this Sacrifice has been felt in all ages to be characteristic of the New Testament, however it may have been reduced and explained away by those who have undertaken to interpret the New Testament. If we accept its language in the simplest and obvious sense, another announcement was at least as distinctive of it, and was no less closely connected with its claim to be intended for all nations. The commonest, vulgarest people were told that the Spirit of the Father in Heaven would be with them to raise, reform, and educate their spirits, to emancipate them from their animal and sensual nature, to deliver them from the suspicion, malice and vanity which set them at enmity with each other and made the pursuit of selfish ends the business of their lives. No words can be more distinct than those which contain this assurance. The presence of such a Spirit is declared to be the very bond of the Universal Society which was to be composed of such heterogeneous elements, that which alone could prevent them from breaking loose from each other, and becoming more hostile than ever. These statements lie on the surface of the record, so that the man who runs may read them. Yet they evidently belong to its inmost essence. If there is a Society for men as men, they, according to the teaching of the Apostles, explain the possibility of it. Accordingly the *people* of Christendom, when they have felt the social impulse strongly, when they have become impatient of class divisions, have turned to this language, have recognised in it a message addressed to them. On the other hand, the learned men have been anxious to construe it in some other than its apparent sense, to explain that it could not interfere with the authority of teachers who had better means than wayfarers of judging what was true in belief and right in action. Whether these advantages were derived from some external advantages of position or culture, or from the divine gifts and the inspiration of the Apostles descending upon them, might be disputed. There was an agreement to this extent, though one not precluding the bitterest controversies between those who entered into it, that the popular belief is a dangerous one, sure to issue in an outbreak of enthusiasm which must be dangerous to all organisation, civil or ecclesiastical. This was the feeling of the divines as well as of the philosophers in England during the last century. Enthusiasm was their horror. That must in all ways be checked. Hume's method of checking it by establishing a religion in which he did not believe I have referred to before; it was accepted by numbers who denounced his skepticism, as a desirable and judicious expedient. For they had evidence—clear evidence—from the facts of their own days, as well as from the testimonies of history, that very wild incoherent acts were perpetrated by individuals and sects who supposed that they had possession of this divine gift; to that persuasion might be traced the contempt of learning which had characterised the followers of Ziska in Bohemia, the contempt of law and its restraints which had characterised the Anabaptists in Munster. These appeared sufficient reasons for making efforts—desperate efforts—to prove that the Apostles did not mean that this was a gift for men in all ages; that it was in fact exhausted, for all practical and important purposes, in the miracles which they were enabled to perform. To shew how necessary these were for their work, how strong the evidence was that they were performed in that age, how little any subsequent age could assert the same privilege, was a chief object of those who aspired to connect scholarship with Christianity. Protestants indeed were obliged to combat the traditions of the Latin Church in favour of the continuance of miraculous powers; but as against what were called the enthusiastical delusions, they might generally calculate on the co-operation of their opponents.

So it was in the 18th century. A great change has taken place in ours. As in the 13th century, the popular conviction has sensibly modified if not overpowered the opinions of the learned. Our fashionable language is in many respects the very reverse of that which was adopted by our forefathers. We do not denounce enthusiasm. We are wont to speak of it as a great power, indispensable for the study of any subject, for energy to fulfil any task. The reaction has been so vehement that, as was sure to be the case, another is setting in. There is seen to be much affectation in the talk about enthusiasm, that the *talk* cannot promote energy either in study or action. Motives, it is supposed, such as Hobbes deemed the only powerful ones, are necessary to stimulate both. Rewards and punishments of some kind are said to be the only securities for diligence in one kind of work or another.

But however fashions of speech may alter among the wise or the unwise, the great movements of the world go on. There is in every land a people demanding to be recognised under that name, not as a set of castes; there is a demand for a fellowship which shall not be confined by boundaries of space or even of time, which shall unite us to men in the most distant regions of earth, which shall unite us to our ancestors and to our posterity. States may do their utmost to assert their authority; but can they satisfy these requirements? Ecclesiastics may put forth their highest pretensions; can they control these aspirations?

Both confess their inability. They say, "We are rent asunder by sects." These, cry the Statesmen, make it most difficult to educate the people of a country; these, cry the Churchmen, destroy the unity which we declare to be the special characteristic of Christian life. Yet what deliverance is there from these sects? The States have tried persecution and have failed, have tried toleration and have failed. The Latin and Greek Churches have tried excommunication, and sects have been the result of it. Protestants have followed in their wake, behold what they have accomplished! There remain two courses. One is to ignore all that the sects have been inculcating; to cultivate indifference; to decide that we can know nothing of the invisible world. I have not denied before—I shall not deny—the many pleas which there appear to be for this course, or the number of philo-sophical men who recommend it, or the attraction which it may well have for the body of citizens in every country weary with the contentions of its religious par-ties. I would only ask whether it is possible; whether what you have disposed of under one name is not certain to appear under another; whether as we become acquainted with different lands and seek for living intercourse with the inhabi-tants of them, we are not obliged to perceive how thoughts of the invisible world have mingled with all their thoughts of the visible, so that you cannot extinguish one except at the risk of extinguishing the other? In an age which demands the freest scope for thinking, you wish to draw a broader, deeper line of demarcation between the subjects which it may approach and those which it must avoid than the most dogmatical priest or ruler of consciences was ever able to draw. We may confidently affirm that if it were drawn in this day as in former days hosts of new sects would spring up to efface it, and would obtain power over the hearts of the people everywhere just *because* they effaced it.

The other alternative is that which I have just spoken of. We may believe ac-tually, as we have professed in words to believe, that there is a Spirit guiding and educating the thoughts of us and of all men awakening us to activity when we are most inclined to be slothful, keeping us at one when we are most inclined to be divided. Instead of shrinking from this assertion as one that is likely to exalt the vulgar against the cultivated, we may announce it to the most vulgar because we desire for them the highest culture; to the learned because we wish them to know what Humanity really is, and how they may be instruments in bringing forth that which is latent in the most brutal. So the first may feel all arrogance, self-conceit, refusal to learn, all unsocial tempers, a rebellion against a divine Teacher who would make them capable of receiving illumination and diffusing it; so the second, when their zeal in study and discovery is flagging, may recognise an Inspirer; may perceive that he is a detecter of the frauds which they practice on themselves, of the excuses which they make for not fairly grappling with facts and giving all weight to evidence. Then as to common morality. It was a great blunder in the teachers of the last century, first to tell poor men that they must not rob and cheat, and that they ought to be good husbands and fathers; and when they said they had found a counsellor nearer to themselves who resisted their inclination to rob and cheat, who inspired them with a desire to be good husbands and fathers, then to reply, "There is no such counsellor for you; there was One who enabled the Apostles to do strange acts, but He has left the earth long ago." It was a fearful blunder, for it led these poor men to rejoin, "Well, and why should not we perform strange acts too? We did prize the Helper who enabled us to do common acts, to care for our neighbours, to be honest and just in our dealings; but since you say that there is no other sign of His presence but the doing of that which is uncommon, we will try to work wonders." So the enemies of spiritual guidance became the abettors of the impostures and insincerities which they intended to put down.

But whatever may have been the case then, the circumstances of our time shew how certain it is that Society in the most civilised lands will perish through the frauds of rich men as well as poor men—of the most refined and the most outwardly religious—if there is not some power which can create a habit of honesty, which can resist the secret temptations of flagrant dishonesty in men whom neither the terrors of law nor of public opinion can hinder from bringing disgrace on themselves and ruin on their fellow-citizens. Such discoveries give us stronger reasons for asking whether the news of such a Power which came to men centuries ago must be discarded as false, whether they may not be accepted in a more complete sense than they have ever been?

There are other facts which the sight of the streets in every civilised capital brings home to us, which are brought much more vividly home to those earnest men who have penetrated into the dwellings within those streets. Much, very much as been done, much more might be done, for the improvement of those streets and dwellings by mechanical contrivances, by medical knowledge, by wise legislation. But there are habits in men and women which may set at naught the effects of all mechanical contrivances, of all medical knowledge, of the wisest legislation. They cannot be reformed by any of these; till they are reformed they will produce ever more crimes, ever fresh misery. Who can work this reformation? Threats of punishment cannot, promises of reward cannot. Is there not some demand for the old faith in a Spirit to regenerate social life as well as individual life, to overcome the sources of death, ultimately to raise men out of death itself?

We want—I cannot say how much we want—the labours of physiologists, of statesmen, of men with every kind of gift, to co-operate for the removal of the plagues that torment Humanity. We want them; most thankful we should be that so many of them are ready to meet the want. Who has inspired them? Who has taught them to labour for an end which is not a selfish one? I wish they would ask themselves that question. I have tried to find an answer to it in this Lecture. I have sought for the source of that Humanity, of that human morality, which I see and admire in one man or another. I have sought for the source of the habit, the temper, the character, which I believe is struggling in every man with those impulses to self-indulgence and self-aggrandisement which I find in myself, which the wisest observers have detected in our nature. I cannot discover any defence of this morality, any security for the performance of it or the development of it, any power of combating that which is opposed to it, except in that Spirit to whom the Apostles attributed every gift which they possessed, but to which they traced as habitually the consistency and harmony of the Society that was meant for all men. The phrases which confess this presence cannot be the power that we want if those phrases are true. They speak of that which is not measured by our notions or apprehensions of it, they promise that clearer revelation of it by which we hope to see the weakness of our apprehensions detected, all that is strong in them expanded.

There is however a notion current among men of letters and men of business—not unsanctioned by divines—that the portion of the New Testament which has been supposed to contain its canon of morality is wholly unsuited to the conditions of modern society, though it may be accepted as a respectable and venerable document if it is reduced into figures and denied all connexion with ordinary practice. "The Sermon on the Mount speaks," it is said, "of those to whom it is addressed being perfect as the Father in Heaven is perfect. Of course, therefore, it only suggests what are technically called *counsels of perfection* to men who are disposed to quit the business of the earth and devote themselves to the contemplation of a future world. It leaves ordinary crimes which men are prone to commit, in order to warn the select class against purely internal evils. It bids that class abstain as much from seeking the protection of law as from self-defence by arms. It teaches them to depend on divine help such as is afforded to ravens, not to work for their bread. It encourages indiscriminate almsgiving which we know to be so mischievous. It forbids us to exercise any criticism on the acts and opinions of our fellow-men. In every particular it sets at naught the most established maxims of modern civilisation, all that has been proved to be most important for the well-being of our community." If these statements are true, the doctrine which I have endeavoured to establish in the Lecture is overthrown. I am therefore very anxious to examine whether they are true.

1. That the command—*Be ye perfect as your Father in Heaven is perfect,* taken in connexion with the previous words—*He maketh the sun to shine upon the just and the unjust and the good and the evil,* instead of recognising a class of devotees

was the first complete proclamation of a Universal Morality, I have maintained already. All dreams of such "counsels of perfection" as lead to the separation of men into classes, of just and unjust, of good and evil, are shattered by that sentence. Unless there is some way in which the disciples of Christ can care for the just and the unjust, for the good and evil, can care for men as men, they are declared to be not like their Father in Heaven. Accordingly the strongest denunciations of the Sermon are directed against the sect of Jews which was following *these* counsels of perfection. Such were the counsels of the Scribes and Pharisees—schemes for cultivating a righteousness which should make them eligible for higher rewards than other men. Those rewards, so the Sermon everywhere declares, could not be the rewards which the Father who seeth in secret bestows. His reward is that likeness to Himself, the unselfish Being, which such self-seeking makes impossible.

2. Instead of such crimes as adultery or murder being spoken of as if they belonged only to the outside world, the disciples are expressly reminded that they are just as liable to fall into them as any men; that the propensities which lead to them exist in every human being and may at any time be developed into acts. The acts are subject to the cognisance of the law. If it meddles with anything besides acts it becomes mischievous and cruel. Yet the lawgiver feels that there is something behind which is producing the acts: if there was any power which could reach that something, which could prevent the commission of the acts, what trouble he would be saved, how thankful he would be! Christ tells men the good news that they may have a will in accordance with the law, that they may overcome that in themselves which leads them to violate it. An *esoteric* morality surely in the strict sense of that adjective; but universal *because* esoteric—applying to the inner life of all men, to the man himself. To talk of this as superfine morality, a morality for the specially religious, is to pervert language grossly. It is only a morality for them so far as they acknowledge themselves to be like all other men. It is a message to all men that they may be right and true, for God would make them so.

3. "If any man ask thy cloak, let him have thy coat also" is supposed to interfere with the principles of justice. I apprehend that we interfere with the principles of justice when we take other men's coats or cloaks, not when we give up our own. A man of great genius in our day, Victor Hugo, has perceived the immense power which a literal compliance with this command might exercise in the reformation of a criminal. The hero of the *Misérables* is changed from a ruffian into one of the noblest of men precisely by this kind of conduct in the Bishop from whom he stole a pair of candlesticks. A beautiful illustration surely of the way in which the interests of law and of social order may be promoted by one who does not consider that they exist to promote *his* advantage or secure *his* property; that a man is worth more than these. He benefits the individual and the community equally because he does not prefer himself to both.

4. There is however one great exaggeration and perversion of the words "If he

compel thee to go with him one mile, go with him twain," which this excellent Bishop sanctioned in his practice. He seems to have read, "If a criminal tell thee one lie, tell him two." So his virtue confirmed the offender in one of his most characteristic vices. Apply that doctrine to the passage in which the disciples of Christ are told not to turn away from him that asks. The whole principle of the Sermon being that the man is to be like his Father in Heaven, we must learn what this precept means from the sentence: "Your Father in Heaven will not give those who ask Him for bread a stone, for a fish a serpent." He will not do men an injury merely to please them. If I regard a beggar as a fellow-man, as a brother, I shall conform to the same rule. I shall not give him what would make him idle and brutal. I do turn away from him if to get rid of him or to please myself I degrade him. What then if it has been proved by criminal statistics or by political economy that indiscriminate almsgiving is most mischievous? That proof determines this application of the principle in the Sermon on the Mount; it shews what would be an unbrotherly act. It does not alter the principle unless statistics and political economy have proved that all men are *not* brothers. No national morality rises to *that* principle. But its own principle of neighbourhood needs the deeper and more universal one to sustain it. Maintain the *meum* and *tuum* if you can; but the *tuum* will be effaced by the *meum* if there is not some principle which is capable of defending humanity against selfishness. In that case political economy will never be able to defend itself against the natural instincts of monopoly, let its maxims be as much accepted as they may.

5. Christ's disciples, it is supposed, were told that they need not work because they were commanded not to be anxious and restless about the results of their work. If I wanted evidence that this Sermon belongs to the circumstances of our time this passage and the objections to it would supply the evidence. We have fallen into the notion that we shall work more energetically with our hands and with our brains, because we are continually fretting ourselves about what will come of our work, what pence or praises we shall get by it. And yet every one of us knows in his inmost heart that this fretting destroys the honesty of his work and the effects of the work. If we could be free from this perpetual fever, if we could work from an internal impulse, not under the pressure of external motives, if we could work as freemen not as galley slaves, what a difference it would make to the health of our bodies and of our spirits and to all our influence upon Society! If it were not a falsehood to tell the student of a University, or the tiller of the ground, or the woman in a factory, You have a Father in heaven who cares for *you* at least as much as for the sparrows, who will sustain your life—your human and your animal life—no less than that which He has given them, what a new spring of hope there would be for them in their most solitary hours, what a sense of fellowship! Is it wonderful that this part of the discourse should be more out of harmony with the temper of a restless excited age than any other, and yet that none should be so necessary for an age? And what a curious illustration it is of our current notions that we should be supposed to need this kind of inward

help and strength less than a former age, *because* our occupations are so multiplied, *because* we have so many new mechanical aids which earlier times had not for fulfilling them!

6. Precisely the same twofold remark is applied to the command not *to judge lest ye be judged,* not *to take the mote out of other men's eyes while a beam is in our own.* None can be so tormenting to all of us of every school and sect and profession; none seems so necessary if Society—human Society—is not to be extinguished by the jealousies and enmities of schools, sects and professions. If there is a Social Morality this must be its leading maxim. If there is a Personal Morality this must be its leading maxim. Here they coincide. The distinctions of the just and the unjust, of the good and the evil, which are as much recognised in fact by those who reject the words as by those who attach the most importance to them, cannot be discovered by the study of other men's lives, by prying into their acts and their motives. I can only be a true critic when I am my own critic; when I distinguish between the powers which are fighting in me for ascendency, which are claiming me for their servant. And when I enter into this criticism I perceive how treacherous it will be if there is not a Judge over me who detects what I cannot detect, who shews me my evil that He may lead me out of it. When I ask who this Judge is, the old words come back to me. I find that the internal teacher, who appears to take me apart from my kind, is in very deed that Spirit of the Father in Heaven who unites me to my kind, who shews me that the highest blessings are those which I share with it, that the worst curse is to lose fellowship with it and therefore with Him.

I shall have more to say on this subject in my final Lecture. I will conclude the present with two remarks. The first has reference to the passive or feminine character which has often been ascribed to the Sermon on the Mount. It has been thought to discourage all the qualities which have been most conspicuous in heroes who have struggled for freedom; to commend the submission which is sought for by tyrants and paid by slaves. Since I have spoken to you of the message concerning a Father in Heaven as being exactly that which encountered the image of a Man God upon earth, you will understand how far I can accept this statement. The Sermon on the Mount was expressly designed to prepare those who heard it for opposition and persecution, for the courage which could defy both and endure to the end. That object is manifest upon the surface of it. The notion that it is hostile to courage springs from the opinion that what sustains courage is a sense of self-importance, and therefore that whatever undermines this sense weakens courage. That unquestionably is a favourite tenet in this day. The incapacity of this self-seeking, bragging spirit to resist any great oppressor will, I believe, be made manifest by the circumstances of our time. When Imperialism comes forth in its full force to demand our homage, we may find that *we* demand something to oppose it which we have lost. And then we may understand as we never did before, that the free and brave Spirit is the Spirit of charity and truth, the Spirit who fights in us with our selfishness; a Spirit which makes men feminine, if feminine means courteous, deferential, free from brutal and insolent pretensions; but which also gives women manliness, if manliness means the vigour to live for the cause of Humanity and die for it.

The other remark has reference to what I said in a former Lecture about Cardinal Virtues. I said I believed there might be such virtues, and I quoted the words of the Apostle concerning faith, hope, and charity, I did not say more lest I should mislead you. There is in some a notion that Cardinal Virtues mean certain specially grand and exceptional virtues which entitle certain men to specially grand and exceptional rewards hereafter. Cardinal Virtues in this sense are identical with those Counsels of Perfection to which I have just referred. You will judge therefore how little I can admire them or associate them with Universal Morality. But a Cardinal Virtue may signify just what its etymology would suggest. It may be the hinge on which other virtues turn, without which they would have no coherence, no vitality. If that force is given to the phrase, there can be no doubt that the Sermon on the Mount does set forth the Cardinal Virtue. Self-sacrifice is that upon which all its precepts hinge. Without this the faith, hope, and charity of the Apostle would be mere idle names, they would have no relation to the practice of life. But Sacrifice leads us again to the original principle of the Discourse—"Be like your Father in Heaven." Men are only bidden to exhibit this grand principle of morality in their acts, they are only able to exhibit it, because He has given the example of it. The paradox is amazing, but it is the Christian paradox, the Human paradox. The fuller illustration of it must be reserved for the last Lecture of this course.

CHAPTER 5

Dialogues between a Clergyman and a Layman on Family Worship

THE REGENERATE AND THE UNREGENERATE*

Layman. Some words of yours just before we parted last week recall me to the subject of your own inconsistencies as an English clergyman. I must not be put off that scent by your proposal to invest me with honours certainly quite unsought for and unmerited. Before you spoke of family faith and of what I as an infidel might do to restore it, you observed that individual Christianity would gain much if Regeneration were not spoken of as belonging to a class. Now do you not speak of it in your Baptismal service and Catechism as belonging to a class? Are not the regenerate the baptized? Are not the unregenerate the unbaptized?

Clergyman. The baptized include, I conceive, a great many classes whom language and distance of place keep apart, who are utterly unlike in customs, opinions, government. Among them would be found Greeks, Latins, Armenians; servants of the Pope, protesters against the Pope; Lutherans, Calvinists, Zwinglians; Episcopalians, Presbyterians; Italians, Germans, Spaniards, Americans of the North and Americans of the South.

Layman. A motley gathering, certainly, to make up a Holy Catholic Church!

Clergyman. No doubt. The question is, how you would distinguish them; where you can find some marks which shall serve to shew which form the Church and which are shut out from it. Shall it be a geographical sign? Shall it be difference of speech? Shall it be complexion? Shall it be a certain census of wealth, the payment of rates or taxes perhaps to some sovereign? Shall it be rank?

Layman. Every sect would repudiate these as the notes of a Church. Every one

*From *Dialogues between a Clergyman and a Layman on Family Worship* (Cambridge and London: Macmillan and Co., 1862), Dialogue 4, 49–63.

181

would assert certain opinions, be they what they may, to be essential character-istics of it.

Clergyman. You are right. That is the demand of a Sect. A Church must, I con-ceive, stand on a different ground.

Layman. On what ground?

Clergyman. On that which our friends the Calvinists were so vehement in de-claring to be the only one, "The will of God choosing men into His family, call-ing them to be His sons and daughters."

Layman. But how is that will made known?

Clergyman. That I could not have guessed. The words, *Go ye into all the world and preach the Gospel to every creature, baptizing them into the Name of the Father and of the Son and of the Holy Ghost,* guided the Apostles and those who followed them to the knowledge of the sign which was to mark the family. On that com-mand, as I believe, they acted. A Christendom has grown up. You and I have been claimed as portions of it.

Layman. But you say that the Baptism signifies something to you and also to me?

Clergyman. Just so. I say that it signifies to each of us what he is; what God has made him.

Layman. And you believe me to be what my Baptism tells me that I am?

Clergyman. It has been the main object of my conversations to persuade you that you cannot be anything less than what it says you are.

Layman. That is, according to the baptismal service, "regenerate;" and ac-cording to the Catechism, "a member of Christ, a child of God, an inheritor of the kingdom of heaven."

Clergyman. Even so; and what I intended by the remark which you quote at the beginning of this dialogue is, that I should be a much better individual Chris-tian than I am if I habitually and at every moment remembered that this is my state, and if I habitually and at every moment remembered that I have in myself that which indisposes me to believe in this state and to act as if I were in it; or to use more theological language, all unregenerate tendencies and impulses; all the impulses that belong to me merely as a child of Adam. And I also meant that it hinders me greatly from exercising this recollection and the moral vigilance which would accompany it, to be trying to prove that I am one of a class; and therefore different from other people or better than other people. My baptism ought continually to keep the truth of my own state in my remembrance. It can-not, except by the grossest perversion of its nature and object,—only when dif-ferent signs of my own contrivance are introduced by the side of it and as the sub-stitute for it—lead me to that pharisaical presumption.

Layman. It does and must lead those who follow the teaching of the Catechism to suppose that they are better than other people.

Clergyman. Why?

Layman. Because they were "made in their baptism members of Christ and children of God." All who are not baptized—Quakers for instance—are therefore not members of Christ and children of God. Every troublesome school-girl, every baptized criminal in Newgate, had a right to think herself better than Mrs. Fry.

Clergyman. You hold that any one teaching this manual is bound to put that construction upon the words?

Layman. Unless he distorts them from their obvious and natural meaning. You ought to recollect that the document is written for the use of children or of simple teachers of children; that it is short; that it is carefully composed. Would such a word as "made" have been adopted if it had not been intended that the child and the child's teacher should give it the force I give it?

Clergyman. In a document short, written for a child or a simple teacher of a child and carefully composed, would a writer contradict himself formally and directly within a few paragraphs?

Layman. He may have done so unconsciously in some chance phrase, but these primary words must rule the interpretation of any other.

Clergyman. How if the chance phrase should occur in a careful, deliberate interpretation of the baptismal Creed, which the child's godfather and godmother promised in its name that it should believe?

Layman. That would be puzzling. Tell me what part of this interpretation you refer to.

Clergyman. The child having rehearsed the Articles of its belief, is asked what it learns from them. The answer is, "First, I learn to believe in God the Father Almighty, who hath made me and all the world. Secondly, In God the Son, who hath redeemed me and all mankind." That is part of the explanation given of the Creed which expresses the meaning and ground of the child's baptism.

Layman. Is there not another part of that explanation?

Clergyman. There is: "Thirdly, In God the Holy Ghost, who sanctifieth me and all the elect people of God."

Layman. There! What does that mean? The troublesome child, the criminal in Newgate, has an assurance that she is one of the elect people of God. What is the assurance? She has been baptized, Mrs. Fry has not been baptized.

Clergyman. I said that I believed the whole of Christendom was called or chosen by God to be a witness to mankind of its redemption. Is not that what the Catechism says? You seemed to think that according to our faith *mankind* was doomed to perdition and that the Church was redeemed out of it. Is that the doctrine which is set forth in this Manual for children? Can we hold it while we adhere to the express terms of that Manual?

Layman. But the troublesome child and the criminal in Newgate are to say that God the Holy Ghost sanctifies them, and that He did not sanctify Mrs. Fry the Quaker.

Clergyman. In what copy of the Catechism have you met with that last clause?

Layman. It is implied in the one which I have met with.

Clergyman. I say that it is not only *not* implied in those words, but that any teacher would be guilty of treason against those words if he added this clause to them, if he did not give the child such an interpretation of them as would make your inference from them ridiculous and impossible.

Layman. What can you mean?

Clergyman. I mean that the teacher ought to say this to the child: "My dear child, you are taught here that God the Holy Ghost is the author of all good which is in you or in any creature whatsoever under Heaven. You are taught that He alone sanctifies people or makes them holy. He will enable you to renounce those words of the devil which your godfathers and godmothers renounced for you. They are such works as St. Paul describes in the verses I read to you out of the Epistle to the Galatians—malice, bitterness, uncleanness. He will enable you to do all the good works, the works which St. Paul speaks of in the same place— meekness, gentleness, loving-kindness. Remember therefore that you are fighting against this Spirit who is always with you, when you do any of these bad works, when you fail in those good works. Remember that this will be so always, all your life through. Whatever good works you do will be the fruits of God's Holy Spirit; whatever evil works you do will be from resisting God's Holy Spirit. Your Baptism tells you this. Your Baptism marks you out as chosen and sealed of God to carry this witness with you wherever you go. And therefore whenever you see a person who shews you gentleness and loving-kindness, who calls forth gentleness and loving-kindness in you, who resists the works of the devil in you, I tell you, the Bible tells you, the Church tells you, that you are to say, that person is acting under the inspiration of God's Holy Spirit, and cannot be acting by any other inspiration than His."

Layman. But still Mrs. Fry was not baptized.

Clergyman. That was her business, not mine. She might think me and all the rest of Christendom utterly unspiritual; I am not bound therefore to think her so.

Layman. But you spoke of Baptism as a sign which God has given to us that we are His witnesses.

Clergyman. Certainly I said so. Not a sign which He has given us that others are *not* His witnesses. The blessing of Baptism is that it refers all to His will and choice, nothing whatever to our judgment. If I set up my judgment or presume to measure His acts by it, I contradict the witness of my baptism. It is no longer the sign of His purpose; it is merely the badge of my profession.

Layman. Still I must come back to my old text. That word *made* stands written; no logical or rhetorical subtleties can evade the force of it.

Clergyman. I quite agree with you. Logical and rhetorical subtleties are singularly out of place in the interpretation of a manual for little children. But do you think I shall commit the folly and crime of resorting to them, if, having perused the whole document and derived those lessons from the most distinct and authoritative part of it which I have just set forth to you, I resolve that this word *cannot* have a signification which is directly in the teeth of those lessons?

Layman. Provided you can find any other. I do not think you can.

Clergyman. Your mother used to speak to you of a natural birth, and a birth from above?

Layman. Certainly. That distinction was continually present to her mind.

Clergyman. Was it not a true distinction?

Layman. For theologians I suppose yes.

Clergyman. I mean not for theologians. For you and me and every man?

Layman. That is what you have been trying to make out; I suppose you are satisfied with your own success.

Clergyman. I am not the least satisfied unless you have gone along with me. But I am certain that you have. I am certain that you are as conscious of the struggle of a lower nature in you against higher impulses and instincts, as I am.

Layman. That struggle you will find spoken of just as much in heathen books as in Christian.

Clergyman. I am saying so. It belongs to man as man. Some may be more conscious of it than others. Those who have been most conscious of it have been the best and wisest men. But still it is in all.

Layman. Well?

Clergyman. Supposing then there were a revelation of a God who had taken part with these higher instincts and impulses in men, who had Himself inspired them, who had *justified* them, saying, "This higher thing in the man is the true man. This is my child . . ."

Layman. I grant you the supposition. I do not know whither it is leading us.

Clergyman. Suppose again that He who had given this revelation, had given a sign and pledge that He recognises this in the man as the true man, that whatever is fighting against this He regards as the man's enemy and as His enemy.

Layman. This may or may not be the explanation of the worth of Baptism; but we are talking about that special word in the Catechism, *made.*

Clergyman. If there is this distinction and if Baptism involves this distinction, may it not be of very great importance to signify in the strongest manner possible, that the child is not a member of Christ and a child of God in virtue of its natural birth, that God has *made* it what it is by another operation, by another kind of birth? May it not be exceedingly difficult to guard by *any* form of speech against two opposite dangers: the first, of losing sight of this distinction and merging the spiritual in the natural birth; the second, of diminishing the universality of the blessing and confining it to certain persons? There have been times when I have felt the last danger much more than the first; when I have feared so much to narrow the Redemption of Mankind, that I have used language which might easily convey the impression that men as natural creatures were sons of God. Then I have tried to find a more comprehensive phrase than the one of the Catechism, and have secretly or openly murmured against that. But the greatness of my own mistake has been brought home to me by some strong inward experience. I have felt that I was not really more universal, but was cheating men of a conviction which is of the most radical and universal kind, cheating them also of the message of God which has met that conviction. Then I have come back to this word *made,* and while fully admitting how open it is to misapprehension, have been led to doubt whether I could invent any other, which would not be open to much greater misapprehension. Therefore, leaving my brethren to take what liberties they think justifiable with the language of this document, all the liberty I ask for myself is, that I may give it that sense which is most in accordance with the intention of the writer, as indicated and expressed by himself in other passages of his own composition.

Layman. Let this be as it may. There is another difficulty in which you have become involved by the tone you have taken in our conversation. How you can extricate yourself from that I do not see. You have said, that the natural birth and the spiritual birth are to be carefully distinguished, that Baptism is the great support of this distinction. And yet you have spoken of the family as—I do not know how to express it properly—a sort of ecclesiastical or divine institution. Surely Baptism puts a kind of contempt upon the human family. You, M. or N., are the child of certain parents upon earth. That is your natural state. That belongs to you as a descendant from Adam. Your Christian name tells you of a different parentage and a different family. Can any child help making this reflection; or if the child does not, must not the man ask it? "These family bonds and attachments, do they not belong to the natural earthly condition out of which I have been raised? Would it not be a very high perfection if I could strictly follow the command of hating father and mother for the sake of Christ? If I cannot attain that height, may I not make some approximation towards it? Must not my Christian or baptized life be all throughout antagonistic to this life of child and parent, of brother and sister?"

Clergyman. You think you see tokens in history that that has been the feeling of religious people in different ages?

Layman. What else means all the history of Monkhood and Nunhood in the east and the west? What mean the separations of families which spring up whenever any strong religious feeling is awakened in wife, or son, or daughter? What means the priestly influence in Protestant as well as Romish countries? Talk of reviving the family through theology, or theology through the family! why it often strikes me that they are the deadliest of all enemies!

Clergyman. These are facts upon which I earnestly wish to enter, and to examine them with your help. I believe you will have terrible charges to bring against us Clergymen in all lands, charges which we must confess with shame and confusion of face. Before I come to those which belong to us officially as priests, I will tell you, for myself individually, that whenever I look back upon my life and upon the causes which I have for profound repentance in it, those which concern these family relations stand out with a breadth and aggravation which scarcely attach to any others. If the Spirit of God convinces us, as our Lord says, of sin, I am certain that He convinces us of these sins. They connect themselves with all others. They seem in some sense to lie beneath all others. At the same time, I can also bear witness that the meaning of Christian theology has presented itself to me through these revelations, and as the eternal ground of them, in such a way that but for them all books of Divinity, all ordinances of the Church, even the Bible itself, would have been to me without significance or power. But most of all have these relations explained to me the force of those words of Christ, about hating father and mother, wife and child. There are words appended to those which you have forgotten, *And his own life (or soul) also.* I believe we shall sacrifice father and mother, wife and child, to our own life or soul, till we sacrifice them all together to Christ. Then He bids them, them and all the affections that belong to them, live again; not upon the ground of self, not upon the ground of our own life or soul, but upon His own divine ground. The accusation which you will be able to make good against the priests of Christendom elsewhere and here, is, that they have not understood this, that they have sacrificed themselves, and have encouraged wives and daughters to sacrifice husbands and fathers, husbands and fathers to sacrifice wives and daughters—to their own lives or souls, and not to Christ. The soul has taken the place of Christ. And woe to the family, woe to the Church, woe to humanity and divinity when this is so!

THE METHOD OF PRAYER*

Layman. When I first spoke to you about family worship, I had a dim, half-formed notion that you might suggest to me some ingenious compromise with my conscience—some universal prayer in which Jew, Turk, Pagan, and Infidel might join. I confess I had heard many suggestions of the kind from others, had made many attempts myself, and that the results were not satisfactory. The terms could never be quite sufficiently vague. They tended continually to the formula, "O God, if there be a God, save my soul, if I have a soul;" and whatever faith may be embodied in that petition, it is not a faith which seems to demand a very definite expression, or which one cares to propagate even in one's home-circle.

Clergyman. I think there *is* faith embodied in that prayer as well as in the one which Bp. Atterbury quoted as a rebuke to the layman who spoke of it at some dinner-table, "O God, I am going to be very busy to-day. If I forget Thee, do not Thou forget me." Believing that we have a Father, every feeling after Him by every man must seem to me sacred and significant. Whether the man thinks he has a soul or not, the dream that it is possible for him to look up to a Being above himself who may save him, is proof of something much *more* than that he has a soul; it is a proof that he *is* a spirit. That spirit cannot conceive a God, cannot make a God. It cries to Him if He is, to reveal Himself—to reveal Himself by

---

*From *Dialogues between a Clergyman and a Layman on Family Worship* (Cambridge and London: Macmillan and Co., 1862), Dialogue 11, 179–98.

saving that spirit from its darkness, ignorance, degradation. My conviction is, that He has heard that prayer and the other. He has not forgotten us, though in the midst of our business or our idleness we have forgotten Him.

Layman. Your notion, however, of a universal prayer is not of an invocation to a "Jehovah, Jove, or Lord"?

Clergyman. I own I do not want a Jewish religion *plus* a heathen religion *plus* a Christian religion. Nor do I want, by eliminating what is peculiar in each of these faiths, to bring forth an *Être Suprème* who does nothing, thinks nothing, is nothing; who merely represents what is *not* true in the different systems, that which has been the source of their idolatry—the notion that God is created by His creatures. I do need that the "Father of all, in every age, in every clime adored," should make it manifest why He has been so adored; should show us whether He is a Father or no; whether He is a Father of a herd of animals who are without wills, who have no power to do right or do wrong, or of a family of spirits whom He has made in His own image. Accepting the revelation in Christ as the revelation of His Son, I find that need satisfied. Therefore I deem our Lord's prayer more universal than Pope's prayer.

Layman. If you would stop at our Lord's prayer, Unitarians would not complain. Even Deists would not complain, since Christ's own Name is not introduced into it. But you have insisted on the mysteries of the Trinity and of the Atonement as implied in the very nature of prayer, as demanding in some manner or other an expression in our prayers. To reconcile these demands with the "After this manner pray ye" of the Sermon on the Mount, appears to me difficult.

Clergyman. You remember how our conversation began?

Layman. You mean with my statement of the perplexity which I felt about my mother's consistency in teaching me the Lord's Prayer, while she regarded me merely as a child of Adam?

Clergyman. Precisely. My endeavour has been to show you that she did not regard you merely as a child of Adam, however an imperfect theory which struggled with her deeper convictions—her inward faith—may have led her sometimes to say so; that she had a right to teach you the Lord's Prayer; that she did teach it you in sincerity and truth.

Layman. You suppose that her belief in Christ as the Son of God and as the sacrifice for men, was her justification for making me repeat that form of words as I knelt by her.

Clergyman. I am sure she would not have taught them you if she had felt them to be only a form of words. I am satisfied she never said "*Our* Father" herself without thinking of you as well as of herself. She did not expect you as a child to know the reason which warranted any one in using that awful name. As in all other cases, the fact is announced first. Our after discipline and education is to bring forth the interpretation of the fact, and by that interpretation to increase, not lessen, its awe and wonder.

Layman. A strange view of things certainly to a person whose mind has been running, as mine has, in the groove of modern speculations. I fancied that Christian mysteries belonged to the period of infancy, that they still clung about the hearts of women, that he who puts on the manly gown casts them off—except from deference to custom and tradition, from a tenderness to that which was once believed, or from a dark apprehension that a mere void of nothingness may lie below. You appear to suppose that it is manhood more than childhood, manhood even more than womanhood, which craves these mysteries as a rock and resting-place; that all the conflicts of unbelief are driving us not from them but to them; that we need them lest civilization should return to brutality; that we need them lest in place of a more universal fellowship, we should be split into smaller sects and parties; lest at last every one should be for himself, and no God for us all!

Clergyman. You have expressed truly my hopes and my fears. It is under the pressure of such hopes and such fears that one learns to pray, that our prayers become not solitary prayers, but family prayers, universal prayers; and yet that each one really in his prayer attains a sense of his personal life and his personal obligations which he never could realize while his only cry was, "Save my soul if I have a soul."

Layman. And you still think that our Lord's form is the best form, that after this manner we are to pray in manhood as in childhood, with our own family and with the human family?

Clergyman. I can discover no other method but that. I cannot complain, as some do, of our being continually reminded of the form of words itself. The recurrence of it in our Church prayers does not grate on my ears, but recalls me to the sense of what all prayer is. Still we know too well that it may become a mere charm. We do not pray after this manner if we suppose that certain blessings or indulgences follow from a repetition of the sounds. Each petition ought to be realized in its own power and significance. Then I believe it will be a manual indeed, like no other in the world; an education of our spirits respecting our highest and most ordinary necessities; a wonderful illumination respecting the Eternal and the Temporal, and their necessary union; a discovery of the common blessings which all men have need of; a deliverance from the selfishness and superstition which lead men in pursuit of separate and dividing objects; a perpetual admonition that our Father in heaven knows better what we want than we know ourselves, and that prayer is reasonable, blessed, necessary, because He does.

Layman. Your object then would be to construct your family prayers upon this model?

Clergyman. I dislike the word *construct.* I believe we may ask God Himself to teach us how to work, to speak, to think; it cannot be strange that I should suppose He may teach us how to pray. The sudden extemporaneous gushes of a human spirit, if they are indeed gushes, may carry great powers with them because there may be great truth in them, because they may spring from a deep ground, and may not express only what the speaker feels and needs, but what the man in him feels and needs; therefore may find a response in you or me or any man. But the most meditated prayers, those in which the man considers what he needs as a man, and seeks to be delivered from the cravings which separate him from his fellow-men, these surely may import as much of divine teaching, as real an inspiration.

Layman. Inspiration!

Clergyman. Yes; I must use the word. I am certain I cannot talk of prayers as your mother would have talked of them, I cannot mean by them what she would have meant by them, if I do not use it. The coldness and deadness which you complain of in our family worship would not exist if the person who wrote the prayers and who utters the prayers had not been afraid to say, "I cannot think, I cannot pray, I can do nothing which a man ought to do without an inspiration." It is not vanity to think that God will inspire me when I am praying, when I am working, when I am studying. It is the root of all vanity to suppose I can be anything or do anything if He leaves me to myself!

Layman. People will tremble for the Scriptures and their inspiration if you use this language.

Clergyman. Let them tremble. It is well that they should tremble at their own unreal thoughts about the Bible and about themselves. They never will understand Apostles and Prophets, they never will reverence Apostles and Prophets, they never will believe Apostles and Prophets, till they confess that the Holy Ghost who spoke by them has not forsaken us, that we are baptized into His Name, that we are able to perceive anything, hope for anything, love anything, only because He works with us and in us.

Layman. Will not that opinion bring back the notion of gifts of tongues, with all the other dreams that upset the mind of a man so honest and true as Edward Irving?

Clergyman. No: it is the one deliverance from these dangers. It is that which alone can prevent their continual recurrence at any period when men awake out of the torpor of a customary belief, and begin to think that the words spoken in Scripture are not spoken in a double sense but are words of truth. If the presence of the Holy Spirit is not confessed to have been denoted once by the sign of the gift of tongues that men might recognise His presence always, in all exercises of thought, in all communications with each other—specially and as the ground of all other exercises, in communion with God Himself—there will be a continual craving for a repetition of the signs, a desire for sensible phenomena, which will destroy spiritual order and spiritual life under the pretence of vindicating them. What a lesson is contained in Irving's submission of his judgment and conscience to the interruption of some woman, to the decree of some self-exalted man, when he had such a lofty sense of his own calling as a minister of God! If the Spirit is not recognized as the Spirit of order, the Author of family order, the Quickener and Inspirer of all steady, orderly, harmonious acts, He will be confounded with the spirits of confusion and disorder, even by those who like Irving are smitten with the most vehement passion for ecclesiastical organization, and would sacrifice almost anything for the sake of that.

Layman. Your boast of inspiration, then? . . .

Clergyman. Boast of inspiration! Boast of weakness of will, incapacity of judgment, poverty of thought!

Layman. Well, then, your belief that God inspires those who are weak of will, incapable of judgment, poor in thought, does not hinder you from adhering to a certain method?

Clergyman. It makes me feel the blessing and necessity of a method, the terrible bondage of "chance desires," the imperfection of "unchartered freedom."

Layman. To go back, then, to the point from which we deviated, you suppose that family prayers might be cast in the mould of the Lord's Prayer?

Clergyman. I always lament that I have not made more use of its different clauses as guides to my own thoughts; if I had, I should have found my days linked much more closely to each other; my devotion would have been less barren, my family sympathies much more alive.

Layman. I am not sure that I understand you.

Clergyman. You may suppose that we have talked enough of the first words, *Our Father which art in Heaven*—those upon which all the others turn. And yet if we tried—say on each Sunday—to reflect, what would happen if some one came to us, according to the vision of Richter, saying, "These words are a lie; you have no Father"? and if we all believed what he said; we might press more directly home upon ourselves these questions, "*Are* they a lie? Am I prepared once for all to say that they are—to act on the hypothesis? If not, are they *true?* What follows if they are? What can I do that they may not be a lie to me, to my family, to all mankind? Who can hinder me and my family and all mankind from coming into that condition in which they shall be the mere repetition of sounds, which are for us utterly dead? Who shall hinder the dissolution of all human ties which will ensue *then?* Who can hinder the dissolution of human ties which is approaching *now?* Shall I ask the State, the Press, the Hangman, to give me aid, or shall I ask this Father who is in heaven?"

Layman. Are those Sabbath musings?

Clergyman. None drive me so much to seek for Rest where rest may be found—rest for me and my family and the universe.

Layman. Will *Hallowed be thy Name* help us for the week-day work of the world?

Clergyman. I can tell you what need I experience every week-day for help of the kind it might afford me, if I cannot exhibit any signs of the good I have gained from it. Some false name of God, some dark superstition concerning Him, is every day and hour striving to take the place of the Father in my mind, striving to banish His image from it. The confusions I see in the world, the death I see in the world, suggest some of these names to me. My own practice, my own injustice to my children, my want of affection and sincerity to my neighbours, canonize many more. And so I make gods after the standard of the appearances of things and of my acts, and the standard which might enable me to judge of those appearances rightly, and to reform my acts, disappears. I cannot keep the Name which Christ has revealed to me distinct from other counterfeit names; therefore I am forced to ask God that He will keep it apart; that He will hallow His own Name.

Layman. By Name you understand attributes?

Clergyman. His *Name,* as I find it used in the devotions of the Bible—as I use it in my own—saves me from the inversion, misery, and profaneness of "attributing" my conceptions to Him who alone gives me the power of conceiving. Oh! if one could get a learned Oxford logician to think of his own name—of that Sir-name which his fathers bore, of the Christian name which denotes him as a distinct person—that name which he received when the water of baptism was poured on him—if he would think that this is a nearer road to God than he can find through Aldrich or Whately or Mill—what a difference it might make to him and to us, to our human life and our human studies as well as to our theology!

Layman. Can I pass from *"Thy kingdom come,"* to the reading of the *Times* newspaper?

Clergyman. I know no preparation for that reading which will avail us except that prayer, as I know no commentary on that prayer so wonderful and so awful as that reading. "People tell me, Father of all, that Thou hadst a kingdom once in this world; that Thou didst deliver the Israelites out of bondage and reign over them. Other people tell me that that is all a delusion; that Thou hadst no kingdom then, only a certain Semitic people fancied that Thou hadst. Is that so? Or dost Thou reign now? Hast Thou a kingdom over these Frenchmen, these Italians, these Americans of the North and South, these Turks, Greeks, Russians? Have they succeeded in establishing their Popes, Emperors, Presidents in place of Thee? Hast thou no kingdom over these streets of ours, over these boys that we are training for prisons, over these girls that we are nursing into harlots? If Thou hast not, how is it that the universe holds together; that there is any law, any freedom, any national life, any relations of father and son, of husband and wife, of brother and sister? If Thou hast, O arise! Let not us have the upper hand. Let us not boast that we are the authors of the life and civilization which by our pride and selfishness we are destroying. For the comfortless troubles' sake of the needy, for the deep sighing of the poor, for the deliverance of the rich from the evils which they bring upon themselves, let thy kingdom come!" Could such a prayer be more real to any man in the fourth or sixth or tenth centuries than to us whose principal studies are in the *Times* newspaper?

Layman. I have a difficulty in distinguishing this petition from the one which follows it. Do you feel as if that awakened in you a distinct train of thoughts, and as if those thoughts had to do with our time?

Clergyman. I do not deny that it is impossible to separate the idea of a kingdom of God over men from a kingdom over the wills and spirits of men. It is the very distinction of the kingdom of heaven as we considered it before, that its dominion does extend into the region whence all the forces that act upon material and outward things proceed. But if you remember the questions by which men have been tormented respecting Will and Necessity, if you reflect that these questions, though they have given rise to so many bewilderments of school-logic, nevertheless exist in the heart of every man, and come forth in the strange doubts and questionings of every child; if your own experience tells you how they disturb resolution and impeded action, how still "I dare not waits upon I would" in the feeble man, how the strong man, as he throws off that feebleness and says "I will," becomes often the murderer and the tyrant; is it nothing in every stage of our lives, from infancy to old age, to be able to say, "*Thy will be done in earth as it is in heaven*"? What mountains of false prayer and sacrifice, of dark superstition, and of cumbrous reasoning, are thrown down by those childlike words!

Layman. The next always puzzles me. Does not God give us our daily bread without our asking? And does He give us more because we ask?

Clergyman. No; perhaps less. If I ask for the sufficient bread, the bread day by day, I ask that I may not have that fulness of bread, that rank superfluity which destroys my life, which makes me unfit to do my work as a man, disinclined to be a man. Again, the *Times* newspaper comes in with the divinity of its facts, if not of its leading articles. I read of millionaires, of swindlers, of starving operatives; I feel there is something utterly wrong in society as I see it. I find that no agrarian laws, no revolutions for equality, have set things right. Yet I see that agrarian experiments and revolutions for equality must be and will be the effect of this state of things; nay that great overthrows of a fictitious civilization have been the means by which men have been taught that they cannot make laws their own way, that there are laws which bind them and to which they must submit. I do not know what I can do that society may move in a more reasonable and right course. I am sure that I and every one ought to do something. But what we do, often—so the oracle of *The Times* tells us—aggravates the evil; we work against the laws of the universe instead of with them. That I may do what I am meant to do for myself and others, that I may go with the laws of the Universe and not against them; that I may not have bread without toiling for it, and that I may encourage others to toil for it; I am driven to pray, *Father, give us all day by day our daily bread.*

Layman. What a terrific sentence is contained in the next clause! How it seems to contradict everything that you have said about all the good that is in us having its origin in the unconditional love and grace of God! *Forgive us our trespasses,* AS *we forgive them that trespass against us.* We are to earn God's forgiveness by our forgiveness. Our forgiveness is to be the measure of His. The language makes me shudder, even while I confess a certain retributive justice in it!

Clergyman. It would make me shudder, and I should not have your sense of

its retributive justice if I were not praying to a Father in heaven, if I had not begun by learning what His Name is, His Kingdom, His Will. Believing that the
Son of God, the express Image of the Father prayed to that Father for the men
who were committing the greatest crime that was ever committed upon earth,
"Forgive them;" believing that His Kingdom is the Kingdom of forgiveness, the
Kingdom which has always been at war with the unforgiving spirit in the hearts
of men; believing that when He ascended on high He sent forth His Spirit to
preach forgiveness to all nations, beginning at Jerusalem; believing that He knew
what the Will of His Father was, and that He did His Will; I cannot doubt that
all the forgiveness which is in me or in any man, proceeds from the forgiveness
of our Father in heaven. And when I ask Him to forgive us our trespasses, as we
forgive them that trespass against us, I confess to Him that I have in me, that we
have in all of us, an inclination *not* to forgive, a disposition to take vengeance
upon each other for the wrongs we have received or fancy we have received from
each other. And feeling this in myself, and knowing how incapable it makes me
of apprehending His free, full, immeasurable forgiveness, how it forces me to
think of Him as like myself, to confuse my darkness with His light, therefore I
ask Him according to His great promise, to send His Spirit of forgiveness into all
hearts; so that the forgiveness which we receive from Him may be a real and perpetual spring of forgiveness in us. The law is,—we know it and experience it,—
that we can only receive His forgiveness vitally and effectually as we forgive others. The reason is, that He forgives us one and all for Christ's sake; that it is a
universal forgiveness, and that each must recognise it as such if he would enter
into it for himself.

Layman. Does our Father in very deed *lead us into temptation?* Is it only by
asking Him *not* to lead us that we escape the mischiefs which He Himself would
cause us?

Clergyman. I know for myself that I am tempted every hour by every event
which befalls me, by sudden occurrences, by daily routine, by prosperity and ad-
versity, by friendships and enmities, by solitude and society, to do wrong acts, to
think base thoughts, to fall into evil states of mind. Am I led into these circumstances by a foe? Has the devil created the universe in which I dwell? Has he ordered all things that shall conduce most to my ruin? It is my temptation, it is
yours to think so. I have no way out of it but by crying, "Father, I believe that all
these arrangements of my life are Thine. I believe that none of the evil which
arises out of them is Thine. Thou art leading me into the circumstances. Lead
me not into the temptation which the circumstances of themselves acting on my
evil disposition would cause me! But hold me up, hold us all up continually by
Thy hand, and *deliver us from the evil!*"

Layman. If you separate that prayer from the last, you come back, if I reckon
rightly, to Sunday again. The week is completed.

Clergyman. I do not much care whether I join it with the prayer against temptation, or contemplate it by itself. It is a famous prayer to end a week with. It is

a famous prayer to begin a week with. It points to the work of God; it points to the rest of God. It points to the work of man; it points to the rest of man. The work of the Father of all, if Christ's revelation is true, His highest and most glorious work, has been to fight with evil, and to deliver out of it those of His creatures who having wills and being therefore capable of evil, have fallen into evil, and who by that fall have made all the involuntary creation other than it ought to be. The rest of God was in looking upon His creation as He formed it, and lo! it was very good! His highest rest is in looking upon His Son, the First-born of many brethren, the Head of all Creation, the Redeemer of it from its misery and death. Man has been called to the work of fighting with evil, of fighting with it from first to last in the name of God and His goodness. Man has been called to the rest of believing in God's Righteousness, His order, His Truth in the midst of unrighteousness, disorder, untruth. Men since the Incarnation and Ascension of Christ have been called to a more tremendous conflict with evil in its high places, evil assuming the very nature and character of God, boasting that it is God. Men since the Incarnation and Ascension of Christ have been called to a higher rest in the assurance that God has prevailed over evil in their nature, that they are admitted to enter into communion with Him through the finished Sacrifice. There remains still a Sabbath-keeping for God and Man; that full revelation of the sons of God of which St. Paul speaks, which shall be the redemption of the whole travailing creation from its burden and bondage, the complete answer to the prayer, *Deliver us from evil.*

CHAPTER 6

Conflict in Church
and Society

TRACTS ON CHRISTIAN SOCIALISM,
TRACT 1*

Somebody.—CHRISTIAN SOCIALISM! I never saw that adjective united to that substantive before. Do you seriously believe that a Socialist can be a Christian, or a Christian a Socialist?

Nobody. I seriously believe that Christianity is the only foundation of Socialism, and that a true Socialism is the necessary result of a sound Christianity.

S. Sound and true! One understands those words very well. True Socialism is your socialism, not that of Owen, Fourier, Louis Blanc, or any other Englishman, Frenchman, German. Sound Christianity is your Christianity, not that of any church, sect, school, or divine hitherto known in Christendom.

N. The socialism I speak of is that of Owen, Fourier, Louis Blanc, and of the Englishmen, Frenchmen, Germans, who have fraternized with them or produced systems of their own.

S. A sufficient warrant for the other half of my proposition. Your Christianity then, I presume, is that of Owen, Louis Blanc, Fourier? A rather peculiar species of a very comprehensive genus! But to waive that point for the present. Your Socialism is that of a hundred different men, at strife with each other!

N. All these men, if I understand them rightly, are attempting to compass the same end. They differ about the means of compassing it.

S. The same end? Happiness I suppose. Socialists and Anti-socialists are probably agreed so far.

N. The watchword of the Socialist is CO-OPERATION; the watchword of the

---

*Dialogue between Somebody (a person of respectability) and Nobody (the writer), Tracts on Christian Socialism, No. 1 ([London]: George Bell, [1850]), 12 pp.

Anti-socialist is COMPETITION. Any one who recognises the principle of co-operation as a stronger and truer principle than that of competition, has a right to the honour or the disgrace of being called a Socialist.

S. Let me understand you. There is some considerable difference, I presume, between you and the persons you have named. You do not approve of all their statements?

N. I differ with them one and all, widely, fundamentally.

S. But your difference has respect solely to the means by which they accomplish their ends. You think their machinery defective or mischievous?

N. By no means. Their machinery I understand but imperfectly. Parts of it may, I conceive, be useful in any circumstances, large portions of it may be applicable in some circumstances, the greater part of it, I should think, taken by itself, is innocent. I am speaking perhaps at random; for, as I said, I am not minutely conversant with any of these systems. But I wish to assure you as strongly as I can, that it is not in the machinery which these men have invented that I find the causes of my dissent from them.

S. Where then? For you have given in your adhesion to the principle. You have intimated that you consider their anti-competitive doctrine a godly doctrine.

N. I have arrived at that conviction, and I mean to maintain it.

S. The end being good and the means innocent, I see not through what loophole or crevice, evil can have crept in.

N. I should wish for many reasons that you might perceive it. The lesson may be good for other cases besides this one. I will therefore try to point out the crevice.

S. I will strain my eyes and see what I can see.

N. The authors of these social systems felt that there was something wrong in the present condition of the world. They found that rivalship or competition was recognised very generally indeed by almost all classes of persons in all the concerns of life as the law which was to govern it. They found that a society which seemed to be built upon this principle, assumed Christianity as a faith sent from Heaven, that the institutions of this society implied this faith and were more or less leavened by it. The old scheme of the world, they said, must be done away with. But Christianity was part of this old scheme, what was to be done with *it?*

S. There can be no doubt about the conclusion from such premises.

N. But there was a doubt about the conclusion. Only a few could bring themselves at once and decidedly to adopt it. The rest were content to say "Christianity is at all events not that which we want now. It may be true or it may be false. But the social problem which we are considering must be solved without its help."

S. Was it possible to rest in this negative opinion?

N. I think not. The next step in the process made retreat or advance inevitable. If this was not the method of improving the condition of the world, another must be tried. Then co-operative systems were elaborated: some with much greater skill, experience, knowledge of the human faculties than others;—all with a certain amount of sagacity,—all with some insight into existing evils. One or other of these systems was to be the cure for the miseries of the world. Upon one or other it was to be reorganized.

S. To be sure. Who could expect any other issue when once men entered upon the career which you seem to think so hopeful a one.

N. A further consequence soon followed. A great machinery was to be the means of reforming society. Can a machinery, it was asked, reform society? The practical course must be defended by a theory. A broad maxim must be put forth or there seems to be no defence for the particular project. What was that maxim? Not a very new one. A maxim upon which people had acted for a long time, which moralists had often sanctioned along with many assertions quite inconsistent with it, a maxim which seemed to have the very strongest justification from experience, which might be made the foundation of the greatest tolerance and compassion for human infirmities. "We have a right," said they, "to believe that men can be made blessed by a certain set of circumstances, for man is the creature of circumstances."

S. Your Socialist friends will not have a very high notion of your orthodoxy, if you repudiate that fundamental article of their creed.

N. I fear not. But then they do not want my alliance here. They have three-fourths of the world on their side. All the stoutest asserters of competition agree with them in their worship of circumstances. There is nothing in any of the maxims of the most corrupt system the world has even seen to make this tenet unpalatable. But it is just here that they find the breach with Christianity, which had been continually widening, has become irreconcilable. Christianity evidently contemplates men as something else than the creatures of circumstances. If divines do not perceive that fact, our Owenites, with a much clearer and juster instinct, do perceive it. Therefore they say, "Christianity and our system must be for ever at war till one has either banished the other, or reduced it into a tributary."

S. By what charms do you hope to persuade Socialists to cast aside their favourite dogma and to embrace one the most directly opposed to it?

N. I have no charms for the purpose. Possibly experience may have some. One and another scheme of co-operation has been tried—

S. There at last I am at one with you—has been tried and has come to nothing. Tried too on what a scale! The revolution of a whole nation, undertaken for the sake of organizing labour, of establishing co-operation. And what is the result? Why we with our competitive principle laugh you to scorn! You have tried to set aside the laws of the universe and they have been found too strong for you. The old doctrine of gravitation was not refined enough for your tastes. You must have a new universe constructed without gravitation, upon some sublimer method. Alas! alas! poor Phaeton, Louis Blanc! he had the chariot of the sun for a single day. What a drive he made of it, Ovid and the French *ouvriers* can tell. But I do not see why the poor doctrine of circumstances is to be charged with this calamity. Your own beautiful maxim must surely bear its moiety,—more than its moiety—of the blame.

N. You cannot be more anxious than I am that all the experiments and all the failures of honest and dishonest men who have tried to embody that maxim in practice should be fairly reported, carefully examined, earnestly reflected upon. But you must permit me to say that your triumph is a little premature. There may be other Phaetons besides M. Louis Blanc. There may be a principle which sets up a hundred different coaches to run along that same road and commits each to a driver, sometimes not much more experienced, always with much less benevolent intentions than the derided member of the Paris provisional government. People may have their own tastes. I would rather be driven in that chariot or any other by Louis Blanc than by Moses and Son. In plain language, if the year of revolutions produced poor fruits, I cannot yet perceive that the year of reactions has produced any better. If the supporters of co-operation made some strange plunges and some tremendous downfalls, I believe the progress to perdition under your competitive system is sufficiently steady and rapid to gratify the most fervent wishes of those who seek for the destruction of order, and above all, of those who would make England a by-word among the nations. Thousands and tens of thousands of tailors, needlewomen, bootmakers, dock-workers, Spitalfields weavers, are saying to us, "Hold your tongues, gentlemen, about Louis Blanc and French revolutionists. Be silent in the name of common sense, if not of common modesty, till you have settled your accounts with us, till you have proved that your everlasting law of society does not mean a law of mutual destruction."

S. I ought to have been prepared for that burst of declamation. Those *Morning Chronicle* Letters have, I know, driven some sober men out of their senses. Those who were ranters before, they have of course taught to rant more furiously. I wish the feet of those commissioners had been lamed, their tongues blistered, their hands withered, before they collected those stories and published them, which now torment us wherever we go, and lead people to turn away from all quiet and legitimate views of economical science.

N. To keep facts out of sight is certainly very important for the interests of science. Since, however, your imprecation comes too late, and the facts have found their way to the ears of at least a portion of the public, you must prepare for a conflict, with all the disadvantages of position which I fully agree with you, this unexpected reinforcement to the ranks of the enemy necessarily causes you.

S. It is your hope then, that under cover the wild cry against competition, which these letters are leading inconsiderate people to raise, the blunders of your co-operative doctors may escape detection, and that a new experiment of the same kind may be begun in happy forgetfulness of the events which happened so long as two years ago?

N. On the contrary, as I said just now, it seems to me that these new revelations lay us under the strongest obligation to examine why different schemes for resisting that competitive tendency which most people seem to think may be excessive, have come to nought.

S. Certainly a very important and desirable inquiry, in which even my humble help may not be without its use to you.

N. I shall be most glad of it. You will, I think, join with me in acknowledging that the main cause cannot be a want of diligence, experience, knowledge, in those who have produced co-operative systems.

S. Certainly. If any amount of philosophical acuteness and systematizing power could have triumphed over the essential, radical falsehood of your notion, I should think from all I have heard that Fourier, to speak of no other, would have succeeded in giving it an almost perfect form and embodiment. I am perfectly willing to admit the ability of some Socialists in producing constitutions, only, as Mr. Carlyle says of the National Assembly Constitution, "they will not march."

N. After what you said just now, I suppose I need not doubt your assent to my next proposition, that a revolution, with all the opportunities which it affords for an experiment on a large scale and on a cleared ground, would not enable these constitutions to march. The difficulty of bringing them into play is not less in such circumstances than in peaceful times, but greater.

S. Still I am with you. I did not want the year 1848 to convince me of that fact. I am told it has been effectual with many who did.

N. I have every reason to think so. I conceive the most intelligent Socialists of all schools, both in France and England, expect less and less from revolutions. They may think as I do, that the outrages of the competitive system are likely to produce them, and to give them a most malignant character. I do not fancy they desire to see one in any country, or believe that it would be a means of advancing their doctrine.

S. That certainly makes them less formidable. Mere theorists one can afford to despise.

N. The phrase "mere theorists," you are aware, has sometimes been bestowed upon those who are not supporters of co-operation. I do not see that it has much worth in any one's mouth, or for any purpose. You and I, however, are trying to escape from it by considering facts. They have led me to one more conclusion, to which also I expect your assent. The co-operative teachers have failed, because they have not found a power which is adequate to resist the power of competition.

S. Bravo!

N. They have set up their systems as the means of keeping men fellow-workers, as the means of preventing them from becoming rivals, whereas the systems, supposing them to be the best and wisest in the world, presume some influence which is not to be found in themselves.

S. Or anywhere else.

N. That is precisely the question, the one with which I started. I hold that there is an influence adequate to resist competition, adequate to keep men fel-low-workers; that this influence has been latent in the old world, which Social-ists have wished to destroy; that in seeking to get rid of this influence, or to ig-nore it, they have inevitably given their adversaries a triumph, which will become greater and more insolent with every new struggle, till they succeed in completely realizing their own half-truth, till they make the principle which is always threat-ening to break up society the one governing power within it.

S. Of course I foresaw that you would come at last to this point. But you must remember that you have not in the least removed the difficulty, which your So-cialist friends, as you confess, have felt so strongly; that this Christian influence has been recognised and apparently at work for eighteen centuries, and yet that competition is as rampant as ever—you and they think more rampant than in any former generation.

N. I should not have stated that difficulty so strongly if I had not believed that it was one which must be fairly encountered.

S. I have foretold already the way in which you will encounter it. There has been a Christianity in the world, but not a sound one, not yours.

N. You are a little mistaken in this case, as in the former one, when you sup-posed that I had a Socialism of my own which was unlike that of all other per-sons. I hold that there has been a sound Christianity in the world, and that it has been the power which has kept society from the dissolution with which the com-petitive principle has been perpetually threatening it. I hold that this Christian-ity has been sound, because it has not been mine or yours, but has been a Gospel from Heaven concerning the relation in which God stands to His creatures, con-cerning the true law under which He has constituted them, and concerning the false, selfish tendency in you and me, which is ever rebelling against that law. I hold that that Christianity has become unsound just in proportion as it has be-come mine or yours, as men have ceased to connect it with the whole order of the world and of human life, and have made it a scheme or method for obtain-ing selfish prizes which men are to compete for, just as they do for the things of earth. So it has become mingled with that maxim of selfish rivalry which is its deadly opponent. So the two have blended themselves together in strange disor-der. So men have identified the one with the other. So they have believed that if one perishes, both must perish. If Christians have ceased to understand what their great foe is, and are actually playing into his hands, and fighting on his side, is there anything in the fact that competition is every day growing stronger, to contradict the proposition which I have maintained?

S. I have noticed for some time, in a certain class of French Socialists, the rem-nants or relics, I believe, of the St. Simonian fanatics, a disposition to invent some religious or ecclesiastical cover for their scheme. It seems as if they thought they could invert the poet's method. They have used all means to move Acheron in vain, therefore, they will see if they cannot persuade the powers above. Socialism *plus* Christianity is not an English novelty, whatever you may think.

N. I rejoice to think that it is not. There is, as you say, a very strong and evident feeling among the most thoughtful and earnest Frenchmen that, if every cooperation is to establish itself in the world, it must have some spiritual power to influence and direct its movements. There is a conviction more and more strongly, if blindly, working in their minds, and expressing itself in their language, that this spiritual influence must have some very close connection with that old Christian influence, which at one time they desired to banish altogether.

S. Which said Christian influence must be entirely remodelled and constructed for Socialist uses.

N. I grant you that a Christianity, which is merely brought in to help out the weakness of a system formed in the eighteenth or nineteenth century, will be a very poor, weak Christianity indeed. I do not believe that these French reformers, if they are as honest as I hope some of them are, can ever be content with such a feeble and paltry creation. They want a ground to stand upon, not a Corinthian capital, to make their edifice look more stately and graceful. And if they begin to look earnestly at the Bible history, at the creeds of the Christian Church, at the records of it from the Day of Pentecost to this time, I believe they will find more and more, that they have the ground there, the only one upon which they can stand or work. They will not read in the Divine book of a great strife of individual competitors, but of a Divine family, expanding itself into a Divine nation, of a universal society growing out of that nation, recognising and preserving both the forms of human fellowship out of which it was unfolded.

S. Stop a moment. Your "facts" have already demolished the connection between Socialism and Christianity, which you are seeking to establish by them. Christianity begins from a family and a nation, Socialism begins with the abolition of both! Remember, your Socialism is that of Owen, Fourier, and Louis Blanc.

N. I said that I agreed with Owen, Fourier, and Louis Blanc, in holding cooperation to be the social principle, and competition the dividing, destructive principle. I agree with them because I discover an order through all society, which seems to me to have its natural and necessary expression in united work, and its natural and necessary destruction in individual rivalship. The men to whom you allude hope to create such an order—to build the universe upon it. I find it existing, I desire only to bring it to light, to act as if it existed. From this primary difference all others which you have detected between them and me proceed. But surely I am not less a Socialist than they are in consequence of this difference; I am more of one. I assume that to *be* the only possible condition of society which they wish to *make* the condition of it.

S. If that is your notion, I do not see why you should want Christianity or any other power as a help, or make-weight in your system. Let "the only possible condition of society" alone. Why in the name of wonder can it not maintain itself?

N. If Christianity means a certain scheme for bribing or terrifying men into compliance with certain rules and maxims, your objection would be irresistible.

That I am aware is the modern notion of it,—the only one perhaps, which is compatible with the competition doctrine. The older view of the Church, as a fellowship constituted by God Himself, in a divine and human Person, by Whom it is upheld, by Whom it is preserved from the dismemberment with which the selfish tendencies of our nature are always threatening it, is the one to which I have already confessed my adherence.

S. You have substituted the word "Church" for the word "Christianity." I can easily conceive the Church in our days becoming another name for a great system of Communism. No one can have noticed the fraternal embracings of certain ultramontane Catholics and certain cismontane Cosmopolitans, without being prepared at least for an attempt to bring about such a result. But I should have supposed Protestant Christianity had different and humbler aims. I do not, however, deny that the age of reformation had its Communism. Possibly the Peasant War and the Anabaptist movement might furnish you with some useful precedents.

N. Most useful hints and warnings may be gathered, I believe, both from that movement and from those Romanist movements in past and present times to which you have alluded. If the Church forgets that it is a Christian Church, a Church united in a Person, who is the living lord of all human society, if it supposes that it is a great machine guided by a human hand, or a great sect of persons specially selected from the rest of the universe, it has a tendency to become a great or a small communist body; and in an age which is struggling for fellowship, and must obtain it by one means or another, it will probably become so. A very tremendous issue I allow; one which no man who studies history, and studies the present condition of the world, can contemplate without trembling. All the democratical tendencies of this age may be recruited and reinforced by that which was falsest and most godless in the superstitions of former ages.

S. M. de Montalembert has, however, disclaimed this alliance. He evidently thinks that the old superstitions can do better for themselves without the modern democracy. His manful denunciation of Socialism will do much to make sensible people content with his Catholicism. The Protestantism of Englishmen who make overtures to Socialism, will not be equally respected.

N. I do not complain of M. de Montalembert. I think he is an honest, as he is unquestionably a most able man. In the horror which he expresses the crimes of the Red Republicans, I heartily sympathize; his attempt to identify those crimes with the co-operative principle, I could easily pardon as the ordinary effect of an orator's passion, and of his indifference to distinctions which quiet men are obliged to take notice of. But that injustice has a still better excuse. This earnest Romanist sees that Romanism must be swallowed up by democracy if it cannot find some new help against democracy. He has never contemplated the Church except in connection with the age of the Crusades. The gospel and the history of Christianity are to him a brilliant, beautiful embodiment of the Romantic spirit. He loves the poor as poor; as means, that is to say, of calling forth and exhibiting the virtues, the self-sacrifice, the saintship of the rich. Although, therefore, the Mammon worshipping spirit of our time is naturally hateful to him, he must ally himself with those who are possessed by it, because he sees that they in their fear for their idol are willing to seek help from traditions in which they do not believe; to maintain themselves by the machinery of a system which till a little while ago they scorned. Though he knows that the greatness of the period which he admires arose from co-operation, not from competition, he must denounce co-operation and practically glorify competition, because the one talks of emancipating the labourer, and the other leaves him to the alms of the faithful. He must know, if he will reflect, that these alms, were they multiplied a thousandfold, could not save hundreds of thousands of his countrymen and countrywomen from abject misery of body and soul. But he does not reflect. What vulgar things are institutions for making chemises which can be connected with no delicate fingers, which can lead to no canonization! How can one whose heart is in the times of chivalry meddle with such matters? He is perfectly sincere in his dislike, not of the excesses of Socialism, but of Socialism itself. One is glad to see the noblest, purest specimen of such a character. It must do good to England as well as France.

  S. How to England?

  N. By showing our young men what they can be, and what they cannot be. *Here* there is no play for romance; the habits of all classes alike forbid it. Manchester, Oxford, Cambridge, Belgravia, St. Giles's, are equally unprepared for crusading middle-age experiments. Let us understand it well. Our Church must apply herself to the task of raising the poor into men; she cannot go on, as M. de Montalembert would have his Church do, treating them merely as poor. This is the true trial of our respective strengths. Can we do *that?* I maintain that if we are standing upon the eternal rock, if we are not merely part of a great ecclesiastical system, we can. I believe the Communion of Saints is not for one time, but for every time; that it was intended equally to be the blessing of the twelfth century and of the nineteenth.

  S. There are, however, wise and devout people who think that you too are in danger of becoming mere reproducers of a by-gone system; there are others who think you are in still greater peril from the rationalistic, pantheistic, eclectical notions of this day.

  N. Both fears, I believe, are reasonable, though great mistakes may be made respecting the persons who are causing the dangers, still greater about the means of averting them. As long as our Christianity is content with what you call humble aims, that is to say, as long as it is willing to be regarded merely as the dogma of an established sect, which is not to interfere with the movements of human society at all, which is to leave it to regulate itself upon the most selfish, tyrannical, hateful maxims, and only to prevent the sufferers from disturbing its movements; so long the most vague dreams of the fancy, which have a show of freedom, or the most terrible despotism, which has a show of government, will be preferred to it. And if these vague dreams of the fancy should be able, through any strange combination of circumstances, to ally themselves with that old despotism, if the first can borrow from the last a look of substance, and the last can receive back in exchange a semblance of liberty, the lie which is made up of these incongruous elements may be for a while powerful, though not powerful enough, as I think, to defy the direct simple Mammon worship. But the hour of struggle will be a fearful one!

S. You think that if Mr. Owen or M. Proudhon can be brought to a good understanding with the Archbishop of Canterbury and the Bishop of London, this formidable combination may be resisted by a still more compact and harmonious one?

N. I have no such dream. These tracts on Christian Socialism, will not be addressed to men in high places, nor to the organizers of new worlds. They will be addressed to common Englishmen and Englishwomen, to the members of the different classes of which English society consists, to professional men, to tradesmen, and working men, to those of whom the writers know something, and to whom they may speak without presumption.

S. With the modest ambition of converting a nation of competing shopkeepers into a family of loving Christians; a Society of Friends probably, or a Moravian *Unitas Fratrum.*

N. Not with the least wish to *form* a Society of Friends, or of United Brethren. These experiments have been made, and have, as I conceive, failed, for the same reason, which must cause the failure of Owenite and Phalansterian combinations, that they sought to create a new state of things, instead of proclaiming what that state of things is which God has made, and which we are trying to set at nought. We may be able to show your nation of competitive shopkeepers, that trade had its origin in another principle and power altogether from that which they are worshipping, and that the manufacturing and commercial prosperity of England is in as much peril from suicide now, as it was of being overlaid by fond nurses in its infancy, or of being flogged to death by prohibitive schoolmasters in its boyhood.

S. Do you mean merely to talk against the present state of the world, or is your reformed system ready for use and exhibition?

N. We should contradict all I have been saying to you, if we hoped to reform the world by a system.

S. Well, never mind words. What do I care whether it is called a system in your nomenclature, or anything else? Do you mean something or nothing? If you mean something, what is it?

N. I objected to the word "System" merely because I thought it would mislead you. It might make you fancy that we should propose a great combination for reorganizing all the trades of the cities, and the agriculture of the country. If we supposed we were the authors of the principle of association, and fellow-work, that would be our natural course. As we suppose it to be the principle upon which farmers and tradesmen would act if they were not drawn aside by false and ruinous notions into false and ruinous practices, a small experiment of association may be in our judgment much more effective than a greater one. It may illustrate better what simplicity and honesty can do, if we are willing to be simple and honest.

S. What an *if!*

N. A great one of course, and yet every appeal to the conscience of men and women goes upon that "if." You are not bound to lie, and destroy one another, unless you choose—that is all we can say; that is all any persons who have protested against any great abuse, and have succeeded in removing it, ever have said. If you do choose, why then—so it must be.

S. Why must people be tormented with such alternatives now more than any other time within the last three centuries?

N. Ask Moses and Son; ask the tailors; ask the needle—

S. The *Morning Chronicle* again!

N. I know it is a disagreeable allusion. But if you accuse us of being idle, visionary dreamers who abhor statistics, we must plainly tell you that our object will be to deal with the commonplace details of human misery, to inquire not how the world may be cut into parallellograms, but how you and I may buy our coats without sinning against God, and abetting the destruction of our fellow-creatures; to show how our little acts of inconsideration may cause far more physical and moral evil than great crimes; to point out a way in which habitual acts of deliberation and reflection upon our relations to our brethren may avert or relieve wretchedness, which grand charities, magnificent subscription-lists leave untouched or perhaps aggravate.

S. How do you purpose to prove that you are the persons who are the fittest to undertake this mission?

N. We do not purpose to prove it.

S. How do you know that any one will listen to you?

N. We do not know it.

S. Have you enlisted any powerful supporters?

N. None at all.

S. You count upon some help from the periodical press?

N. We have no reason to expect the least.

S. Not even from the religious newspapers?

N. From them, one and all, utter contempt or violent denunciations.

S. A brilliant prospect certainly!

N. The old prospect. "If this counsel, or this work be of man, it will come to nought;" if it be of God, slopsellers, philosophers, economists, the whole trading world, the whole religious world "cannot overthrow it, for they will be found fighting against God."

HATRED NECESSARY TO LOVE*

"Do not I hate them, O Lord, that hate Thee? And am not I grieved with those that rise up against Thee?"

—Psalm 139:12

The Psalmist answers his own question: *"Yea, I hate them right sore, even as though they were mine enemies."* We should most of us reply quite differently. We should say, "Hate them! We hate nothing. We try to obey Christ's command, *Love thy neighbour as thyself."*

"There is a way which seemeth right to a man, but the end of it is the way of death." I believe that this plausible, self-complacent language of ours indicates that we are in exceeding danger of wandering into that dark road, if we are not walking in it already. We think that we are far more gentle, humane, charitable, than David was. If we have courage to consider what he meant and what we mean, I fear we shall find that we are as much behind him in these specially Christian graces as in those which we may perhaps allow that he possessed, zeal and earnestness.

I. The force of the sentence evidently turns upon the word *Thee.* Who were those that hated God? Who rose up against Him? If we know what David believed of God, we shall be at no loss to understand. He did not, like the Heathen, ask the sky or the sea or the air to teach him of God. They did teach him much. They spoke to him of peace in the midst of strife; of permanence in the midst of change. They led him to think of One who might be the source of peace amidst the strifes of human beings, who remained the same amidst all changes in human thought and feeling. There must be something that abides; so said Nature to Man. "What is it?" was the question which the heart asked of itself, and trembled to hear the answer. "Is it a thing or a person, a friend to be embraced or an enemy to be fled from? Anyhow I must be closely connected with this presence. It must be very near me,—nearer to me than to all this universe. Else why is this witness in me of a right which I am to follow, of a truth which is to be in my inward parts? But if He is so near, wherefore is He hidden? If I cannot find Him out, is it impossible that He should make Himself known?" "He *has* made Himself known;" this was the faith of David. "He *has* declared Himself to me as my Guide and Teacher and Friend, as my Judge and King; as the Guide and Teacher and Friend, the Judge and King of my nation. *He teacheth my hands to war and my fingers to fight.* He is the source of my strength, my freedom, my hope. In Him are the springs of my life; from Him comes the discernment of justice and equity; the wisdom to rule, the wisdom to obey. From Him comes the unity of my nation; it exists only as a nation in Him."

This David believed. The more clear his mind became, the less it was dark-

---

*Sermon for the Fifth Sunday in Lent (April 10, 1859), from *Sermons Preached in Lincoln's Inn Chapel,* 6 vols. (London and New York: Macmillan and Co., 1892), 5:269–79.

ened by sensuality, superstition, or self-glorification, the more freely and bravely he was acting,—the more he believed this. He knew that there was a Divine Presence with him. It was no trick, no fantasy. If he confounded that Presence with himself, if he supposed it was created by the spirit which confessed it, all did become trick and imposture within him. But when he clave to this Righteous Living Judge and Lawgiver, when he acknowledged His guidance and desired that all the movements of his life should be ruled by Him, then did he himself and his fellow-men and the world around come forth out of mist and shadow into the sunlight. Everything was seen in its true proportions. Hear how he speaks in the Psalm from which the text is taken. "*O Lord, thou hast searched me out, and known me; thou knowest my downsitting and my uprising; thou understandest my thought long before; thou art about my path and about my bed, and spyest out all my ways. For lo, there is not a word in my tongue but thou, O Lord, knowest it altogether. Thou hast fashioned me behind and before, and laid thine hand upon me. Such knowledge is too wonderful for me; it is high; I cannot attain unto it.*" Think of these words. A Being near to a creature who is formed in His image makes him aware of His presence. He was seeking after the Ruler of his spirit, if haply he might find Him, and lo! He is there close to him, looking into the depths of his being, kindling the very desires which He satisfies. What awe lies in such a discovery! "*It is too high for me; I cannot attain to it.*" Yet what rest! What a sense of standing upon an eternal foundation, of being fixed upon a rock against which the waves may beat horribly, but which they will not shake. "He is not there because my teachers tell me so, because my fathers left me records of His existence. Thanks be to Him for the teachers! Thanks be to Him for the records of Himself! For they testify of that which is, of that which does not depend upon them, but upon which they depend. He is not there because I believe Him. My faith is given by Him. It is but the answer in me to the truth which calls it forth. When I lose my faith I come into waters where no ground is, or I find myself on a drifting sand. But that very experience shows me, as nothing else can, that my faith did not form the rock on which I am standing; no! nor the faiths of a thousand generations. My faith fails whenever I begin to put it in place of God. Nor is it by my acts of obedience to this Righteous Ruler of my inner self that I establish Him on His throne. My disobedience testifies of Him as my obedience does. The sense of separation from Him and all the disorders which follow from it show me that He is, and what manner of Being He is. The disbelief and disobedience of men generally, and all that flows from this disbelief and disobedience,—the cowardice, superstition, falsehood, tyranny, lust, cruelty which are setting the universe at war and making it a cage and habitation of unclean beasts,—these tell me of the goodness and truth and graciousness against which they are contending, and which shall destroy them at last."

II. And "*do not I hate those things, O Lord, which hate Thee; am not I grieved with those that rise up against Thee?*" You will tell me that he hated actual flesh-and-blood men, Moabites and Hagarenes, Goliaths and Sauls. Well! I do not care to dispute it. He hated whatever rose up against righteousness and truth in the earth, whatever sought to set up a lie. I cannot tell to what degree the particular man or the particular nation was the object of his aversion. To some extent I am sure it was, because I find that to some extent, probably to a much greater extent, it is so with us. But I am sure, just so far as he hated men or nations because they rose up against the God of Truth and Goodness, just so far he was hating the untruth and unrighteousness of these nations; just so far he was hating the same untruth and unrighteousness in himself. Their enemies were his enemies. He felt that there were deadly powers which were working deadly mischief in God's world. He who was about his path and his bed, and spying out his ways, showed him what they were. He felt them plaguing his own heart, tormenting him every moment, withdrawing him from trust and obedience, dragging him into a whirlpool of contradictory thoughts, words, acts. In the inmost region of his being he had to encounter these principalities of spiritual wickedness. In those high places he had to wrestle with them; there he was trained to hate them; to hate them from a thorough knowledge of their intense essential vileness. This hatred grew just in proportion to the degree in which he believed, trusted, delighted in a Being of absolute purity and perfection. The dimmer his vision was of such a Being, the more tolerant he was of that which opposed his nation and resisted his will. The more sure he was that God is, and that He is the Lord of man, and that He seeks to establish righteousness and truth in the earth, the more vehemently and savagely he abhorred whatever he saw which denied God and aimed at keeping the earth an abode of deceit and wrong. When he forgot God's name and disbelieved in His mercy, he could be meek and gentle with the butchers of the world and the chosen race; when his heart was thoroughly possessed with the Divine Spirit, "*he hated them right sore, even as though they were his enemies.*"

III. And can it be then, brethren, that the blessing of our Christian profession consists in this, that we have acquired a patience of whatever hates God and rises up against Him, which David had not? Assuredly our Christian profession then does not mean the following the example of our Saviour Christ, and being like Him? It is something the most opposite of this. For do you discover in Him any sign of *this* patience, *this* tolerance? You are told that when He was reviled, "*He reviled not again; when He suffered, He threatened not;*" you hear that He bore the contradiction of sinners against Himself; you hear that He ate and drank with publicans and sinners, whom the religious men of the day considered it a defilement to approach. But do you not hear of His making a scourge of small things and driving out of the Temple those who sold and bought there? Do you not find Him denouncing the Scribes and Pharisees as hypocrites and whited sepulchres? "*Do not I hate them that hate Thee, O Father; am I not grieved with them that rise up against Thee?*" was the language of the Master far more fully than of the servant; it expressed far more thoroughly the spirit of His life. He was engaged in a conflict to blood against evil, in a death-struggle whether it should put out the light of the world, or whether that light should prevail against it. And since He ascended on high He has been carrying on the same death-struggle in His Church and members, a struggle in which He tells us we must all engage, on one side or the other. What means then this notion which we seem to have taken up, that we are better than our forefathers because we hate less strenuously? Does it mean that there is nothing left in the world which deserves to be hated? Does it mean that Christianity or refinement, or civilization or science, or mechanical achievements, or aesthetics, or anything else we reverence, has put an end to pride and malice or cruelty? Does it mean that there are no scandals and abominations in the nation? no fierce party-spirit, no lying, in the Church? Does it mean that men are everywhere worshipping the God of Truth and Love? that they are not worshipping the Evil Spirit of Falsehood and Ill-Will? No one dreams this dream; no one doubts the existence of that which ought not to exist,—of that which is contrary to the good of man and the character of God. Our kindness and gentleness have this root. We are used to these things: we suppose they cannot be helped; we think God is indifferent to them. That is to say, we have ceased to believe in a God of Truth and Love; we do not suppose that what is evil is rising up against Him.

As for our hating less those who rise up against *us,* or those who dislike our notions, religious, political, or philosophical, I cannot see the evidence of it. We cannot, thanks be to God, indulge our desire for the suppression of the opinions that contradict ours as we once did. Earnest men have fought and bled that we might not have that power, any of us. We are obliged at present to limit ourselves to bitter words, dark insinuations, the destruction of each other's characters, to the undermining of moral freedom in the land. But withdraw for an instant the legal restraints upon our mutual animosities; give any one sect or party the opportunity of indulging to the full its passions against the rest; and it would be seen how much excuse we have for boasting of our charity—even of our toleration.

IV. And that bitterness on behalf of our own notions and dogmas,—that desire to crush whatever and whoever runs counter to them,—can, I believe, only be overcome by a very earnest cultivation of the other temper,—of that which we have denounced in David. Determine to hate that which rises up in you against God,—that first, that chiefly,—and you will hate, along with your indifference, cowardice, meanness,—all this conceit of your own poor judgment, this dislike of opposition to it, this unwillingness to have your thoughts probed to the quick. The intense certainty that there is a God of Truth and without iniquity, and that He must mean to sweep all falsehood and all injustice from this earth, will make you desire, above all things, that He should search you and try your ways,—that He should detect whatever in you is yours and not His, and should burn that with unquenchable fire. The acknowledgment of a God who was revealed in Jesus Christ,—a God in whom is light and no darkness at all,—will compel us to desire that no traditions of the past, no conceits of our own minds, may shut Him out from us. The acknowledgment of a God who beareth all things, hopeth all things, endureth all things,—who has been long-suffering with all His creatures and long-suffering with us,—will make us tremble to deal harshly with the struggles and doubts—how much more with the convictions—of our fellow-beings. Believing that God's Spirit, the Spirit of Truth, is the only Guide to Truth, and that He is seeking to guide us in the right way, how we must fear to check His mighty operations upon our own spirit or upon the spirit of any with whom we are in contact! How we must desire that we may be His instruments, not His foes, and therefore that we may partake of His own grace and gentleness!

And so with this hatred, deeply and inwardly cherished, will come the true, and not the imaginary charity,—the genuine, not the bastard toleration. To detect the right meaning, the sound faith, the divine inspiration which is latent under confused, rough angry words, directed against ourselves,—even against principles which are dearer to us than ourselves,—will be a duty which we learn at the Cross,—a faculty which only Christ can impart to us. We shall exercise it just because we believe Truth to be all-important, falsehood accursed; just because we love the one and hate the other. We shall remember that God honoured Job,—who complained bitterly and spoke words like the east wind, and was determined that he would know the meaning of the Divine judgments,—more than the three friends who pretended to justify Him, and in fact only showed their want of sympathy with His purposes of mercy and goodness. Whatever is contrary to that mercy and goodness, which are parts of His being, we shall desire to hate more and more,—therefore to bear more and more with all that merely crosses our tastes and inclinations and judgments.

Brethren, these are lessons which I think are not quite out of place at the beginning of a general election. In spite of the mingling and confusion of parties amongst us, and the uncertainty about leaders—perhaps about principles,—I suspect we shall find excuses enough for denouncing one another, if not for hating one another. To interpose general maxims about goodwill and forbearance at such times is mere idleness; every one accepts them, no one gives heed to them. I would press another exhortation upon you; I would beseech you to give full scope to your hatred. I am sure you will need it. For you will be tempted to do things that are hateful in the sight of God, and that you should do your utmost to make hateful in the sight of men. Those frauds which candidates use to disguise their meaning, to pass themselves off as intending that which they do not intend,—to obtain suffrages from two opposite quarters,—do they not deserve to be hated with a perfect hatred? Is not every slander against any opponent, every encouragement which you give to tongues and pens less scrupulous than your own, part of a hateful system? Is not the trafficking with party-symbols and ambiguous phrases, which may import everything or nothing, hateful? Is not the trafficking with sacred names for low purposes more profane and hateful still? Is not everything which tends to bewilder the consciences, to degrade the moral nature of those whose support you seek, to be hated as an insult to the God of Truth, to the God who seeks truth in His creatures? Do not all these deceitful words and acts go to make up a frightful sum of falsehood, to destroy the land which we pretend that we wish to save? Must not they bring God's curse upon us? Oh! for a more burning rage in us all against that which makes our professions ridiculous, our acts and words destructive of sincerity in ourselves and in all whom they influence! And since we are so unfit to search each other, because we have so many hidden falsehoods of our own, let us rejoice while we tremble that God has promised to search us and try us, and see what wicked way there is in us, and lead us in His true and everlasting way!